D0173752

Lizzy Disney

lizzydisney.co.uk

CHRIS ADRIAN • AYANA MATHIS • JACKSON TAYLOR • DANYEL SMITH • JUSTIN TORRES • TAYLOR PLIMPTON

THE WRITER'S FOUNDRY MFA

www.sjcny.edu/mfa

to be, not to seem.

GRANTA

12 Addison Avenue, London WI1 4QR | email editorial@granta.com
To subscribe go to www.granta.com, or call 020 8955 7011 in the United Kingdom,
845-267-3031 (toll-free 866-438-6150) in the United States

ISSUE 130: WINTER 2015

GUEST EDITOR	Ian Jack
MANAGING EDITOR	Yuka Igarashi
ONLINE AND POETRY EDITOR	Rachael Allen
DESIGNER	Daniela Silva
EDITORIAL ASSISTANTS	Luke Neima, Francisco Vilhena
MARKETING AND SUBSCRIPTIONS	David Robinson
PUBLICITY	Aidan O'Neill
TO ADVERTISE CONTACT	Kate Rochester, katerochester@granta.com
FINANCE	Morgan Graver
SALES	Iain Chapple, Katie Hayward
IT MANAGER	Mark Williams
PRODUCTION ASSOCIATE	Sarah Wasley
PROOFS	David Atkinson, Amber Dowell, Katherine Fry, Jessica Kelly, Vimbai Shire
CONTRIBUTING EDITORS	Daniel Alarcón, Anne Carson, Mohsin Hamid, Isabel Hilton, A.M. Homes, Janet Malcolm, Adam Nicolson, Edmund White
PUBLISHER AND EDITOR	Sigrid Rausing

OUR THANKS TO
Ahsan Akbar and Michael Collins in London
Urvashi Butalia, Chandrahas Choudhury and Nandini Mehta in Delhi

(your words here)

There's a long history of writing women (*writers*) off. It's time to right that wrong, to get relevant not relegated.

Visualizing is for the work. **Galvanizing** is for getting the work out there. We can see your words here. So can publishers, agents + scholars. **Can you?**

Until it's just about the art.
Submit your literary work now.

PEN + BRUSH

PRAIRIE**SCHOONER**

BOOK
prize
series

2014 Winners

PRIZES
$3,000 and publication through the University of Nebraska Press for one book of short fiction and one book of poetry.

ELIGIBILITY
The Prairie Schooner Book Prize Series welcomes manuscripts from all writers, including non-U.S. citizens writing in English, and those who have previously published volumes of short fiction and poetry. No past or present paid employee of *Prairie Schooner* or the University of Nebraska Press or current faculty or students at the University of Nebraska will be eligible for the prizes.

JUDGING
Semi-finalists will be chosen by members of the Prairie Schooner Book Prize Series National Advisory Board. Final manuscripts will be chosen by the Editor-in-Chief, **Kwame Dawes**.

HOW TO SEND
We accept electronic submissions as well as hard copy submissions.

WHEN TO SEND
Submissions will be accepted between **January 15** and **March 15, 2015**.

For submission guidelines or to submit online, visit prairieschooner.unl.edu.

CONTENTS

Introduction

This is the second *Granta* devoted to India. The first was published in 1997 to coincide with the fiftieth anniversary of the country's independence, though that was really no more than an excuse. To me, as *Granta*'s then editor, the issue's real purpose was to try to capture a country that was beginning to change fundamentally, preparing to say goodbye to its old self. There was a gathering sense of expectation. Modernity beckoned. Bill Gates was reported to have said that after the Chinese, South Indians were the smartest people in the world. Every Indian villager, it was also said, knew Gates's name. In one of that issue's pieces, in which the writer Trevor Fishlock went looking for any remaining traces of Gandhi's influence on the country, a marine engineer told him: 'We are growing. People want to work and learn. We are taxiing on the runway. We will leave America behind. Nothing will stop us becoming the greatest economic power in the world.'

When I first came to India as a reporter in 1976, nobody could have taken such a prediction seriously; it would have been placed in the same box of eccentricities as the claim, sometimes made by the kind of excitable Hindu patriot that the visitor encountered on railway trains, that ancient India – the India of the Mahabharata – had invented the helicopter and discovered the theory of relativity. That was the mythic past. On a train in the seventies, the future looked less glorious. As likely as not, we would be hauled by a steam locomotive; through the dirty carriage window we would see smoke unrolling over fields that were irrigated, planted and harvested by human labour, with no other assistance outside of a camel or a bullock. Rusting buses and swarms of bicycles waited at the level-crossing gates. On cross-country journeys night fell with a completeness not seen in Europe since the nineteenth century; once the last urban street had been left behind, the traveller peered out into an unelectrified gloom alleviated only by oil lamps and cooking fires. The Indian economy – the statistical abstraction that formed the backdrop to these scenes –

lay becalmed in what was known as 'the Hindu rate of growth', which for thirty years averaged a yearly increase in GDP that kept it only slightly ahead of the rise in population. India began to lag further and further behind its rivals to the east. In 1960, South Korea's per capita income was about four times bigger than India's but in 1990 it was twenty times as big.

What kind of literature in English did India produce at this time? It was often printed on rough grey paper bound between fragile covers. At a station bookstall the traveller might find a paperback of a novel by R.K. Narayan or a collection of poems by Tagore. The better bookstores in the big cities would stock Nirad Chaudhuri's *Autobiography of an Unknown Indian* and perhaps a story by Mulk Raj Anand or the Indian-by-marriage novelist Ruth Prawer Jhabvala. But these writers had small audiences (even Tagore had, beyond Bengal) compared to the writers who lived abroad and became known as interpreters of India. Sometimes these writers were Indian by ancestry or birth – V.S. Naipaul and Ved Mehta; often they were English – Paul Scott, J.G. Farrell; sometimes they were English and dead – E.M. Forster, Rudyard Kipling. A visitor who wanted to understand the history of India would turn to good books written by English authors such as Gillian Tindall, Geoffrey Moorhouse, John Keay and, later, William Dalrymple. Even the most important national narrative of all, the story of the state's foundation, had foreigners as its most popular chroniclers. *Freedom at Midnight*, a racy account of independence and partition by Dominique Lapierre and Larry Collins, respectively French and American, became a must-read paperback for the Indian middle class during the mid 1970s. Nobody in India had thought to write like this, though English was long established as an Indian language and both Indian readers and Indian writers were familiar with its literary forms. The Bengali writer Bankimchandra Chattopadhyay published the first novel written by an Indian in English in 1864. The first English non-fiction by an Indian, in the form of Sake Dean Mahomed's *Travels*, appeared even earlier, in 1794. And yet well into the second half of the last century India remained largely content to see itself as others saw it. There was official grumbling about the Western media 'obsession' with poverty and squalor – Louis Malle's documentary TV series, *Phantom India*, attracted the greatest censure – and many Indian readers of Naipaul angrily contested his bleak analysis of their society. But the outsider version prevailed; its voice was stronger and more fluent than the writing that came out of India, and it was left to film-makers such as Satyajit Ray to illuminate the country's life from the inside.

In 1980 Anita Desai became the first India-born and India-domiciled writer to have a novel selected for the Booker shortlist, her *Clear Light of Day*, but the big change came after Salman Rushdie published *Midnight's Children* the following year. The charge could be laid against him that, as a product of an English private school and an ancient English university who had settled in London, he too was an outsider. But he had grown up in Bombay and didn't approach his subject with a stranger's eye. A new post-imperial generation recognized themselves in a novel that brilliantly evoked the India in which they'd come of age, and its worldwide success encouraged young Indian writers to see that their country not only offered important things to describe but also that they might be the best people to describe them.

At first, the impulse was almost entirely confined to fiction – the novel was the thing – but by the late 1990s one or two writers were publishing non-fiction that had a decidedly literary ambition. *Granta*'s India issue of 1997 introduced Arundhati Roy to Western readers with the first published extract from her novel, *The God of Small Things*, which later won the Booker. But just as importantly it published pieces by Urvashi Butalia and Suketu Mehta, both in their different ways reportorial, that laid the foundations for their fine books on partition and Bombay. In the years since, most forms of narrative non-fiction have found gifted practitioners in India. Pankaj Mishra, Samanth Subramanian, Aman Sethi, Basharat Peer, Ramachandra Guha: these are just a few of the names whose work has punctured the West's near-monopoly on reportage, biography, popular history, the travel account and the memoir. *The Caravan*, a Delhi magazine devoted to long-form journalism, provided a platform for these writers after its relaunch in 2010 and deserves credit for persevering with a form that outside America has always had a small audience. As for Arundhati Roy, having published a prizewinning and best-selling novel, she promptly gave up fiction to become a polemical reporter and social activist. It would be wrong to make too much of that – to see her as exemplifying a trend. Nonetheless, it suggests that in India as elsewhere some questions are too urgent to be left to the novelist.

None of this eruption of literary non-fiction was very likely, if you believe in the general idea of a 'national psyche' and V.S. Naipaul's view of a specifically Indian one. In *India: A Wounded Civilization*, Naipaul writes that 'the Indian way of experiencing' means that 'the outer world matters only in so far as it affects the inner'. He was criticizing the self-absorption he saw in Gandhi's autobiography, *The Story of My Experiments with Truth* and other rather worse autobiographies, which made their writers blind to landscape, architecture, other people and the weather. This was a typical Naipaulian generalization (Sam Miller has more to say about it in his piece for this issue) but perhaps it once contained a grain of truth. Even so, it was far from the only handicap. Another was the uncertainty that Indian writers in English felt about their audience – who were their readers, where did they live? To be published in London and New York was thought to be a necessary seal of approval, but how much did the European or North American reader know or care about India? How much contextualizing knowledge could a writer take for granted? 'One critique of Indian writing in English is that we translate too much,' wrote Amitava Kumar in *The Caravan* in May 2014. 'Not simply that the humble samosa is described as a savoury food-item but that the narrative, like the menu in small Indian restaurants abroad, remains limited to the same familiar items. All too often, our writing is an act of translation on behalf of the West.'

This seems to me much less true than it once was. And if you were to ask what has caused the change, I would have to answer: 'Mainly money.' Whatever the other results of India's economic liberalization, which began in 1991, it has enormously expanded the middle class and its disposable income. People can afford books. Books can offer a deeper understanding of a society in flux, which is trying to make sense of its past and present – deeper, that is, than the passing excitements of the mainstream media. They can also be fun. India has developed a bustling publishing industry, where once a few respectable imprints specialized in educational titles and refined works of socio-economic history. The Indian writer need no longer look over his shoulder at his imagined audience abroad; many if not most of his readers are much closer – are Indian like him and need no telling about samosas.

Publishing is prone to fashion, and an idea has got about that interesting fiction no longer comes out of India but that all its new non-fiction is tremendously good. Like all absolute ideas, this is nonsense. As well as reportage, history and memoir, this issue of *Granta* has fiction that stands comparison with anything in the past – lively poetry, too, and in the work of Gauri Gill and Rajesh Vangad a depictive art of memorable originality.

When I was travelling by train through India thirty and more years ago, so much of India's present life was unimaginable. The change has been swift and is sometimes hard to take in. Patna, the capital of the eastern state of Bihar, for example: it was then a byword for all kinds of corruption and cruelty, usually described with the portmanteau adjective 'backward'. In 1983, I had my appendix removed there in an emergency operation at a private hospital staffed by Christian nurses. 'Thank God you weren't taken to the state hospital,' said a knowledgeable friend in Delhi. 'You would never have come out alive.'

Now I'm going to Patna again. Of all the things it needed – decent sanitation, drinkable water, honest policemen – who would have guessed the latest aspect of its public life? To a city where I once bought *Treasure Island* as the most interesting book in a bookshop, I am returning for the Patna Literary Festival. ∎

Ian Jack, November 2014

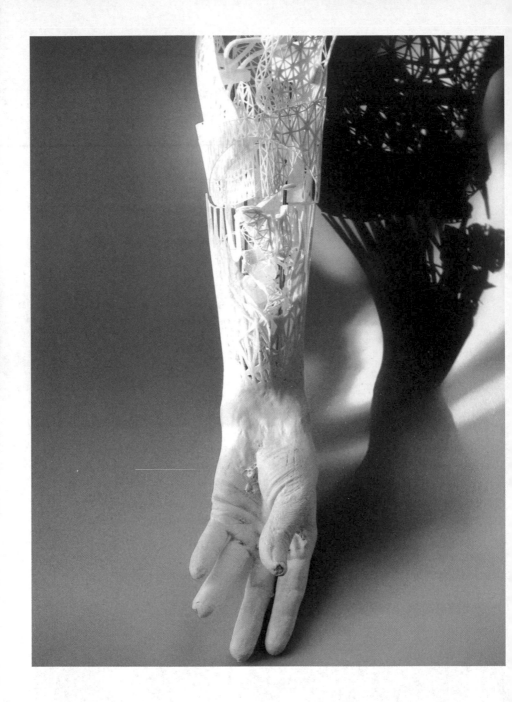

D_I Arm, 2012

DRONE

Hari Kunzru

I

It is, of course, the tallest tower. In the slums below, people orient themselves by it as they carve their way through the warren of chawls. Rich men have been building tall on this hill for centuries, but no one will ever reach as high again. The owner of this hundred-storey pinnacle has bought the air rights around its peak, for sums so vast that the men who own the adjacent fifty- and sixty-storey erections feel quite sanguine about the cap he has placed upon their desires.

For now. Perhaps *ever* is too strong a word.

This is the house of the Seth, who has learned, in his century and a half of life, to appreciate the beauty of layering. A man of taste knows that when you change, you should always leave a trace. The common people have short memories. One needs to remind them, to keep things before their eyes.

Eighty years ago, when he built his house, the Seth loved Italy. He loved, in particular, the rolling hills and cypress trees of Tuscany as they appeared in the background of portraits of aristocratic Renaissance warlords. He owned pictures like this and saw no reason he shouldn't go further. He had no interest in physically occupying any part of Tuscany, or indeed anywhere else in blighted Europe. It was the fantastical chivalric Tuscany of the portraits he desired. Urbino, as he called his house, was to be both a landscape and a castle within that landscape, a crag with a view of a palace and a palace with a view of a crag. A waterfall would tumble down its sides. And so it rose, the work of one of the great perspectival architects of the era, four impossibly elongated Palladian facades, which, from the point of view of the neighbours (and the shack-dwellers far below), broke into passages of Italian landscape, incorporating flocks of birds and a cataract that gushed white water. In certain weather conditions, a line of robed angels modelled on the Seth's third wife could be seen ascending a set of spiralling golden stairs.

The apsara house, the slum boys called it. The sexy-sexy house.

Later, the political climate changed. Italy was not the sign of a true patriot, a real Indian. Unlike a lesser man, who would simply have pulled the thing down and built again, the Seth melted Urbino, like an ice sculpture left out in the sun, impressing the new order onto the upper floors. On top of the old palace, now angel-less and renamed Adityavarnam, is a Sun Temple built of red sandstone, in the shape of a chariot with a high-pointed shikhara and massive carved wheels. A saffron flag flutters at its peak. Below it, on the middle floors, are the quarters of the earthly members of the Seth's household. The lower storeys, a maze of slimy rock and rotting Italianate columns, contain garages for his vehicles and giant kitchens for festival days, on which it is the Seth's custom to feed the poor.

Today the temple courtyard is packed. Priests, businessmen, figures from the world of entertainment and the military. Godmen of every shape and size yawn their way through the ceremony, naked to the waist or swathed in orange robes, bald, bearded, scratching themselves, adjusting their topknots. Every orthodox sect is represented, holy figures of every order and foundation dozily gripping tridents and checking their messages. Most are not visibly augmented, but modesty hasn't prevented the addition of a little aura here and there; a snake or two, a discreetly open third eye. Whatever other embellishments or accessories they're sporting, everyone has a prominent caste mark on his forehead, incorporated into whatever tilak is customary for his sect.

The caste marks of the executives are less conspicuous. By law they must be displayed, even by such powerful men as these, but not everybody's origins are exalted. Some are best concealed by a terminal or an artfully curled lock of hair. The executives crane forward, generically handsome, furrowing their Napoleonic brows, their powerful forearms tensed as they press their palms against crossed silk-suited thighs. Most of their interpersonal augmentations have been muted, but even with the volume down, their relentless focus on growth is a palpable force in the air.

Of the various interests represented, the military men are the most visibly moved by the actions of the officiating priests, who are pouring libations of milk onto a large pile of weapons. More than one handkerchief is removed from a dress uniform pocket. Medals tinkle on imperceptibly quivering chests. The police chief stares glassily, his optics occupied with monitoring the crowd down below. High-ranking state administrators inhale the scent of burning sandalwood, their noses twitching with jealousy and awe. Though the Seth is famously ascetic, he does everything with pomp and extravagance. Down into the slums rolls the incredible scent. The sandalwood is not synthetic. It is real. The Seth owns one of the very last natural groves, in a secret location in the hills far to the south. And to win blessings it is being burned, piece by piece, on a sacrificial fire.

The Seth's wealth has deep and ramified sources. He is the lord of change, the emperor of process. He controls everything from raw materials to staggeringly abstract forms of intellectual property. So entangled is he in the global economy that it is impossible to imagine how he could be excised. Things have to flow through the Seth, through the cosmic corporate person he has conjured out of his navel.

The Seth is deep in the food chain, the hydro-cycle. He is a converter, a changer of speeds and states. Though his companies produce almost a quarter of the synthetic food consumed on the planet, he does not touch it himself. No algal protein or vat-grown muscle fibre passes his lips. In his household they eat wild line-caught fish; they eat lamb, fed on grass. The Seth himself, being pious, does not touch meat, but his vegetables come from soil that is protected from contamination with forensic care. He no longer sports the silk suits and Michelangelesque body of his Italianate years. These days he has the appearance of an austere seeker, wearing homespun cloth and quenching his thirst with water flown from high above the Himalayan snowline.

The Seth's servants sometimes adapt the old quip about the Mahatma, about the cost of keeping their master in his holy poverty. This does not trouble him. He is a believer in the virtuous path of *artha*, which he likes to translate to foreign business contacts as 'enlightened self-interest'. As long as the getting of wealth and position is conducted in accordance with Vedic principles, it is not merely legitimate, but noble. In this dark age of vice, as the universe hurtles towards its obliteration and eventual cyclical rebirth, the Seth stands against entropy. His great age, though not unprecedented, seems to him a cause for celebration. As does his fortune. But of all his achievements, the greatest is his daughter, Parvati. She is his most perfect creation. Today, in her name, he is making a donation of sacred weapons to a strategic ashram high in the mountains at Gomukh, once the source of Holy Mother Ganga.

Of the Seth's twenty-seven children, Parvati is by far the youngest. Her mother, the Seth's seventh wife, was headhunted from an isolated rural community, where she'd grown up under the supervision of a disciplinarian aunt. Only after compliance with stringent genetic and astrological tests did the Seth's agent offer her the position of vessel. She was, of course, a virgin, whose pristine caste background demonstrated, on the part of her ancestors, an impeccable lack of interest in the wider world.

Since the moment of her conception, Parvati has existed in a controlled, monitored environment. The biological matter that makes up her body has flowed in from the purest sources. Networked into medical scanners that watch over her vital signs as she sleeps, she is also bathed in the luminous attention of her guru, her yoga coach, several tutors and a warm nebulous presence known as Chhotu, a transmigration of a favourite Pomeranian that now exists in her sensorium as a repertoire of gestures, a nuzzling, a pleading, the scrabble of tiny paws on her skin.

Measurements and calibrations. Golden ratios and means. Her handspan, the distance between her shoulder blades, the various facial angles and relations – all converging on the best, the finest and most desirable. The Seth is a great believer in optimization. There are certain visual traits he finds appealing in a woman. There are others that remind him pleasantly of himself. He is moulding a family aesthetic, a brand that can be passed on. Only the very oldest families are in a position to do this. It is what differentiates them from new money.

Take her ear, for example. Take the gorgeous curve of her ear. The sinuous curve. The instantly recognizable curve of his daughter's ear.

Everyone with any income is tall now. Everyone has a fair complexion and lustrous hair. Everyone has perfect skin and teeth and eyes that sparkle like polished gemstones. Any old parvenu could sculpt a child with blandly beautiful features, based on whichever actress or sportsman he wishes to use as a model. It takes a connoisseur to signal an inheritance – this distinctive nose, that strangely shaped eyebrow, deviations from the ideal that act as a signal to other genetic aristocrats that a pedigree is at work. Of all his children, only Parvati has the Seth's full set of selected traits. She is the vehicle of his sense of futurity, of hopes whose scale sometimes unnerves him; so he locks them away, these hopes, and only allows himself to see them in glimpses, segmented, like a giant statue of a reclining deity housed in a colonnaded hall.

The Seth can command the loyalty, or at least the respect, of everyone who counts in the city. Were some terrorist to place a bomb inside this compound, the whole nation would descend into chaos. His speech is brief and dignified. He thanks everyone for attending. He seeks the blessing of God on the noble endeavours of the Committee to Restore Holy Mother Ganga, and expresses the hope that its humble efforts will bear fruit. Until the day comes when the river starts to flow again, the vital task of protecting her source against enemies of dharma must continue. The Seth is proud to do what he can to assist the brave jawans in their mission to guard the strategically vital ashram. He hopes his offering will be accepted.

This is supposed to be Ramrajya, the kingdom of God. In this perfect nation, every aspect of life, from the highest to the lowest, is operating in accordance with the moral law. There is a place for everyone, and everyone knows their place. The Seth's guests – the gurus and soldiers and administrators and captains of industry – are the flowers of civilization, the brightest and the best. Their wives and daughters are chaste and obedient. Their wisdom and munificence are celebrated by the crowds in the streets below, who love them like parents. And yet the river doesn't flow. It hasn't flowed for a hundred years. At Varanasi the ghats tower over the dry riverbed. An oily, polluted stream runs through a rubble of garbage and human remains. If this were Ramrajya, wouldn't the waters flow?

The Seth gives a sign to the head priest, who rings a bell and begins to chant.

Adi Shakti Namo Namah Sarab Shakti Namo Namah Prithum Bhagvati Namo Namah Kundalini Mata Shakti Namo Namah

The girl obediently follows her cue, takes a chakra from the pile and raises it over her head. There she is, the personification of his power. His beautiful daughter, the very emanation of his godforce.

He likes to be close to her as she is going about her day, to hover as a presence on her shoulder as she dresses up and plays with her toys, to lie next to her in bed as she sleeps.

She must know he is there.

For a long time, something about Parvati has preoccupied him. His security has become interested in traffic between Adityavarnam and an obscure sector of his business holdings, a company conducting mineral extraction in the unadministered periphery. Someone or something in his household is spending a lot of time on this small company's network. Antivirals have determined that the origin of the traffic is his daughter. He can think of no conceivable reason why she should be interested in mining. Perhaps it is educational. An economics project. Geology. It is a small thing, but in the Seth's experience, small things are not necessarily without consequence.

2

If this is not the worst place in the world, then it comes close. When the wind rises, it lifts the dust into great roiling clouds, which sweep over the enormous open pit and blot out the sun. The dust coats the skin of the miners. It works its way into their nostrils, their throats. The darkness is terrifying. Sometimes it is impossible to see a hand in front of your face, or the rung of a ladder. Men lose their footing and fall.

There used to be a forest here, dense and green. There used to be a river. Now the nearest trees are a hundred miles away; there is nothing to block the howling wind. Even inside the arcologies they must feel it, as it scours the outer shells with sand and rocks. They must feel the vibration, hear a low rumble like white noise. For the miners, living in their ramshackle encampment, a dust storm means flying debris, structures torn from their moorings and thrown into the maw of the pit. Smashed skulls. Respirators torn away from faces, mouths and nostrils filling with suffocating dust. When the wind blows, the sun is just a faint glow above a red-shifted landscape of scurrying wraiths in masks and goggles.

The wind blows men into the pit, down past the place where the sandy soil turns to blue-black mud, to land like broken dolls in the maze of duckboards and ladders and claim markers at the bottom. The miners live and die caked in this mud. It is their livelihood, their destiny. Sweltering blue-black men, slipping and sliding down into the pit to fill baskets with the mud which covers them, heavy baskets that must be lifted onto their backs and ported to the surface, up the ladders, up the narrow and treacherous paths cut into the walls.

If a friend chooses to bring up your bones, that's his business. No stranger is going to bother about a corpse. The miners are poor men. They are so poor that, apart from the few who have been augmented, or who can afford to pay the toll at one of the winches, they must carry their loads unassisted, using the strength of their backs and legs. They know what it means to be exhausted, to lie down at the lip of the pit, gasping through their masks, tasting metal. They know the feel of mud caked on skin, the way it splits into crazed patterns as it dries, like land in time of drought.

All the land is in drought. A satellite view shows the mine eaten out of the bend in the dry river, like a cancer on its jaw.

The miners take the mud for washing. They must pay for this. Water is precious, almost as precious as the particles washed out of the mud. The men who run the washers are foreigners. They wear hazmat suits and expensive ventilators. They don't want to share the air of this place, not if they can help it. Pity the miner who disagrees about weight, or accuses one of the washers of using too coarse a mesh; they have their niche in this ecology and guard it with the viciousness of small men who know that they are only a step above the mud. It is waiting for them, the mud. Waiting to drag them down. So their suits are ostentatiously white. They flash fancy guns and chakras. There is no law here to stop them killing. In a place such as this, the only protection available to a small man is the ability to inspire fear.

The miners sprawl in the dust, waiting for their loads to be called. When their numbers are processed, the mud goes through the machine. They stand by the tank with their tins, praying to their various gods. Santa Muerte, Lakshmi Devi. Let it be pure, let it be heavy. The atmosphere is tense. The miners look like beggars, children at an orphanage. Everyone knows the washers are cheating them. Everyone knows that when the waste mud is rewashed, late at night, it will turn out not to be waste at all.

The mud is rich in a rare earth, which yields a metal necessary to make certain electrical components. The metal is not decorative. It is dull and grey. It has no iconography, no trail of songs and stories. Yet upon it such a huge structure has been built, such a pyramid of machines and money, that it is worth more than gold or platinum. There is no alternative; this hole in the dry land is one of the few sources left. The metal is the only thing here the great powers care about. No one wants to administer the territory or organize the people. The last state of which this land formed part still exists, but only on paper. In reality this is what international law terms a Special Economic Zone.

When the mud has been washed, the miners take their little tins of precious dust to the dealers, who sit behind their perimeters some way from the mine workings. The miners must negotiate to cross. They must participate in network identification and trust protocols to demonstrate that they are not a threat. The perimeters are not physical, though some have visual markers. They are enforced by drones and chakras. The air is thick with them. After a storm, the ground is crunchy underfoot with little electronic corpses.

The dealers have many layers of protection. Some have crawlers, which disarm their clients and hold them in place to be scanned and swabbed. There are cages and holding tanks. There are intelligent weapons, set to operate with full autonomy. This poses no legal problem. All laws have been suspended here, all norms. At every scale, a Special Economic Zone is in a state of continual, undeclared war, the war of each against each

The dealers, mostly women, are from the capital. They are fat and glossy, eating from hygienically sealed packages, breathing the controlled atmosphere of their pods. The miners hand over their tins through an airlock. No physical contact ever takes place. Some of the dealers work for Indians. Others for the Chinese. Most are linked to the militias, to the CAAC or the AFLC or the CPPA or the CPPA(M) or CPPA(ML) or any of the dozen other factions that depend on mining revenue to continue their obscure insurgencies. Some militias own washers. The largest have airstrips. The water tankers that serve the mine are battered limping things, on their third or fourth owners. Thirty years ago they were making runs across the American desert states. Fifteen years ago they were in Central Asia. Now they're here. They pay to land. It's worth the risk – the price of water is fifty times what it is on the coast, near the desalination plants.

Only the toughest pilots stay the night. Most are turning round their birds before they've even drained their tanks. To get in and out, they must use contaminated airspace, low and vulnerable. The higher air is reserved for the great powers and they have satellite defences. So the tanker pilots pull back their sticks and judder upwards, squinting at their instrumentation in case some obstacle appears ahead.

On the ground it's worse. Teeming, swarming. The camp is saturated with replicators. Every system at every scale – from the miners' ramshackle living pods to the exotic viral strains proliferating in their blood – is in flux. Repair swarms, security swarms, rogue medical processes. The encampment's street plan, its architecture, the very bodies of its inhabitants – all are mutating at a pace that is frequently visible even to the unaugmented eye. When the mineral rush started, about five years ago, after this area fell out of the control of the last group that could style itself a government, miners laid out a street grid. Now the parts of the camp that still possess streets have melted into a maze of winding, crooked alleys, like those of medieval cities. The areas that don't have streets – where swarming and replication have intensified to catastrophic levels – resemble anthills, though the force and abstraction of their overlays makes observation tricky. A mess of sensory fragments. Hybrid phenomena, organic and inorganic jumbled up together. The miners have names for these places. Hives, Eggs, Who-Can-Tells. In most places where the rule of law holds sway, they are termed 'mutabilities' and suppressed. There are people in some of them. What used to be people.

Mutabilities. Tunnels. Gropes. Names for uncertain zones, with complex powers of attraction. The camp is full of them. Formations can appear overnight, capturing raw materials and biomass, then disappear just as quickly, overcome by some counter-process, some alternate will-to-form. Some of these events are more or less under the control – or at least guidance – of some person or faction. Others appear spontaneous. Opinion in the camp is usually divided about causality, as it is about most things. The only constant is waste. Once the water has been recovered, and usable raw materials fed back or scavenged, there are only two outputs of this filthy midden – radiant energy and dust.

His name is hard to pronounce. It is a name from a small language. No one cares about his name.

We will call him Jai.

Jai is beautiful. His blue-black skin, his high strong voice. He wields his shovel like a child's toy. He is nineteen years old. Is he different from the other miners? No, he is exactly the same. He has no mystery of birth or parentage. He is a human, a man.

Somehow Jai is untouched by this place. It's as if the mud refuses to stick to him. In the midst of the daily struggle he appears as clean and bright as a city boy, though Jai has never seen a city. He has no family or friends. He is part of no tribe or community that he can remember. He has already seen most of the bad things that humans can do to each other, and since he finds them unremarkable, they do not frighten him unduly.

When Jai walks about, there's a cloud over his head, a plume of tiny drones and flyers. They come from far away, carried on the wind. They seem drawn to him. Are people somewhere paying attention? Perhaps not. The drones are mostly low-grade personal devices. They have optics and sometimes haptics, but there may not be anyone watching or feeling. There are many more eyes than people in the world; everyone knows that even in their most intimate moments, there's a chance that they're being observed, if not by another human, then by some algorithm trained to sift through the feeds for porn or lulz or evidence of crime. Jai, like everyone else, carries on his shoulder an invisible They, a formless little gremlin composed of the combined potential attention of an unknown number of people and machines. None, millions. Privacy is a quaint word, like 'chivalry' or 'superego'. Some say the need for it is an evolutionary relic, a kink that's being ironed out by the forces of order, but for others, the feeling of being preyed upon, of hosting a parasite, can be hard to handle without medication.

Perhaps all that's watching Jai is a glitch. Perhaps some common process has got stuck, dragged a lot of flyers down into a sort of sinkhole of attention. They could be dead machines, a frozen botnet marking time by watching the unremarkable doings of a poor and unremarkable young man. Around the world, people set eyes off on journeys. Go find something to look at. Not that, this. Not this, that. Floating about on solar-cell gossamer. Some are directed, others almost completely autonomous, trained to go in search of some particular kink or flavour. The famous put up security; otherwise they'd live in a swarm of angry voyeuristic bees.

Who can say why a young miner should generate a cloud of drones? But as Jai walks about, the sight is unusual enough for other miners to remark on it. They have nicknames for him. Starboy. Mister Clean. He tries to ignore the swarm, to blot out its high-pitched whine.

One reset and it'll probably vanish. That's what most people in the encampment think. Others aren't so sure. A couple of times Jai has been attacked. Hard to say why. Other miners jealous of his celebrity, wanting to divert the swarm's attention to or away from themselves.

One evening, he goes to buy himself an arm. It's a common enough transaction. Most people on earth are augmented. You can increase your strength, overclock your reaction time or your lung capacity, multiply your attention span. You can cosmetically alter your face, reskin your body in the latest colours. You can augment your perception, overlaying the hideous environment of your mining camp with a pristine rainforest or an educational maze or a hypersexual forest of organs and limbs. Elsewhere in the world, people have changed themselves in ways these miners can only dream about. The rich are fantastical creatures, young gods living in a customized world, generating themselves and their environment out of the stuff of their desires. Not this, that. Not that, this. For the less fortunate there are wealth-sims and optical overlays that make cramped living spaces feel spacious, cosmetically luxurious. You may be exhausted and feeding yourself textured algae, but you're doing it in a marble throne room.

Jai, like everyone, worries that he's falling behind. Other miners stimulate their muscle growth, or use cheap mechanical prosthetics with docks for attaching tools. One or two have elaborate biomechanical grafts, though these many-armed, monstrously sized men are usually enslaved by the militias and are so psychologically alienated that they can't properly be called human any more. Jai is young and strong. He has the body he was born with, a body which has been constructed entirely by chance, without selection or surgery or fetal therapies, with a variable food supply, patchy shelter and unrestricted exposure to diseases and swarms of all kinds. He is miraculously healthy, but can't seem to make enough money to survive. Sometimes he goes hungry. He struggles to pay the water boys.

The prosthetician is based in a highly entropic zone of the camp, the informal red-light district known as the Cages. It's a quarter that has spawned a hundred slang terms for process, words for every type and quality of peak, dip, spread and intensification. As Jai squeezes through a decaying alley, a flock of what look like geese with glandes instead of heads skitter past him. Who knows where they came from, but they're ubiquitous in the Cages. The miners call them 'dickchickens'. Whores grafted into the walls display available orifices or scroll out stims that grab the crotch or flicker and bounce off the eye like thrown business cards. Even the architecture is pink, moist to the touch; when it comes to overlays, miners tend to want the hard stuff. Cheap and heavy. Margaritaville. Pussytown. Jai is assaulted by a confusion of tacky skins and feelies, which override his permissions, come congaing through his field of vision, trying to trick him into giving out his credit strings. Phantom pudenda flourish and bloom. Semen spatters the optics of his sensorium. He is brushed by nipples, hair, lubricated hands.

He squeezes himself through a rectal crack into the limbmongers' colony, the swarm of drones battering round him, thick and black. It fills the narrow alley. Machines get stuck underfoot or mashed into the deliquescent walls. The largest are the size of small birds, the tiniest mere hoverflies, with little iridescent solar sails for wings. As he is finally enclosed by the prosthetician's stall, sheltered behind his firewall, the swarm forms a clicking, skittering crust on the transparent shell, jostling for a sight line.

The limbmonger is a sallow man with a double ridge of bone on his forehead and a cage of carbon fibre around his jaw, the platform for some kind of sensorium. As he shows Jai his wares he's probably multitasking, climbing pre-thaw Everest or swapping feelies of cats. He has a telltale absence to his manner, a blankness. Of the various devices on offer, there's only one Jai can afford, a contraption with a battered shovel, a claw, and some kind of twitch control that the man swears works perfectly, but which only seems to react intermittently to Jai's instructing left shoulder.

He's not sure what to do. It's a terrible deal, but he badly wants it to work out. Even functioning poorly, the device will halve the time it takes for him to fill a basket, and it can be fixed to a rope to act as a winch, sparing him much hard climbing. The limbmonger assures him he has clean instruments and a freshly debugged operating bay. What could go wrong? So Jai pays and lets the chair settle round him. The prosthetician sprays his upper body with antiseptic phages. As the man goes to work, Jai hums a low syllable. He lengthens the sound, spooling it out of his diaphragm. When the anaesthesia kicks in around his chest, the syllable drains away until it's no louder than a whisper.

At first all is black. Then he hears a tone, single, constant, running through him, resonating in the cavities of his body. This is the tonic. Every note he will hear in his life, every note of his life that he will hear, has its meaning only in relationship to this tonic. All this unfolds in his mind with the clarity and force of prophecy, but when he wakes he remembers nothing. Just a high white sound lingering at the edge of his consciousness.

Round white oval, gridded jaw. The prosthetician is leaning over him, testing the connections. When he sees Jai is conscious he dims the light. Jai feels as if each muscle has been individually beaten, tenderized. His nervous system is sending decontextualized nastiness across his sensorium. Nausea, tinnitus, sensations of being grazed or scalded. The man gives him a drink of water and plugs him into a sim, where he spends a couple of hours running through a set-up routine. Stretch out, grasp, swivel. The damn thing has adverts. He has to bat away upgrade offers, 'free' trials of antivirals. The arm is unfamiliar, a dragging weight that doesn't feel comfortably counterbalanced. The prosthetician wants to sell him some kind of active harness but he can't afford it. He goes away filled with misgiving.

The next day he uses the arm to dig. It leaks. He does his best to patch the hydraulics but as the day goes on, more problems develop. The arm is jerky, unresponsive, barely usable. He clips onto a cable but when he gets to the top the thing dies altogether and he has to pay the winchman to be detached.

In a rage, he ejects the arm and throws it to the ground. The terminals in his chest and neck are red-raw. Sitting by the lip of the mine, he sells the piece of junk to a recycler, whose swarm arrives, eats it and carries the particles away. He tries not to look up, but can't help himself. There it is, the watching cloud, a flock of little black pixels darkening his personal sky.

He makes his way through the filthy camp back to his shack, the smells of cooking, sewage and algal run-off commingling unpleasantly in his nostrils. He has to shield his eyes from the saffron glare of the Indian arcology, its curved glass peak reflecting the setting sun at his back. As night falls, he begins to feel sick and shivery. He falls into a fitful sleep.

The high white sound returns. The tonic wavers, warping and shivering and falling off. It takes on a queasy plucked rhythm, like a folk song played on an ektara.

In the morning he wakes feeling sick, and as he vomits into a bag, he's suddenly swamped by a girl singing a pop song in a foreign language. A few words loop moronically in his ears, then she warps into a contact button, which hovers for several seconds before he can banish it. The thing is grainy, corrupt, some kind of virus hidden in whatever code the limbmonger hacked together to install the arm. It's a hybrid fever – digital and biological. His temperature is high; the terminals on his shoulder are tender to the touch. Every minute or two another earworm strikes, sometimes with fragments of visual overlay. There's an intermittent feelie, noisy and out of sync, which roils his face and abdomen, worsening the nausea. The light is hurting his eyes and he realizes that he's covered in dust. During the night someone or something has eaten part of his shelter. More than half the wall is gone, along with part of the dome. The dust is everywhere. God knows what it's brought in with it. He is lying exposed to the sky. Here and there insects and scavenger formations are at work, attacking the surface of his sleeping bag, carrying off his food. As he staggers around, trying to seal the breach, he notices a regimented swarm on his neighbour's roof, busily reinforcing its canopy. They are trailing a sac of raw material, much of which appears to be the same colour as his shelter's missing skin.

He feels too sick to do anything about it, too sick to go to work. The signal comes for a water delivery, but he's too weak to walk, let alone fight his way through the crowd at the airstrip. The virus proliferates, uses his body's strength to propagate itself. Ten copies, a thousand copies, a hundred million. It wants him to network, to find its next host, but he's too contagious; everyone and everything rejects him. Of course he used his last credit on the arm. He has no money for a doctor. At last he connects with a freeware triage, which tells him that he's in critical condition, and offers him treatments that cost more than he earns in a year. His firewall is crumbling. Offers run right through him, subprime bids for his organs, corporate indentures. *Your fatal condition cured in return for ten years' labour: new life just a click away.* The organ dealers say they replace whatever they take with high-grade implants, but everyone knows they put in trash.

Cursing the prosthetician's filthy operating bay, he falls deeper and deeper into trance.

He knows what is coming. Cold sweats and phantom synaesthetic pain. Soon, in an hour or two, he will experience massive central nervous system failure and then death. After that, rampant looting. Cannibal phages running over his skin, swarms taking whatever's left of his shelter and possessions. This is what the death of the poor looks like. Absolute annihilation. Tomorrow, no one will even remember he was here.

He drags himself to the door of his hut, to take a last look at the light. Overhead the plume swarms and wheels, eyes trained down on him. The dust begins to silt up against his side in a little dune. ■

Vijaykant Chauhan, Saharanpur, 2014
Courtesy of the author

LOVE JIHAD

Aman Sethi

Every few days, Vijaykant Chauhan WhatsApps me a photograph of himself. He appears on the screen of my phone as if dressed for battle. The photographs are invariably cramped scenes of crowds gathered along one of North India's anonymous street corners. Chauhan is right in front: a thickset, mustachioed man in his late thirties, clad in faux-army fatigues, a camouflage-print baseball cap and sunglasses.

He stands with his fists tightly bunched, arms upraised. Occasionally the police make an appearance – their faces creased by patient smiles, their hands held close to their chests, palms facing outwards, in gestures of pacification.

These are photographs of protests, celebrations, rallies and, most often, 'cultural programmes': neighbourhood events usually organized under the patronage of the local political representative to promote good values in society.

Onlookers peer out from the margins, their faces inscrutable amid all the posing and scuffling, shouting and jostling. In Punjab, a pink-cheeked boy, standing under a sign that reads SHOE STORE, stares at Chauhan astride a motorcycle festooned with the national flag and a garlanded plastic bust of pre-independence revolutionary Bhagat Singh. In Saharanpur, a young girl, dressed as Mother India in a tricolour sari and a paper crown, stands on a stage with her hand raised in benediction while Chauhan – down on one knee on a stage scattered with tricolour flags and sparkly confetti – aims a shotgun into the unseen audience. A bright pink party cracker peeks out from Chauhan's pocket, suggesting that this particular programme ends in a celebration of nationalist fervour and happy popping sounds.

Then, last week, I received a photograph of Chauhan posed beside a scooter laden with slabs of raw meat.

'What's up, Chauhan-ji?' I asked, when I called him up that afternoon. 'Why is a crowd gathered around a hunk of meat?'

'We found that meat secreted under the scooter's seat,' Chauhan said. 'Proof that cow flesh is still freely traded in these parts.'

Beef, Chauhan reminded me, was an affront to Hindus. 'Our strength, Aman-ji, comes from four pillars: our cows, our temples, our ancient culture and our girls. Anyone who attacks any one of these pillars should be put to death.'

I chanced upon Chauhan while on assignment for my newspaper, the *Business Standard*, in Saharanpur, a trading town in western Uttar Pradesh. In the summer of 2014, the Hindu nationalist Bharatiya Janata Party (BJP) and its controversial leader, Narendra Modi, had swept the general elections in a campaign that addressed the two presumed weaknesses of the ruling Indian National Congress – the faltering national economy, and the Congress's alleged appeasement of minorities in the garb of secularism.

All summer long, Modi had dismissed accusations of orchestrating a communal riot that left over a thousand dead in his home state of Gujarat in 2002. He said he was saddened by the loss of life in the manner of an occupant of a car involved in an accident. 'Someone else is driving a car and we're sitting behind,' he said. 'Even then if a puppy comes under the wheel, will it be painful or not? Of course it is.' He deflected attention away from the topic with rousing speeches about the need for jobs, progress and development. In the meantime, his lieutenants reached out to men like Chauhan to stage rallies, mobilize crowds and organize cultural events to consolidate the diverse Hindu spectrum against their Muslim neighbours.

If Uttar Pradesh were a country, it would be the fifth most populous in the world. China, India, the US, Indonesia and then Uttar Pradesh, on a par with Brazil and some way above Pakistan, Russia and Japan. More than 200 million people live here, a fifth of whom are Muslim. The rest are mostly Hindu, and divided broadly between three mutually antagonistic caste groups: the upper-caste Brahmins and Thakurs; the lower-caste Dalits; and the 'Other Backward Classes' like the Yadavs. While castes were once divided by hereditary occupations like priests, warriors, traders, animal herders and manual scavengers, years of lower-caste political mobilization and emancipation have blurred these hierarchies.

For the last two decades, Uttar Pradesh's regional parties have formed state governments by promising state patronage to unusual social coalitions. In 2007, the Dalit politician Mayawati struck an unlikely alliance of Brahmins, Dalits and Muslims to sweep the polls; in 2012, the rival Samajwadi Party forged an alliance of Yadavs and Muslims to oust Mayawati.

As a primarily upper-caste Hindu party, the BJP has historically struggled to build broad alliances in Uttar Pradesh, but in 2014 the party saw an opportunity. In 2013, another communal riot had caused an outbreak of violence throughout the region, and the ruling Samajwadi Party had failed to contain it. Most accounts suggest the state administration played one community against the other – leaving the Hindus alienated and the Muslims fearful.

A year later, with elections round the corner, Amit Shah – Modi's most trusted lieutenant – toured the riot-affected areas in the company of local BJP leaders accused of inciting rioters. Shah himself stands accused of ordering extrajudicial killings in his time as Home Minister of Gujarat. 'This is an election for honour and revenge,' he announced at one point of his whistle-stop campaign tour. 'A man can live without food or sleep . . . but when he is insulted, he cannot live. We have to take revenge for this insult.'

The strategy paid off; the BJP won seventy-one of eighty seats in Uttar Pradesh and 282 of 543 seats across the country. While the politicians were transparently opportunistic in their utterances and their aims, I was interested in the motivations of their followers. Who were these men? What were the lives they returned to when the elections ended?

'Cut my own throat if I'm lying, but I swear to you: around us, right now, all around us, are Hindu women held captive by Muslim husbands,' Vijaykant Chauhan said on our first meeting. 'Islamic terrorists are using the sacred land of Hindustan, the wealth of Hindustan and Hindustan's daughters to breed children who are sent to madrasas, trained in Pakistan and turned into more terrorists who want to destroy India.'

We had been discussing the Uttar Pradesh state elections scheduled for 2017. The BJP leadership had found a new issue to rally their Hindu voters. They called it Love Jihad.

'I coined the phrase. Everyone called me crazy,' Chauhan told me. 'Now they listen to me. I have it all on record. I estimate over 20,000 Hindu women are abducted by Muslims each year, but their parents are too frightened to tell anyone.'

Chauhan describes himself as a foot soldier in the battle to save Hinduism from its enemies. His job, broadly, is to 'spread awareness' of the evil designs of Hinduism's many enemies. He said he had no ties to any political party, but offered 'issue-based support' to formations that supported his causes. He said Love Jihad, or the practice of Muslims seducing Hindu girls with the aim of converting them to Islam, was an existential threat to India. 'They want to make us into a Muslim-majority nation.'

Three months after the general elections, the Rashtriya Swayamsevak Sangh (RSS), a right-wing organization with affiliations to BJP, put Love Jihad on the covers of *Organiser* and *Panchjanya*, their English and Hindi magazines. 'Love Jihad: Reality or Rhetoric?' the *Organiser* cover wondered; the article decided on the side of reality. *Panchjanya* went with a caricature of a clean-shaven man wearing a keffiyeh and sunglasses with red hearts stuck on the lenses: '*Pyaar andha ya dhanda?* (Is love blind, or a business?)'

'It's a big business, there are cash rewards.' Chauhan fiddled with his smartphone to pull up a pamphlet his friends had been WhatsApping each other. The image, purportedly made by unknown Muslim Love Jihadis, called on all followers to take Hindu wives.

'You are ordered and requested to bring more and more non-Muslim girls to our great faith ISLAM,' it read. 'Here is the cash reward list.'

I noted that the author had a particular taste for upper-caste Hindus: bagging a Gujarati Brahmin girl could win a lucky jihadi six lakh rupees, while a Buddhist girl was worth a mere 1.5 lakhs.

'We have not made it ourselves, if that is what you are implying,' Chauhan said, putting the phone away. 'I'll WhatsApp it to you and you can read it at your leisure.'

Vijaykant Chauhan was born to a family of Punjabi artisans who crossed over from Rawalpindi in Pakistan to settle in a refugee camp in Saharanpur. In Rawalpindi, his grandfather had made *ghungroo*, tiny metallic ankle bells worn by subcontinental dancers, and in Saharanpur, his father learned the craft and set up a small business.

In his telling, Chauhan's father was an impoverished and occasionally violent man, and so young Vijaykant spent a lot of time with his grandparents, particularly his maternal grandmother.

'My nani told me stories about the partition, and how entire neighbourhoods butchered each other. When the mob came for my nani, she squeezed herself under a pile of fresh corpses that lay in the local vegetable market. That is how she escaped.'

Vijaykant claims he was an extraordinary student – 'I was perfect' – but was forced out of school in grade seven on an administrative technicality.

'My parents tried to reason with the school, but what did they have? No connections, no money – and so my father put me to work at the shop.'

Vijaykant hated it. He escaped to religious functions organized by the RSS and joined the Bajrang Dal, a particularly violent RSS affiliate implicated in everything from attacking young unmarried couples for holding hands to organizing riots and building bombs.

The RSS and its many affiliates work on what a friend of mine once called the 'life insurance model': the RSS puts out a policy – it could be an agitation against cow slaughter, or the need for a new temple in the place of an old mosque – and leaves it to individual agents to take the initiative, spread the word and find followers who buy into the policy.

'I began my career as a particularly aggressive enforcer for the RSS,' Chauhan said. 'When the Bajrang Dal demanded that the markets close in solidarity with their causes, I made sure all shops downed their shutters immediately.' On the side, he did odd jobs; he worked briefly as an electrician and he helped out at his father's shop. Still, there was always a tiny voice that said, 'I don't have a school degree, my family has no resources, but God has made me for a special purpose.'

In 2004, that purpose was made manifest. Rashid Masood, an influential Muslim politician from Saharanpur, publicly declared that he would not say 'Vande Mataram', as saying a prayer to a deity like Bharat Mata was against his religion.

Chauhan was incensed. Bharat Mata, or Mother India, is the personification of the Indian nation as a female, sari-clad, Hindu deity. She made one of her earliest appearances in *Anandamath*, an 1882 novel by Bankimchandra Chattopadhyay, in which a group of Hindu sages rise up against Muslim overlords loyal to the British Empire.

Chauhan is obsessed with Bharat Mata – she is a frequent subject of his WhatsApp messages. 'Vande Mataram', or 'Hail Thee Mother', a poem from *Anandamath*, was a rallying cry for the independence movement and is accorded the status of India's 'national song', separate from the national anthem. Chauhan has 'Vande Mataram' tattooed on his chest, arms and back.

The morning after Masood's refusal, Chauhan launched Mission Vande Mataram – the aim of which was to get as many people to say 'Vande Mataram' as often as possible.

The following year, Chauhan organized a cultural programme to commemorate his Vande Mataram movement. When the programme sponsors pulled out at the last minute, he sold his house to pay for the arrangements.

'The programme was a super-duper success. We did a play about Bhagat Singh's sacrifices to the nation,' he said. 'Thousands of people came up to me to thank me for reminding them of their sacred duties as patriots. I asked myself, why do I need a house? Why do I need a job? All I need is two rotis a day, which God shall provide. I decided to devote myself to the nation.'

These days, Chauhan lives in a large open cow shelter in Saharanpur. He sleeps on a string cot and spends his time looking after stray cattle and fighting Love Jihad.

One day I visited Chauhan to watch him at work. The shelter is a large airy space with a temple at one end and a feeding pen at the other. A shipping container, sawn in half, serves as his living space, where, Chauhan said, a veterinary surgeon sometimes examines sick cows.

People dropped by in ones and twos; some brought fodder for the cows, and others put some money in the collection box. Reverentially they fed the assorted cows – healthy, injured and infirm – while their children gaped at two caged white rabbits. A middle-aged man walked up to Chauhan towing along a young girl dressed in a pink shalwar kameez. He shouted, 'Vande Mataram'; Chauhan replied in kind.

'She was standing around the market as if she was waiting for someone,' the man said, pointing to the nervous young girl. 'She won't tell me why she's out in the market on a Sunday afternoon.'

'Muslim boys keep buzzing up and down this street on their motorcycles, looking for precisely such girls,' Chauhan said. 'Hello,

hello, what's your name, girl? Does your father know you have come out to the market?'

The girl looked down at her feet.

'See, Aman-ji, she's clearly waiting for a Muslim. This town is full of girls who claim they are going to school, and then go off to service Muslim businessmen who give them money and drop them back in time to catch the school bus home.'

'But she hasn't said a word since you brought her here. How do you know?'

'I have studied this in great detail. Notice she can't look me in the eye. She's been brainwashed.'

Love Jihad made its first appearance in Uttar Pradesh in the 1920s. 'In June 1924, in Meerut, handbills and meetings claimed that various Hindu women were being lured and their pure bodies being violated by lustful and sexually charged Muslim men,' writes historian Charu Gupta in her article 'Hindu Women, Muslim Men: Love Jihad and Conversions', describing a time of intense communal tensions in pre-independence India. Since then, the idea has periodically regained currency when purveyors like Chauhan are granted a fleeting moment of relevance.

My conversations with Chauhan suggested that, for him, Love Jihad is a game of deception that had to be countered by the same coin. After all, why would a Hindu girl willingly fall in love with a Muslim? In the past, Chauhan has stormed district courts to prevent Hindu girls from marrying their Muslim fiancés. In one instance, he claimed he was already married to the girl and produced false papers to stake his claim. 'It is true the papers were false, but the scriptures allow the righteous to adopt falsehood to do good.'

Most Muslim Love Jihadis, Chauhan insisted, disguise themselves as Hindus. A pamphlet doing the rounds in Saharanpur offers an insight into their methods: when girls go to recharge the talk time on their mobile phones, some stores pass on their numbers to Love Jihadis who seduce them via text messages.

If that doesn't work, the Jihadis pose as electricians, auto mechanics and vegetable vendors to gain access to middle-class Hindu homes and seduce their daughters.

The young girl before us at the cow shelter didn't seem brainwashed; she just looked very scared.

'Let's drop her home,' Chauhan said. 'Come along.'

We piled into a battered Hyundai piloted by one of his friends. 'Me? I'm a farmer; actually I'm a farmer turned businessman. Make that a farmer turned real estate agent,' said the driver when I asked him what he did for a living. 'But most importantly, I am a Hindu. I am an admirer of Vijaykant-ji and support him whenever I can.'

The ride takes about fifteen minutes. The girl sits silently in the back seat, occasionally giving directions. We turn into an alley and stop before a woman sleeping in the doorway of a brick hut.

'This your daughter?' Chauhan asked, awakening the woman. 'Do you know where she was? She was waiting for her Muslim boyfriend.'

'I have a fever,' the woman replied.

'I will return in the evening to speak with her father.'

The girl ran to her mother; we got into the car and drove off. As we made our way back to the city I asked Chauhan if he wanted to enter mainstream politics.

'It's not possible,' he said. 'You need money, you need connections. I don't even have a house any more. But I live on the love and support of the people. I am happy.'

Does he wish his life had panned out differently?

'When I was younger, I thought: If I hadn't been thrown out of school I could have become a police officer, or joined the army, or risen to a position where I could serve my people better. But now I feel that God has always had a plan for me; he wants me to fulfil a special purpose.'

'The problem with Chauhan is that he will go back in the evening and speak with the girl's father. And who knows what he will say,' remarked Shandar Ghufran, pulling on a cigarette. Ghufran, a boyish forty-year-old schoolteacher and political activist, has been monitoring the communal polarization in western Uttar Pradesh for some time now. 'This Love Jihad idea has ruptured what remains of Uttar Pradesh's social fabric.'

Across the country, the campaign has imbued all contact between the two communities with the possibility of tragic consequences. In Meerut, for instance, the police had to be called in to confront a mob of right-wing Hindus when a fifteen-year-old Muslim boy had run away with his fourteen-year-old Hindu classmate.

The two children were found in Jaipur, en route to Mumbai to become Bollywood singers. The boy, the son of a carpenter, told his friend of his plan to make it big in Mumbai, and she decided to go along with him. By the time the police brought them home, two Muslim-owned shops had been vandalized and a Muslim home was attacked. In Bhopal, in Madhya Pradesh, a Hindu woman insisted that the state's women's commission order a medical examination of her Hindu husband to ensure the foreskin of his penis was intact, when she learned that he had a Muslim lover.

Such incidents, Ghufran said, will continue until the 2017 state elections. Each party will consolidate its base at the cost of the others, ratcheting up the tension in a region primed for conflict. 'Things appear peaceful, but I fear that any single incident could trigger a riot,' he said. 'There is, of course, a history to this.'

In August 2013, three young men – one Muslim and two Hindus – were killed in the course of an altercation in Kawal, a village on the outskirts of Muzaffarnagar. Some say the Hindu boys killed the Muslim in an argument that began as a traffic accident, and others say the argument began over the harassment of a Hindu girl, but all agree that the incident came at a time of rising communal tension.

In the weeks that followed, both the BJP and the Samajwadi Party, then Uttar Pradesh's ruling party, did their best to keep tensions alive by sending their representatives to deliver inflammatory speeches before angry crowds. In the course of the riots that swept the western Uttar Pradesh countryside through the end of September, at least sixty-two people had died, several women were raped and over

50,000 mostly Muslim villagers were displaced from their homes.

A year later, the riot relief camps still dot the villages around Muzaffarnagar.

'We left our village the moment we heard news that a riot had broken out. That was the mistake we made,' recounted Mohammed Aslam, as he sat hunched on a string cot beside a torn tent. 'We should have waited for someone to get killed first.'

The government, Aslam said, does not consider his village to be riot-affected and hence he is ineligible for the riot compensation of 500,000 rupees (five lakhs, about £5,000) per family.

Thus far, 768 families have been granted compensation as per state records, and the Supreme Court has ordered the state government to compensate another 203 people. Yet, the administration is in a bind: they need a framework to distribute the compensation, failing which they could be accused of distributing state money in return for political support. In a state as poor as Uttar Pradesh, living in the putrid environs of a riot relief camp is not sufficient grounds for state-sanctioned relief.

Most of those who received support have sold their homes in their villages and have purchased lands in Muslim-majority settlements. The countryside is slowly reordering itself into Hindu- and Muslim-dominated pockets. Those with nothing are stranded where they stopped running.

Before the riots, Aslam said, he sold plastic crockery from the back of his bicycle. In the late 1980s, his father had gone to Saudi Arabia to work as a labourer and had returned with enough money to build a house, a portion of which was inherited by Aslam.

Four years ago, the household was hit by crisis: two of his daughters, aged seven and four, fell sick when they drank contaminated water from a village drain. Aslam sold his house to pay for their treatment, but both girls died within hours of each other. After that, the family was kept afloat by a monthly loan from a Hindu neighbour, paid back at 5 per cent a month or 60 per cent a year. When the riots rippled through western Uttar Pradesh, Aslam and his family fled to this camp, leaving behind a trail of possessions and IOUs. It's been a year since Aslam worked, let alone considered paying his dues.

'I'm too scared to go back home and I have no money to buy a house anywhere else,' said Aslam. 'I really don't know what to do.'

The retired schoolmaster sat with his head propped up on his palms, his elbows balanced on his knees, his radio by his side. 'It's a year today, isn't it?' he said. 'No one has returned.'

We sat on plastic chairs in his tiny yard at the edge of the Hindu quarter in Lissad, a village in Muzaffarnagar district, and looked out at the abandoned homes around us. At least thirteen Muslims were killed here and several homes torched in the course of the 2013 riots.

'This was once a very busy neighbourhood,' he said. 'That building over there, that was my son's school. He is Hindu, but all his students were Muslims. It's shut now. There are no Muslims in this village.'

'Why haven't they returned?' I asked.

'I don't know, things have changed, I suppose, times have changed,' he replied, as a young man in a tracksuit came to sit beside us. 'I hear some people from the village went to call the Muslims back, but they refused to return.'

Did he miss them?

'What is there to miss?' asked the young man. 'They kept to themselves, we kept to ourselves.'

'You lived together for many years before the riot,' I said. 'What changed?'

The old man stayed silent – I sensed there was something he wanted to say, an explanation he wanted to offer. Perhaps he too was trying to understand why his village had suddenly turned on its neighbours, or how a schoolteacher and his students could be pulled into opposing camps.

'I don't know,' he said, turning his back to me. 'My heart doesn't accept it.'

His young companion looked up. 'Ask the Muslims what changed. We are still here.'

I left the old man to his radio and walked down into the abandoned settlement. The homes had been stripped clean, doors ripped off their frameworks, cupboards broken open. The roofs had caved in in many places, but the walls were mostly intact; some bore telltale signs of fire.

Down an alley of broken homes, I spotted a group of four young Hindu men. 'Come sit, sit, sit,' said one, as he cleaned out a stalk of marijuana and mixed it with tobacco. 'Do you work for a television channel?'

'A newspaper. And what do you do?'

'We?' he said. 'We get high.'

So here's the real issue, they said, between bouts of hysterical laughter. 'Think about it, here we all are, sitting around. And them? They've got five lakhs compensation per house. Do any of these homes look like they are worth five lakhs?'

'Some families? They claimed their sons were living separately. Five sons, twenty-five lakhs.'

'They could buy themselves a BMW with that money.' More laughter.

'An Audi,' suggested the plump young man who said he worked as a hardware technician in Gurgaon, a suburb in Delhi's outskirts.

'They've given our names to the police, though,' said another, a well-built boy in a striped shirt. 'I knew the Muslim boy who did it. I said why have you put my name on the list of rioters? I paid him thirty thousand rupees to strike my name off the report. He said the cops took twenty thousand to do it.'

'My name is still in the police files,' said a third young man whose thick spectacles magnified his slightly dilated pupils. 'The cops asked for a lakh to strike my name. I don't have a lakh, but it doesn't matter.'

'It doesn't matter for him, because he's not applying for a government job, you know,' said the last, a boy who looked about nineteen. 'We all want government jobs. You can't get a government job if you have a pending case. He hasn't gone to college. But wait, you came first in school, didn't you?'

'Yes.' The boy with the spectacles frowned. 'Yes, you could say that.'

The afternoon sun dipped and a mild, early-evening melancholia set in. I sat with them for a while, listening as they ribbed each other, but the fun seemed to have slipped away with the sunshine and everyone seemed preoccupied by the thought of going home to face their parents.

As I got up to leave, the boy with the spectacles spoke up. 'I knew those boys, we played together. But they've gotten out. They've got five lakhs to move to the city, start a business or a shop or something. We are still stuck in this village.'

For years, the Muslim film-maker nursed the possibility that he would – one day – marry his Hindu girlfriend. We met at a dinner organized by a friend in Muzaffarnagar. When I mentioned my work, he called me over for tea the next day. Our conversation about Love Jihad and the repercussions of the Muzaffarnagar riots had prompted a recollection of love and riots at another time and place.

'I saw her on a train,' he recalled, when we met in his studio. 'She was travelling from Dehradun to Ahmedabad, where she lived, while I was going to Mumbai to try to break into the film industry.'

She gave him her phone number, and asked for his.

'But I didn't have a number,' he said. 'I was living out of a cheap hotel room in Mumbai's red-light district.'

So he decided he would visit Ahmedabad every few weeks to see her.

'I would take the overnight train and wait for her at the temple outside her office. She would sneak out at lunchtime, and then again for a few hours after work.'

They'd talk till she left for home and he'd take the train back to Mumbai and wait for the next time they would meet. But when her sister found out about the romance, she wasn't pleased. Loving a Muslim, the sister said, was a path to schizophrenia.

'Their mother had schizophrenia – so her sister's remarks hit home. The logic was that marrying someone outside the Hindu fold would cause some sort of psychic schism.'

The pressure from her family grew, and his trips to see her became less frequent. In February 2002, a train carrying Hindu pilgrims from Uttar Pradesh to Gujarat was set alight, killing fifty-nine people. More than a thousand people, most of whom were Muslim, were killed in the riots that ensued.

'She said it was too dangerous for me to come to Ahmedabad after the riots,' the film-maker said. He took off his spectacles and wiped his eyes. We both sipped our tea. 'We continued to meet, but it wasn't the same.

'She called me after her wedding. Asked me how I was. I said, "Please don't call me. Don't send me news. If you are sad, I shall be sad. If you are happy, I shall still be sad."'

It's been five years since he moved back to Muzaffarnagar. He's married as well now. He loves his wife and his young daughter. Sometimes he is tempted to look back at the whole episode as a shared, youthful folly.

'But it was love,' he said. 'For what it was, for as long as it lasted, it was love.'

I once asked Vijaykant Chauhan if he thought it was possible for a Hindu and a Muslim, with complete knowledge of each other's beliefs, to be in love. My fear, I told him, was that his campaign was fostering suspicion and fear rather than amity and understanding.

'We are not against love, Aman-ji. We are against deception and forcible conversion,' he said. He referred to Muslim Bollywood superstars with Hindu wives. 'In most cases, the women are brainwashed and converted. Like Indira Gandhi.'

'Indira Gandhi?'

'Yes, she was married to Feroze Gandhi – but he was actually Feroze Khan, a Muslim. She was the first victim of Love Jihad.'

'But Feroze Gandhi was Parsi.'

'That's what you think, Aman-ji, that's just what you think. Everyone knows Feroze Gandhi Khan was a Muslim. It's all over the Internet.' ■

Greater Noida, 2014

A DOUBLE-INCOME FAMILY

Deepti Kapoor

Mrs Mehra found Raju through her old friend Mrs Sethi, who herself found him through her own domestic, Sandesh. Raju and Sandesh were from the same terminal village in eastern Uttar Pradesh, and may even have been cousins, though the truth of this is hard to know.

While Mrs Sethi changed her domestic staff often, which is to say that they often left her, often without warning – abruptly, for a cremation or a puja, the same way a husband might leave for a pack of cigarettes – the widow Mrs Mehra was a steadier sort, by nature kind, patient and, above all else, acutely sensitive to the injustices suffered by those less fortunate than she, so much so that Mrs Sethi often predicted the calamities that would befall her, and chided her friend for her laissez-faire attitude towards the help. 'The problem with these people,' she explained one afternoon, high-jumping her eyeballs towards Sandesh while presiding over his table placement retraining, 'is that they just don't appreciate kindness the same way as you or I. Their needs are simpler. Showing kindness is a sign of weakness to them. It's like training a dog. One has to be the master. Don't give them a chance. And don't spare the rod!'

Yet the aforementioned attributes were precisely those that had seen Mrs Mehra retain the services of her previous domestic, Devi, for a full thirteen years. Strong of tattooed forearm and paan-stained of mouth, she had been Mrs Mehra's confidante, bodyguard and pet project for longer than either cared to remember, and it was only the unfortunate circumstance of Mrs Mehra's moving – from south Delhi to one of the vast new satellite townships on the eastern fringes of the metropolis – that had led to their parting at all. Devi, who had four hungry children and an alcoholic husband to support, and whose husband in turn had a second family supported by the weekly misappropriation of Devi's wages, couldn't very well move out with Mrs Mehra, or travel so far each day; such a change to her delicately balanced life (her twenty-four-year-old auto-driver lover was also a factor) would surely send it spiralling out of control. So they said their tearful goodbyes and Devi found herself another employer right away.

It was the death of Mr Mehra that had precipitated the move. He had suffered a heart attack at sixty-four. Afterwards, Mrs Mehra simply couldn't continue in the same apartment: even with exposure to Devi's salty and radioactive chatter, there were just too many memories for her to remain energized in that place. Mrs Mehra's daughter, Aarti, who was married to a dentist in the US and only visited once a year (if that), agreed it was the right thing to do, especially when she heard the figures involved.

It came to pass, then, that Mrs Mehra sold her drab Saket flat for sixteen times its original value, and, with the help of Mr Sethi, used one-eighth of the profits to buy a luxury fourteenth-floor 'Executive Apartment' in Arcadia Mansions Heaven, a highly desirable gated township tiptoeing into the dead sea of Greater Noida.

Only by soaring early one morning through the soft-focus pollution could one appreciate the true scale of this land: hundreds of faceless townships rising up as far as the eye could see, like a fleet of cruise liners run aground, creating a frontier territory both ancient and sickeningly new. Outside each highly secured razor-wire fence, the desiccated ex-farmland wore a dull red hue, dissected by the veins of new tarmac roads, where nothing strayed except water buffalo and wild dogs, and bandits who loitered around the underpasses at night, hoping to divorce returning wedding parties from their gold. Yet within the dewy confines, pert lawns sat pristine, consorting with tennis courts and swimming pools, amid rows and rows of parking bays hosting gleaming new cars, all guarded by black-clad private security officers, drilled into duty with corporate zeal.

As reassuring as this was, Mrs Mehra knew she must secure the services of a live-in domestic asap. So it was with great relief that she received Mrs Sethi's call informing her that Sandesh knew of someone appropriate (Mrs Mehra had stressed they must be over eighteen, since those pesky NGOs had been cracking down on such things). Though he was currently employed in the kitchen of a South Indian restaurant in west Delhi, he was actively seeking a less heated engagement. The only misgiving, that of keeping a man in the house alone with her at night, was allayed at the first sight of Raju, for he barely touched five feet in height and had the most disarming and boyish expression, decorated with goofy teeth and credulous eyes that popped out of his head when his enthusiasm got the better of him.

For two whole years their arrangement went off without a hitch. As the surrounding land slowly filled with construction sites promising a computer-generated, fair-skinned future of malls, a darker, jury-rigged sub-economy of servants, labourers and service providers popped up as a place card.

Clown prince of this territory, Raju became invaluable to Mrs Mehra, so much so that Mrs Mehra, or '*behenji*' as he always called her, began to see him as, well . . . if not exactly family, then as someone she felt a steady affection and responsibility for. She went out of her way to educate him, tried to teach him English as best she could (he was unteachable), clothed him, gently taught him the finer points of personal hygiene, bought him a cheap smartphone so he could remain in contact at all times and generally made sure his health was at its peak. When her own health occasionally failed, he looked after her with tenderness and unflinching devotion, and, for the rest of the time, was the model of decorum and productivity, performing twice as many household duties as Devi ever did, with three times the speed. Moreover, as she informed her daughter during their weekly Skype conversations, besides a hand that was a touch heavy with the salt, his cooking skills were unimpeachable. When it was Mrs Mehra's turn to host the bimonthly kitty party in the tower – for she had, by now, many casual friends – she was praised to the heavens for the excellence of her menu, and when this was passed on to Raju, his chest puffed up like a little robin, so that he went to bed in his cupboard of a room with a surfeit of pride.

And what of his inner world? Well, in his scant leisure time he wandered the pathways of the campus, gazing at the greenness of the lawns and shaking his head in disbelief at the garbage bins shaped like giant frogs, whose mouths gaped as wide as his at the absurdity of it all. He became civic-minded for the sole purpose of watching his used tissues – which Mrs Mehra has pressed upon him for hygiene's sake – fly inside, before sitting on his favourite bench to watch a game of tennis, perpetually confused by the simple complexity, with no small amount of envy for the starched white clothing the players wore. Once or twice it occurred to him that he'd died and been reborn, so different was this world to the village he ran away from at fourteen with nothing but fifty rupees in his pocket. Those had been hard days, sleeping on the floor at the train station, working at chai stalls and cleaning buses, before he found his way into that first kitchen and discovered his talent. Yes, it was a paradisiacal world for him. He stood up at the end of his break and sighed contentedly, and walking past the landscaped pool that was guarded ferociously from the likes of him, he imagined jumping in. One day he confided this last little secret desire to Mrs Mehra, just as he had begun to confide other secrets and pieces of gossip, and to his tearful astonishment she arranged with the warden of her block (who had a religious fondness for widows) for Raju to splash around in the children's pool one quiet summer afternoon so long as she held onto him from the edges to make sure he didn't drown. For that alone, he was her eternal slave.

But late in the second year everything changed. One day he grew quiet and withdrawn. It was clear to Mrs Mehra that something was troubling him but, unlike before, he refused to confide in her, and it took a whole week of gentle cajoling, alongside a mistaken deduction that his haemorrhoids had returned, before she managed to divine the true nature of his discontent: his mother, who had hitherto barely received a mention, had now found him a bride. He was expected to marry in November, only two months away.

Mrs Mehra shared Raju's turmoil like a tiramisu, two spoons for the same bowl. The smooth road ahead now contained as many potholes as the real ones outside. She could see it: marriage, then kids conceived on the wedding night (it was a truth universally acknowledged that villagers were exceptionally fertile), his mind wandering, a family to support, attention divided. It would be a disaster. She called Mrs Sethi later that day to be condoled, and the woman was suitably anguished. She reminded Mrs Mehra about the fate of Sandesh, who had been married a year back against her will. She had provided him with both condoms and the contraceptive pill before the wedding night, and to her continued revulsion sternly demonstrated application of the former with the aid of a cucumber, but to no avail. Sandesh and his new wife agreed that the pill was most likely poison, while the condom defeated the point of everything. When she gave birth to the first son nine months later, Sandesh moved out of the servants' quarters (whose dimensions had been significantly reduced on account of a kitchen extension) to a rented room nearby, and only worked thirteen-hour days thereon. 'It was a disaster,' Mrs Sethi concluded. 'I would have been better off hiring a eunuch.'

For his part, Raju had no desire to marry. He liked his bachelor life, enjoyed his work, and his innate need for companionship was satisfied by the combination of Mrs Mehra and Dilip, a Bihari servant of similar age who worked in one of the adjacent towers, and whom he'd become friendly with during his bench-sitting days. If one were to steal a glance at his smartphone, as Mrs Mehra once did, this voyeur would find a photo library full to bursting with much-prized selfies showing Dilip and Raju reclining hand in hand on the grass, or posing shirtless with each other in their respective quarters.

No, marriage was the last thing on Raju's mind, but marry he would, for though he had previously severed almost all ties, he could not oppose his mother on this matter. A brief word about his mother: she was also a widow. Raju's father, whom he had no memory of, died in a traffic accident of his own creation while blind drunk in the road in 1994. Raju's mother, an angular, formidable woman who ruled her family with a clenched jaw, was driven by a great fear of the world and a need to survive. She had two other sons who were layabouts, who lifted not a single finger in house or field, but rather than chastise them for this, she encouraged their behaviour wholesale, seeing it as their natural masculine right. In fact, she looked on Raju's own work ethic and strange urban ways as suspect, effeminate even, and poured scorn on him even as he supported the family financially, supplementing her meagre farming income with his own superior wage.

All these swirling factors came together in the choosing of a bride, for once secured in marriage, Raju would be retied to village and family, and never drift off into the great immoral night of the city, while the arrival of a bride in the village house would cut his mother's workload considerably, and her remaining sons would have a servant of their own. The canny woman could see no downside.

Mrs Mehra discussed the situation in great detail with her daughter, now preferring to bend this more enlightened ear rather than the gnarled one of Mrs Sethi. Her daughter commiserated, but insisted there was nothing to be done. To oppose it would be to invite further problems, and perhaps resentment. Her mother should support Raju as much as she could, and 'keep him close by letting him go', words of wisdom she had recently read in a self-help book entitled *At the Heart of Do, Is You*. It was agreed then: Mrs Mehra would assist Raju all she could. So when he came asking for a loan to pay for the wedding itself – for the entire village needed to be fed and goats had to be slaughtered – she went into her Godrej cupboard and pulled out a stack of rupee notes the likes of which Raju had never seen. He would pay it off out of his wages, she said solemnly, remembering with some shame the stack, five hundred times the size, which had been spent on her own child's wedding nine years previously.

The wedding came. Raju left for the village. It was agreed he would be away for eight days. Mrs Mehra spent those eight days in monastic penitence, running over her life with Raju, her life before, that of her daughter, remembering her husband too. As those eight days progressed, she seemed to briefly wake from the slumber she only then realized she was in, enjoyed the silence, enjoyed preparing her own food, making her own tea, so that on the ninth day she waited with some apprehension for Raju to return, thinking how his presence would shatter her new-found equanimity. On the tenth day she woke up with some mild discomfort at having to prepare her own tea, instead of having it delivered to her door. On the eleventh, when the groceries in the fridge ran out, she became a little agitated, and called Raju on the phone, but the phone rang off. On the twelfth day he called himself, and said he was delayed: he was trying to get the train and would be there in two days. Still fearful of Mrs Sethi, Mrs Mehra called her daughter to complain. 'Ma, he's getting married,' Aarti said. 'You know how it is. Let him be. He's just had sex for the first time. He's firing bullets into the headboard!'

'Aarti!' her mother exclaimed. But secretly she remembered her own wedding night, and she was pleased.

Raju returned on the fifteenth day. With renewed vigour, he worked to produce a small feast of masala dosa and idli sambhar. The wedding had been a great success, eight goats had been slaughtered and the bride was not unappealing at all. He produced his phone to show Mrs Mehra her photo, and Mrs Mehra was horrified to see a child's face looking back at her. 'But how old is she?' she nervously exclaimed, and Raju, his grin falling when he saw the look on her

face, ummed and ahhed and replied rather evasively that he was
certain she'd just turned seventeen.

A married man, Raju now spent much of his free time circling
the complex, glued to his phone. It wasn't his wife he was in
dialogue with but his mother, who regularly called to harangue
her useless son about the latest misdeeds of his teenage bride. For
rather than the compliant young thing they thought they'd receive,
the child – formerly known as Preeti, but newly christened Rani to
complement her husband's name – had already caused mayhem in
the family home. Refusing to cook, refusing to clean, sulking in a
corner, crying all night, more stubborn than their own decrepit mule.
Raju's mother had taken to beating Rani with a stick in order to make
her work, and on the occasion the stick did not work she used the
carrot named Raju, ordering him to speak to her as a man, thrusting
the phone under Rani's nose while telling her to obey her husband
or else. Once on the phone she would run into the cane fields and
cry and implore Raju to bring her to the city, to save her from this
domestic servitude, for she hated it more than anything in the world,
and would surely suicide soon.

Raju was caught in an impossible situation, stuck between his
mother, whose breast he had suckled from birth, and his wife, whose
breast he had suckled far more recently. On one hand, he knew his
bachelor days were over, and he thought to himself what a delight
it would be to have her with him every day, how her body gave fire
to his heart and soiled his loin. He was greatly moved by her cries
of distress, which were peppered with tender and loving words. His
wife, he thought. His *life*. No life without wife.

Then he thought of his mother. The sacrifices she had made,
the hard work of her entire life. To rob his mother of her recent
peace, knowing how much she had slaved in the fields – this also
broke his sensitive heart. He forgot all her miserable words. He only
remembered that she was his mother. How could he do this to her?

He turned to *behenji* for advice. He disclosed all the dramas, the ins and outs, and she listened patiently and attentively until it came to the question: Should I bring her here?

I told you so, I told you so, I told you so. This is what Mrs Sethi said. "This is the end for you. Look for a new boy immediately; find a local woman, not a girl, someone old, though they're all devious in their own way.' Mrs Mehra mulled this over, then called her daughter for another perspective.

Aarti ate granola at the breakfast bar and listened with great interest as her mother explained the situation. Rani, she disclosed, was completely uneducated. She had not a day of schooling in her life. 'How can this be?' her daughter asked. Mrs Mehra replied that none of the girls went to school any more because of an incident two years previously when one of their number had fallen in love with a local boy, and together they had eloped to Kolkata. This was an affront to the honour of the village, and naturally education was to blame. So from that day forward it was agreed that no more girls should be educated there.

"That's outrageous,' her daughter said. 'Someone should report them to the police.'

To which Mrs Mehra informed her daughter that several of them *were* the police.

'What country do we live in?' Aarti went on, with the tacit understanding that her house, looking out on the Pacific, was Indian soil. 'Something must be done!'

'But I can't bring her here to live with me.'

'Think of yourself as a Good Samaritan. Think how grateful this girl will be.'

Her mother wavered for a moment, before saying: 'No, it's too much stress.'

And that was that.

Just three days after this verdict, Rani broke her hand. Mystery surrounds the exact circumstances; to this day no one knows what happened aside from those involved, and who they are is itself a mystery. It is enough to say that from this day on Rani could no longer work in the field nor tend to the home. To make quite certain of this fact she went on hunger strike as well, and stood bolt upright like a holy man in the middle of the field, refusing to eat or drink all day long. In the end she had to be dragged back into the family home, tied and beaten, but still she would not break. Upon hearing this (for his mother proudly relayed the sequence of events over the phone) Raju went back to the village – with Mrs Mehra handing out his travel money, adding it to the loan. When he arrived the afternoon of the next day, to the satisfaction of all present, he barged straight into the home and beat her with a stick himself.

And then he wept. He wept over her bruised flesh and fell down in front of her, held her and sobbed and begged to be forgiven, swearing never to let his family hurt her again. His mother looked on in disgust, and Rani never once said a word. Raju called Mrs Mehra that night and told her what had happened, saying that he wanted to bring his wife home.

Mrs Mehra spoke to her daughter, and her daughter became greatly excited. She said: 'Think about it, you can save her. One life that can be saved. We can educate her, find her work. She'll be in heaven.'

'They'll become a double-income family,' Mrs Mehra muttered to herself as a growing revelation.

'Yes! That's right. They'll be a double-income family. And when they have kids of their own we'll make sure they go to a real school and have the kind of future their parents could never dream of. This is the new India. You'll be the heroine of the piece.'

Six weeks then passed.
Six whole weeks since that fateful day.

It was full winter, deathly cold. Outside, the smog obscured the distant city in a sulphurous fug, turning the nearby buildings and construction sites into lighthouses and ghostly ships. The horn from a careening truck bounced between the tower blocks before drifting off despondently into the night's chemical haze.

Mrs Mehra was exhausted. She had lost a good deal of weight, and was certain that beneath the mask of henna, her greying hair had now turned full white. She sat down at the living-room table and switched on the laptop and, while she waited for it to load (for it was a very old laptop), poured out her nightly glass of orange juice, newly fortified with gin.

'She doesn't eat,' she said to the computer screen, exasperated, anguished, shaking her head. 'She doesn't speak, she doesn't utter a single word. She won't look me in the eye.'

The computer finally loaded.

'I try to talk to her and she buries her face behind her shawl. Is she laughing at me?'

She rattled the ice in the glass for succour, and connected to Skype.

'Do you think she might be, you know, retarded?' Aarti asked, upon hearing the update. They had been talking the matter over endlessly these last weeks, and a special bond had developed between them. The Californian sunshine backlit the breakfast bar beautifully.

'I don't know,' Mrs Mehra said with sagging shoulders.

Her face seemed to lurch out of the gloom like one of those deep-sea fish that carried its own light.

'Ma, sit back from the screen! Put on some lights! And for God's sake stop drinking so much orange juice. Anyone would think you had scurvy.'

Mrs Mehra ignored her daughter and continued, as if to herself: 'It's so hard to know with this girl.'

And it was; it was as hard for Mrs Mehra to gauge the child's mental acuity as it was to guess her real age.

'It's the malnutrition, obviously,' her daughter said. She was having blueberry pancakes for breakfast. 'It's stunted all her growth and her brains. But give it time, that's all she needs, time and a little TLC. There's a lotus in there waiting to bloom, I can feel it. One day she'll surprise us all.'

On the train to Delhi all those weeks ago, Rani had sat with her knees to her chest, watching in disbelief at the world as it refused to stop unfolding. Despite the presence of several undesirables, she'd fought her way to the window seat, dragging Raju in her wake; now he sat grinning like an idiot in his ill-fitting shirt and trousers while the rest of the men fixed their eyes on the young bride with the grubby bandage on her hand, who was otherwise resplendent in a bright red shalwar kameez, topped off with a cheap wool sweater Raju had hastily bought for her at the market outside the station. Her feathered forearms were chattelled with bangles, and a bright red sindoor marked the parting in her hair. When she'd applied it that morning it was not with drudgery but joy, and for the first time in a long time she'd thought of her wedding night. Later, her good hand crept along the bench to her husband's own, to the twitchy delight of the ever-observant crowd.

She had few belongings, but Raju dutifully carried each from one train to the next, to the bus and along the final two-mile walk. He watched her face always; it was the only thing he saw: as they had entered Delhi, he'd noticed how it had fallen and she'd turned mute and seemed to recoil in every direction. He knew these feelings. He recalled his own terror-stricken entry into the city eight years before, and allowed himself a private smile, for now he had it all.

But in the intervening six weeks chaos swept through the household. It was true: Rani barely spoke to Mrs Mehra; she hardly ate either, and although the widow's heart melted when the child first walked through the door – the urge to give her a hug checked only by Rani covering her face with her hands as the woman approached – misgivings soon began to arise. For a start the girl just would not come out of her room. Then on the few occasions that she did, in order to enter the kitchen, which had a separate doorway from the servants' room, Mrs Mehra could have sworn she heard giggling and cheerful talk, but when she hurried in to try and engage the girl herself, nothing but a dumbstruck silence was returned.

It was tolerated as culture shock to begin with. Even so, Mrs Mehra grew increasingly frustrated at her young charge, grumbling under her breath as she dusted her vases, muttering about opportunities squandered and generosity wasted. Did Rani not understand the sacrifices her benefactress was making? Did she not see how lucky she was to have landed so squarely on her feet? A million girls would have killed one another for this place. And here she was, being difficult!

Rani wasn't the only cause for concern, for Raju was slipping himself, his chores neglected, his food haphazardly prepared, his free salt hand dynamic as a conductor's, one meal sodium-rich, the next with no seasoning at all. 'She has him right where she wants him,' Mrs Mehra said to herself one day, and was surprised to hear Mrs Sethi in her tone.

Things went really downhill about a month after Rani's arrival when a neighbour stopped by for tea. While Mrs Mehra ducked into the bathroom for her ablutions, the visitor poked her head into the kitchen to find the honeymooners in full view, kissing over a sizzling pilau. She chastised them both herself right there and then, and later warned Mrs Mehra that, though she would keep the incident to herself for now, this kind of behaviour was not conducive to a well-run house.

'Ah, but it's good if she has a little spunk in her,' Aarti said that evening, pooh-poohing the controversy. 'Better that than a prude. Just ignore these women.'

But her mother wasn't so sure. So as she rooted through the cupboard for the duty-free gin her son-in-law had gifted her the year before, faintly hearing the hubbub of Raju's old TV set through the wall, she decided that since Rani's hand had healed, she would send her out into the world.

The bright idea was to pair the child, like wine to cheese, with Mrs Pronoti Das, a twenty-eight-year-old homemaker with creative tendencies and a husband in marketing, the thinking being that an enlightened Bengali household such as hers would be the most perfect finishing school of all. Pronoti herself had welcomed the extra pair of hands, since her domestic had left for her brother's funeral only two days prior and wouldn't return for another six. Pron remarked with a hip giggle how she and her new charge must have been fated for each other – and could even have been sisters in another world. She would supervise Rani in the dusting, the mopping of the floor, the washing, ironing and folding of clothes, the washing of dishes and the preparation of food, all spread into segments and laid out on an Excel spreadsheet for the coming week.

Rani lasted less than two days. Mrs Das, whom Mrs Mehra had never seen so harried, turned up at 5 p.m. on the second, just as the elder woman was pouring her juice, to deposit the girl back from where she came.

'She's impossible!' Pronoti cried. 'Auntie, with respect, you should have warned me. I've never met anyone so stubborn in my life. I don't know what to do with her. I certainly can't have her in my house.'

With that she gave the sullen girl a final dark look, turned on her kitten heels and marched towards the lift. By the time Mrs Mehra had processed the turn of events, Rani was safely back in her room.

It started to give the woman sleepless nights. She lay awake now wondering what she had done to deserve this fate, what great sin had been committed in a previous life. Between Mrs Das and Mrs Aggarwal, the scandalized neighbour, it was only a matter of time before her own name would fall into disrepute. But what could be done about this diabolical girl? She entertained fantasies of chance and coincidence that would magically put an end to things, and (though she would not remember it) in her darkest moments, when her gin-addled brain was sinking into the nothingness of sleep, she recalled a rumour from six months ago about a servant who had 'accidentally' fallen from a twelfth-floor balcony.

Unbeknown to Mrs Mehra, Raju was also lying awake at night, for Rani's demands were leaving his tiny body the worse for wear. Not only that: he was becoming sensible to the pain the current situation was inducing in both mothers of his life. Through the gap in the kitchen door, he had lately taken to spying on Mrs Mehra as she fretfully circled the liquor cabinet, while on his evening errands he endured his mother's pitiful overtures, feeling such pangs of guilt at depriving her of a stable workforce that he wished he could turn into a plastic frog and be done with it once and for all.

The final straw came in early December, when Raju asked for a day's leave so he could go into the market town nearby to purchase Rani a wardrobe of winter clothes. His request, so sheepish it was barely a bleat, was met with defeated acquiescence on Mrs Mehra's part, on the condition that if he must go, his wife should at least complete his own basic chores. Ever the optimist, Raju perked up at this, thinking it the perfect opportunity to end the cold war. 'This is your chance,' he implored his wife, as she cat-stretched on the bed. 'Do it for me.' She smiled enigmatically, and promptly fell back to sleep as he walked out the door.

Raju returned that evening to a scene from a war. There were plates and glasses smashed in the living room, chairs upturned, laundry scattered over the kitchen floor. From the servants' room he heard two screaming voices, and when he dashed in, found Mrs Mehra and Rani jabbing fingers at each other, hurling insults the likes of which Raju could never repeat. What had happened was this: after Raju left for the market, Mrs Mehra had taken herself off for a bracing walk. Despite the cold, she found herself energized, momentarily free of her woes. She stayed out longer than expected, reflecting on life in that apartment, which suddenly seemed so petty and small. Observing two children running in their mittens and winter coats, she understood they were not dissimilar to the girl upstairs, only, unlike her, they had all the privileges in the world. As she set off home she resolved to be more patient and to make things work.

But when she got back inside, the old familiar bitterness wrapped around her, as she saw not a scrap of work had been done. At first she poured a gin and juice to contain her antipathy, but it only served to make matters worse, and by the time she opened her second carton Mrs Mehra was ready to explode. Though she'd made a promise long before never to enter the servants' room, she heaved herself from the table and set off for a showdown.

What she saw inside made her Punjabi blood boil: there was Rani, looking up with a comely smile, expecting her husband through the door, meticulously ironing and folding her vast set of clothes, showing such love and care as she'd never offered to anything in Mrs Mehra's wardrobe.

It happened very quickly after that, and later Mrs Mehra was at a loss to recall the exact sequence of events. She knew it had started with her bursting into tears, and also with her lifting up and hurling the girl's freshly folded garments against the wall. Rani had fought back, of course, and this had produced the mess outside, Mrs Mehra ultimately trying to control the child as she ransacked the place. Raju returned at the moment Mrs Mehra was back in the servants' room, forcibly packing Rani's belongings into a suitcase. When she saw Raju standing agog she yelled: 'That's it, she's gone! You're to take her to the village in the morning. I never want to see her again.'

Rani, expecting her husband to put up a fight, was appalled to hear her husband say: 'Yes, *behenji*. It is time.'

They never had a chance for an official send-off: sometime in the early hours, Rani and her suitcase vanished without a trace.

The next morning Raju and Mrs Mehra sat together in bewilderment. The previous day's violence was still scattered around them. To an outsider it would be an unfathomable scene, these two unlikely companions shipwrecked among the rubble of their lives. Occasionally they looked up at each other and looked down again, but mostly they stared at the table in disbelief. Had it been a dream? What was happening to them? And where was she? Each ran through their private theories. How resourceful was Rani? What would she do? She didn't know anything about the world, Mrs Mehra thought. Raju, on the other hand, wasn't so sure.

By mid-morning they roused themselves to search the campus. But there was no trace, and the guards had no record of her passing by. After a few days of waiting they filed a missing persons report at the police station. The duty officer remarked how there were many abductions for trafficking in these parts, but, though he wouldn't hold out much hope, there was always a chance she would come home.

And she did. Two weeks later the guards called the apartment to inform Mrs Mehra that Rani was downstairs, with two young women and a police officer in tow. 'Send them up,' said Mrs Mehra, with a trepidatious heart.

'What has she done now?' she whispered to Raju, who stood beside her with a quivering mouth.

When the doorbell rang, Mrs Mehra and Raju answered side by side. And there was Rani before them both, fresh and clean and well fed, holding the hand of one of the women, while the other cradled a clipboard in her arms. Both were dressed in Fabindia kurtas and wore their hair, to Mrs Mehra's mind, suspiciously short.

'Is this the house?' Clipboard barked.

Rani nodded meekly and squeezed The Hand, deathly afraid, causing the latter to issue soothing words.

Clipboard turned and nodded manfully at the officer standing behind. With embarrassment he shuffled forward a touch.

'Ma'am, we are with the Childfight NGO,' Clipboard said, bristling with righteous contempt. 'You will have seen us on the national news. I'm here to inform you that we are arresting you, due to your employment and torture of an underage girl.'

'You should be ashamed of yourself!' The Hand suddenly screeched, so that Clipboard had to place a cautionary arm on her friend's shoulder to calm her down.

Mrs Mehra was lost for words. As they took her away, she cast a doleful eye at the unopened Tropicana on the living-room table, and later, while cooling her heels at the station, said that she wished it to be put on the record, among other things, that Mrs Sethi had been right from the start. ■

Shunaka: Blood Count

Shyama, Sister, why
the need for dazed allegiance
to men? We're *canis*
lupus first, *familiaris*
can come later – if it must.

Assurance befits
our kind more than reverence.
Remember, even
Indra – yes, him, lord of rain
and lightning, tsar of heaven –

could not command fore-
mother Sarama, divine
bitch, the dawn-goddess,
the fleet-one, Speech herself – she
that spins words into living

Earth and fades the night
with the glister of her tread.
Yes, Sister, Indra
had to yield, repent and beg
till Sarama agreed, stepped

in, saved his sphere, seat
and skin: those gods, ornery
buggers, would have carved
lush, new planets from his scalp,
had their holy cows (their sweet,

charmed milk, above all)
stayed missing. You know, the time
heaven's herd AWOLed?
All snatched by Panis, dark cave-
dwellers the gods named demons

and consigned beneath
the ground? Seers and minstrels (both
godly and bovine)
hymned the great rescue and her
role – vital, valiant – therein

again and again:
in books five, one, three and four
of the Rig Veda,
in the Atharva, and more.
Later, of course, the bipeds

would try their darnedest
to brand her traitor, faintheart,
Indra's upstart pet;
would try to unspool legend.
But we know. We – mountains, trees,

birds and beasts, time, tide,
and the morning breeze – know she
obtained milk and food
for humans, brought light to earth
and truth to the mortal mind.

(Wear your name in fine
pride, Shyama: you share it with
Sarama's firstborn,
the four-eyed, pied sentinel
on the stairway to heaven.)

Sister, we have lived,
loved, died here, since long before
this land became man's
domain. We take no masters.
We claim no terrain. But men

kill and kill again,
scorch the rivers, rape the earth
and deluge jungles
with death, all to prove manhood.
The blaze that gorged Khandava?

Gorged snake and lion,
oak and sparrow, chital, pine,
chinar, gharial?
Strangled air and loam and stream?
It was gallant Arjuna.

His coronation
gift to the elder brother:
yes, Yuddhishtira –
the essence, they say, of all
that's just and right – who allowed

a forest of lives
to bonfire into birthright;
the king Cousin Shwan
adores – why, I bet he'd trail
the bloke to the ends of hell,

the stupid, trusting
mutt! Can't he see they don't spare
even their fellow
beings, booby-trapping souls
through tortuous, wretched spans

in spiked-iron castes?
Imprint his birth on a man,
call it unchanging
(god's own decree), manacle
his will, his brain in belief –

such a masterly
legerdemain! Grandpa Shwan
(so much cannier
than our cousin) often howled
of Ekalavya, matchless

archer – yet low-born
tribal – whom Drona, guru
to prospective kings,
first rejected as outcast,
despite the lad's striking skill.

Then, Grandpa would bay
(his pitch rising) of the day
Drona – with his horde
of princely pupils – espied
Ekalavya in action.

(And Grandpa's own role
in this sighting still distressed
his heart and larynx:
a dumb witness has control
on squat – least of all the lore.)

Drona, though impressed
by the boy's grit and brilliance,
was mostly aghast:
Arjuna, his favourite,
had to remain unrivalled.

Besides, how could he –
royal preceptor, himself
a loyal Brahmin –
permit low-caste whelps to win?
So he claimed a teacher's fee.

The thumb of his right
hand – an archer's golden arm –
Drona would demand
of the lad: a gruesome price,
sealed in Eka's gore and flesh,

in his buried dream.
I have little more to say
of this strange species
you would serve, whom you esteem
worthy allies for our kind.

Except this: beware
of their wars and victories,
how friends may become
captives or janissaries.
Fetters are not always felt,

nor seen. Dear Sister,
do not bear their sky, it holds
blood – the blood of kin.
Do not share their bread, it reeks
lifeless earth: the final sin.

Art FORUM
SAN FRANCISCO

Art Forum (San Francisco) is a California based non-profit organization committed to promoting the contemporary art forms emerging out of South Asia.

The **Forum** provides the community an opportunity to better understand South Asian culture through performances, dialogue and discussions in collaboration with academic and creative enterprises.

It strives to create interactions between the tribal and the urban, the historic and the modern, the classic and the contemporary, to forge a new understanding of the history and culture of the subcontinent in an international setting.

CONNECTING CULTURES THROUGH PERFORMANCE AND VISUAL ART

Past Programs		Future Programs

- ⚘ Eye on India 2013
- ⚘ Saikat Majumdar in Conversation with Amit Chaudhuri
- ⚘ Eye on India 2014

BAY AREA BOOK FESTIVAL

OAKLAND BOOK FESTIVAL
May 31, 2015

- ⚘ South Asian panel at the Bay Area Book Fest
- ⚘ South Asian panel at the Oakland Book Fest
- ⚘ Eye on India 2015

www.artforumsf.org

Courtesy of the author

PYRE

Amitava Kumar

My mother died in Patna on 7 January 2014. We cremated her two days later on the banks of the Ganga at Konhara Ghat near Patna, more than 150 miles downriver from the burning ghats of Benares where Hindus have cremated their dead since at least the middle of the first millennium BCE. I took notes. During the long fourteen-hour flight to India I dealt with my sorrow by writing in my notebook a brief obituary for a Hindi newspaper that Ma read each morning. I was paying tribute. But once I had arrived in Patna, my reasons for note-taking became more complicated. Grief makes you a stranger to yourself and I was struck by this person that I saw pierced with loss. I was taking notes so that I could remember who I was in those days following my mother's death.

A Hindu cremation is usually held on the day of the death. In Ma's case, there was an inevitable delay. She had wanted me to be the one who lit her funeral pyre but I live in New York: I had boarded a direct flight to Delhi and then taken another plane to Patna. It was evening on the next day by the time I reached there. My family had tried to spare me from distress and hadn't told me that Ma had already died; but, unknown to them, before I left home I'd received a message on Facebook from a distant relative offering condolences. A large crowd stood in the dark outside our house and no one moved or spoke when

I arrived. In the parlour-like space on the ground floor of our house, my father sat on a sofa with other males whom I didn't immediately recognize. I touched my father's feet and he said something about my luck in getting a quick connecting flight from Delhi. I stepped further inside. My two sisters were sitting on a mattress next to a metal box, their faces looking swollen; I embraced them and when I did that the other women in the room, seated on chairs pushed against the wall, began to wail.

A white sheet and strings of marigold covered the rectangular box, but at its foot the renting company had painted in large letters in Hindi: EST. 1967 PHONE 2219692. At first I thought the aluminium box was connected to an electrical outlet but later I found out that the box had space along its sides that had been packed with ice. A square glass window on its cover allowed a view of Ma's face. Her head was resting on a thin yellow pillow with a red flower print. Bits of cotton had been stuffed into her nostrils.

An older cousin took me to another room and told me that the cremation would be held the next morning. I was asked if I wanted to get my head shaved at the ghat just before the ceremony or if I'd prefer to visit a barber's in the morning and be spared the sting of the winter cold. I chose the latter. There could be no cooking fire in the house till the body had been cremated, and a simple vegetarian meal was brought from a relative's house. When most of the visitors had left for the night, my elder sister, whom I call Didi, said that the casket needed to be filled with fresh ice. A widowed aunt remarked that we should remove any jewellery from Ma because otherwise the Doms at the burning ghat, the men from the supposedly untouchable caste who built the pyre and were the custodians of the whole ceremony, would simply snatch it away. They didn't care, she said, and would just tear the flesh to rip off the gold. It was their right.

Ma's nose stud came off easily enough but the earrings were a problem. Her white hair was wrapped around the stud; using a pair of scissors I cut the hair but the earrings seemed stuck to the skin. My younger sister struggled with one of them, and I with the other.

I didn't succeed and someone else had to complete the task. At one point, I found myself saying it was better to use surgical scissors right then so that we didn't have to watch Ma's ears torn by other hands. Didi said of the Doms, using an English term borrowed from her medical books, 'For them, it is just a *cadaver*.' I was unsettled but understood that the Doms were also reflecting an understanding that was drawn from deep within Hinduism: once the spirit has departed from the body, what remains is mere matter, no different from the log of wood on which it is placed. There was maybe a lesson in this for us, that we discard our squeamishness about death, but I felt a great tenderness as I looked down at my mother in that metal box. I caressed her cheeks. They felt cold to the touch, and slightly moist, as if even in death she had kept up her habit of applying lotion. A thin line of red fluid, like betel juice, glistened between her lips.

Having touched Ma's body, I also felt I should wash my hands. I went up to her room. Over the past couple of hours there had been the comfort of shared tears, but now I was alone for the first time. In the room where I had last seen my mother alive and quite well, only a few months earlier, her walking stick was leaning against the wall. Her saris, whose smell would have been familiar to me, hung in the cupboard. Next to the bed were the two pairs of her white sneakers equipped with Velcro straps for her arthritic hands. Standing in front of the bathroom sink, it occurred to me that the bar of Pears soap in the blue plastic dish was the one that Ma had put there just before she died. My first notes in Patna were about these items, which appeared to me like memorials that I knew would soon disappear.

My sisters and I slept that night on mattresses spread on the floor around the aluminium box. On waking up after perhaps four hours of sleep, I saw that my younger sister was awake, sitting quietly with her back to the wall, looking vacant and sad. Under the light of a bulb near a side door, visible through the glass, stood a man with a scarf wrapped around his head. It took me a minute to recognize him. He was from our ancestral village in Champaran and had been a servant in our house in Patna when I was a boy. He had travelled through the night with fresh bamboo that would be used to make the bier on which, according to custom, Ma's body would be carried out of the house and put on the funeral pyre.

When the sun came out after an hour, the rose bushes in the garden were only half visible through the fog, and the fog was still there on the water when we arrived at the river around noon.

That morning, while my sisters were washing Ma's body in preparation for the funeral, my father and I went to get our heads shaved. Papa asked the barber the name of his village; it turned out that the barber's village and ours were in the same district. My father knew a politician from the barber's village. The radio was playing Hindi songs. *Zulfein teri itni ghani, dekh ke inko, yeh sochta hoon . . . Maula mere Maula mere.* The barber was a small, dark man with a limp. He was extremely polite to my father, listening quietly while he talked about inflation and the changes in the economy. At one point, my father said that when he started life in Patna, he could buy a chicken for ten rupees and that now it would be difficult to get an egg for that amount.

I listened to what my father was saying with a rising sense of annoyance. I thought he was being pedantic when I wanted him to be sad – but why exactly? So that I could write down fragments of sentences in a little notebook? I began to see that Papa too was finding comfort by writing his own story of loss. There can be so much pathos in accounting. All the dumb confusion and wild fear of our lives rearranged in tidy rows in a ledger. One set of figures to indicate birth, and another set for death: the concerted attempt to repress the accidents and the pain of the period in between. Entire lives and accompanying histories of loss reduced to neat numbers. My father, with his phenomenal memory, was doing what he knew how to do best. He was saying to everyone in the room that everything had changed but the past was still connected to the present, if only through a narrative about changes in the price of eggs and chicken.

Ma's body had been taken out of the aluminium box by the time Papa and I returned home. Her fingernails and toenails were painted red. She was now draped in a pink Banarasi organza sari and a burgundy shawl with tiny silver bells and a shiny gold pattern of leaves. There were bright new bangles on her arm. Minutes before we left for the burning ghat, my father was brought into the room where Ma's adorned body lay on a stretcher on the floor. He was asked to put orange sindoor in the parting of Ma's hair, repeating the act he had performed on the day he married her. Papa was sobbing by now but he was asked to repeat the gesture thrice. Then all the women in the family, many of them weeping loudly, took turns rubbing the auspicious powder in Ma's hair.

When we were in the car, driving to the Ganga for the cremation, Didi said that my mother was lucky. At her death, Ma had been dressed up in new clothes. Papa had put sindoor on her head, signifying that they were getting married again. Ma was going out as a bride. Had my father died first, none of this would have happened. If Ma were still living, sindoor would have been wiped away from her head. She would be expected to wear white. The women from the family who were now wailing would still be wailing but, if Ma were the widow, these women would have had the task of breaking all the bangles on her wrist before Papa's corpse was taken out of the house.

As I listened to my sister, I understood that even in the midst of profound grief it was necessary to find comfort. One needed solace. It was possible to hold despair at bay by imagining broken bangles and the destiny that my mother had escaped. I would have found the sight of my mother's bare arms unbearable.

I left India nearly three decades ago, and would see my mother only for a few days each year during my visits to Patna. Over the past ten or fifteen years, her health had been declining. She suffered from arthritis and the medicines she took for it had side effects, and sometimes my phone rang with news that she'd fallen asleep in the bathroom or had a seizure on the morning after she had fasted during a festival. I knew that one day the news would be worse and I would be asked to come to Patna. I was fifty years old and had never before attended a funeral. I didn't know what was more surprising, that some of the rituals were new to me, or that they were exactly as I had imagined. That my mother's corpse had been dressed as a bride was new and disconcerting, and I'd have preferred a plainer look; on the other hand, the body placed on the bamboo bier, its canopy covered with an orange sheet of cotton, was a familiar daily sight on the streets of my childhood. In my notebook that night I noted that my contribution to the funeral had been limited to lighting my mother's funeral pyre. In more ways than one, the rituals of death had reminded me that I was an outsider. There were five hundred people at the shraadh dinner. I only knew a few of them. I wouldn't have known how to make arrangements for the food or the priests. Likewise for the shamiana, the community hall where the dinner was held, the notice in the newspapers about the shraadh, even the chairs on which the visitors sat.

There is a remarkable short story by A.K. Ramanujan called 'Annayya's Anthropology' in which the Kannada protagonist, a graduate student at the University of Chicago, makes a terrible discovery while looking at a book in the library. The book is by an American anthropologist whose fieldwork had been done in India; the pictures in the book from Annayya's home town appear familiar to him. One of the photographs illustrates a Hindu cremation and Annayya recognizes in the crowd a cousin who owns a photography studio. This is a picture that appears to have been taken in Annayya's own home in Mysore. The cousin, whose name is Sundararaya, is mentioned in the book's foreword. When Annayya looks more carefully at the corpse in the photograph he sees that it is his father on the pyre. Ramanujan was making a point about the discipline of anthropology, about the ironies of our self-discoveries in the mirror of Western knowledge, but the story tugs at the immigrant's dread that distance will prevent his fulfilment of filial duty.

I had been luckier than Annayya. I had been able to speak to Didi in Patna when Ma was taken to a hospital on the night she died. On WhatsApp, on my phone, a text came from my sister later in the evening, assuring me that Ma was doing better. Then came the call about my flight timings. While the use of social media also meant that I got the news of my mother's death from a near stranger on Facebook, it was also true that technology and modern travel had made it quite easy for me to arrive in Patna in less than twenty hours to cremate my mother. During the prayer ceremonies a priest told me that the reason Hindu customs dictated a mourning period of thirteen days was that it used to take time for all the relatives to be informed and for them to travel to the home of the deceased. But this, he said, putting his hand on his ear, is the age of the mobile phone.

At the ghat, the smoke from the funeral fires mixed with the lingering fog of the winter afternoon. An advance party organized by a cousin's husband had pitched a small shamiana on the bank and arranged a few red plastic chairs next to it. Above the din, a tuneless bhajan played on a loudspeaker. In the crowd, I was led first in one direction and then another. My movements were restrained because of what I was wearing; according to custom, my body was wrapped in two pieces of unstitched cotton. My freshly shaven head was bare. I saw that Ma's body had already been put on the pyre. There was such a press of strangers, many of them beggars and curious children, that I had to ask people loudly to move back. Ma lay on heavy logs and a bed of straw but the priest directed me to pile thinner firewood over the rest of the body. Other family members joined me, adding sticks in the shape of a tent over the corpse.

Ma's face had been left bare. Now the priest told me to put five pieces of sandalwood near my mother's mouth. Some of the sindoor that had been put in Ma's hair had scattered and lodged in her eyebrows and on her eyelids. The Dom who would give me the fire had an X-shaped plaster stuck on his right cheek. He had a dark face and his eyes were bloodshot. His head was wrapped in a brown-and-blue muffler to protect him from the cold; he wore jeans and a thin black jacket and he had about him an air of insouciance that would have bothered my mother, but I liked him. His presence was somehow reassuring, or real, because he was outside the circle of our grief and yet the main doer. He was solemn, but he certainly wasn't sober; his very casualness brought a quotidian touch to the scene, and he accentuated this by haggling about his payment. A maternal uncle's son stood behind me, repeating for my benefit the priest's instructions – this cousin of mine, a few years older than I, had cremated his son recently. The boy had passed away after his liver stopped working, the result of an allergic reaction to medicines that have reportedly been banned outside India. The priest told me to sprinkle *gangajal* again – the endless act of purification with what is in reality polluted water – before the Dom lit a bundle of tall straw for me. Three circles around the pyre. Then followed the ritual that is called *mukhaagni*. I understood suddenly why the priest had given me the five pieces of sandalwood, the size of small Snickers bars, to put near my mother's mouth. In that moment, while performing *mukhaagni* inadequately, inefficiently, even badly, in my grief and bewilderment, the thought passed through my mind: Is this why my mother had wanted me present at her death? *Mukhaagni* – in Sanskrit, *mukha* is 'mouth' and *agni* is 'fire' – means in practice that the male who is closest to the deceased, often the son, sometimes the father, and in some cases, I imagine, the husband, puts fire into the mouth of the person on the pyre.

A cremation on a riverbank in India is by its very nature public, but usually the only mourners present are men. In our case, my sisters and other younger women from the family had accompanied Ma's body. When I turned from the pyre I saw my sisters standing at the edge of the circle. I went to them and put my arms around their shoulders. The flames had risen at once and they hid Ma's body behind an orange curtain. Soon there were fewer people standing around the pyre and the older men, my father's friends, began to settle down on the plastic chairs at a distance of about thirty feet from the pyre. A relative put a shawl around me. Then the Dom said that the fire was burning too quickly, meaning that the fire would go out before the corpse had been incinerated, so a few men from our party took down a part of the shamiana and used it as a screen against the wind.

The fire needed to burn for three hours. Badly managed fires and, sometimes, the plain paucity of firewood – for the pyre requires at least 150 kilos of wood but often as much as four hundred kilos or more – are to be blamed for the partially charred torsos flung into the Ganga. And as wood costs money – 10,000 rupees in our case – the poor in particular can be insufficiently burned. The chief minister of Bihar, Jitan Ram Manjhi, a man from the formerly untouchable Musahar (or rat-eating) caste, told an audience in Patna last year that his family was so poor that when his grandfather died they just threw his body into the river.

I asked Didi why we hadn't taken Ma's body to Patna's electric crematorium, but she only said that Ma wouldn't have wanted it. Didi didn't need to say anything else. I could imagine my mother resisting the idea of being put in a metal tray where other bodies had been laid and pushed inside an oven where electric coils would reduce her to ashes. Her choice, superstitious and irrational as it might be, didn't pose a problem for us. We could afford the more expensive and customary means of disposing of the dead. Nearly three hundred kilos of wood had been purchased for Ma's pyre and, in addition to that, ten kilos of sandalwood. This was one of the many instances during those days when I recognized that we were paying for the comfort of subscribing to tradition. The electric crematorium is often the choice of the poor, costing only about three hundred rupees. I learned that over seven hundred dead are cremated at the electric crematorium at Patna's Bans Ghat each month, and a somewhat smaller number at the more distant Gulbi Ghat electric crematorium. These numbers are only a fraction of the three thousand cremated on traditional pyres at Bans Ghat on average each month. This despite the fact that electric cremation is also quicker, taking only forty-five minutes, except when there is a long wait due to power cuts. There can also be other delays. Back when I was in college, the corpse of a relative of mine, a sweet old lady with a fondness for betel leaf, was taken to the Patna crematorium, but the operator there said that he would be available only after he had watched that day's broadcast of the TV serial *Ramayan*. The mourners waited an extra hour.

While we sat under the shamiana watching the fire do its work, my younger sister Dibu said that she had put perfume on Ma's corpse because fragrances were something Ma liked. Dibu began to talk about how Ma used to put perfume in the new handkerchiefs that she gave away to younger female relatives who visited her. In Bihar, a Hindu woman leaving her home is given a handkerchief with a few grains of rice, a pinch of turmeric, leaves of grass, coins and a sweet laddoo. These items had also been put beside Ma on the pyre, and, I now learned, inside Ma's mouth my sisters had placed a gold leaf. I thought of the priest telling me each time I completed a circle around the pyre that I was to put the fire into my mother's mouth. I didn't, or couldn't. It wasn't so much that I found it odd or appalling that such a custom should exist; instead, I remember being startled that no one had cared to warn me about it. But perhaps I shouldn't have been. Death provided a normalizing context for everything that was being done. No act appeared outlandish because it had a place in the tradition, each Sanskrit verse carrying an intonation of centuries of practice. And if there was any doubt about the efficacy of sacred rituals, everywhere around us banal homilies were being offered to make death appear less strange or devastating. The bhajan that had been playing on the loudspeaker all afternoon was in praise of fire. *Death, you think you have defeated us, but we sing the song of burning firewood.* Even though it was tuneless, and even tasteless, the song turned cremation into a somewhat celebratory act. It struck me that the music disavowed its own macabre nature and made everything acceptable. And now, as the fire burned lower and there was visibly less to burn, I saw that everyone, myself included, had momentarily returned to a sense of the ordinary. This feeling wouldn't last more than a few hours but at that time I felt free from the contagion of tears. I remember complaining about the loud music. Everyone had been fasting since morning and pedas from a local confectioner were taken out of paper boxes. I took a box of pedas to our young Dom but he refused; he didn't want anything sweet to eat. I was handed a packet of salted crackers to pass on to him. Tea was served in small plastic cups. Street dogs and goats wandered past the funeral pyres. Broken strings of marigold, fruit peels and bits of bedding, including blankets and a pillow pulled from the fire, littered the sandy bank. One of my uncles had lost his car keys and people from our group left to look for them.

The Dom had so far used a ten-foot-long bamboo to rearrange the burning logs but when the fire died down he poked around the burning embers with his calloused fingers. I was summoned for another round of prayers and offerings to the fire. The men in my family gave directions to the Dom as he scooped Ma's remains – ash and bones, including a few vertebrae, but other small bones too, white and curiously flat – into a large earthen pot. This pot was wrapped in red cloth and later that evening hung from a high branch on the mango tree outside our house. Its contents were to be immersed in the Ganga at the holy sites upriver: Benares, Prayag and Haridwar. This was a journey my sisters and I would undertake later in the week; but that afternoon, after the pot had been filled, the rest of the half-burnt wood and ash and what might have been a part of the hip bone were flung into the river while the priest chanted prayers. Flower petals, mostly marigold, had been stuffed in polythene bags which had the names of local sari shops printed on them, and at the end everyone took part in casting handfuls of bright petals on the brown waters. I took pictures. The photograph of the yellow marigold floating on the Ganga, rather than my mother's burning pyre, is what I put up on Facebook that evening. ■

© RADHIKA KHIMJI
An Imprint, 2013
from the *Red Stitching* series

SHOES

Anjali Joseph

Is it time to go? These days, I'm sure I need to, and I get up in the night, and get outside to the latrine, but I find I have difficulty beginning.

There's a sense of urgency, but it'll start, then stop. During these excursions, still dreaming I suppose, I believe that I am at home. I mean the house where I grew up. A boy, stumbling into moonlight. In the room where I slept as a child, the walls smelled of ash and cow dung, smoky and rich. If you haven't been in a room plastered in gobar I can't explain. It's sweet, but catches in the back of your throat. Now, in the rains, the smell alters, a growing thing.

My brother and I slept in the corner. His knee in my leg, my sole on his calf, his snoring. The light from the window, and shadows moving near us. Sometimes we listened to our parents' soft noises. He stirred earlier, unclouded; I had to be shaken awake, confused, often angry.

My younger daughter-in-law tells her son, Rohan, to love his brother, to look after him. My brother and I were never told such things. When we fought, if it wasn't out of sight, we were beaten for giving trouble. When we hated each other, which was often, we still slept entangled, resenting it, my knee in his back, his bony elbow in my ribs. There was no sentiment between us, but we would have died for each other.

I remember the offcuts we were given to play with. Small, oddly formed pieces. We learned to plait the leather, or stamp out a flower.

This morning I was polishing the ends of the chappals, varnishing them, checking them. Everything should be perfect. Why so much care for something a man will put between his feet and the ground? But the chappals will be his constant companions. He'll spend more time with them than with his wife. One side of the sole may wear out more, depending on how he walks, so that you could pick up his chappals and observe that he leans a little into his centre, or a little out towards the world. Some people walk quite evenly, but not many, I've noticed, not many. Most of us shuffle along in our own strange way, not giving it attention.

The thing I make is with a man when he's alone, unnoticed. I like that. And he can rely on it. Our chappals aren't like the manufactured ones, stuck with glue; ours will be with you for a long time.

I've never made the perfect pair. There's always something. The scorpion's tail on top of the belt curves differently on one side; there's an asymmetry in the point of the toe, or the design around the upper lining.

I could say it doesn't matter; no one will notice. I could say the only perfect thing is a dead thing, that each pair is like a husband and wife: their imperfections complement each other. At first it's uncomfortable to wear our chappals. They have to be lived with. They will harass the skin between your big and middle toes. You will dip them in water and let them dry in the sun. The varnish will take a while to come off the sole. You'll wear them in, slipping around. Like a tool used over years by the same man, or a child raised by a certain woman, they'll bear the imprint of your habitual bias.

My elder son, who makes the manufactured chappals, has heard all this and isn't interested. They came this Sunday, without Anil, who had a cricket match. My daughter-in-law brought til laddoos for us to take to Pune.

Can you even remember how to make a proper chappal? I asked

my son. I don't know why I feel the need to have these conversations with him.

He nodded and waved one hand slightly. His face is smooth, this son of mine, and his eyes slide around. He's darker than I, looks more like my brother.

Do you remember how? I persisted.

He smiled, but he looked irritated.

What will you teach your son? I asked.

His eyes slid up to mine, then he looked away. He exhaled. I thought I smelled last night's alcohol. His teeth are red, too much gutka.

My wife came with tea and fritters. She put her small hand on his shoulder. He looked up and smiled and his face changed, from sly and angry to abashed, open.

If Prakash had been better in school he would have been like his brother Deepak, I thought, pouring hot tea down my throat. I watched him eat, his fingers shiny with oil. He's strong, taller than I am. He likes his work, in the workshop with the other men, and drink, and songs on the radio. I don't know what else he gets up to. His wife is a practical woman, she wouldn't complain. And their Anil? He's not like my other grandsons in the city, but he's a good boy, straightforward. When his cousins come here he shows them things: the pond to swim in, or they take the bus to the fort. They look up to him, but they also turn their heads to each other and smile. His mother is always with him. They on the other hand live alone in a way. They go to school in a bus. They have their uniform, their routine. They are city children, more fearful, but sharper.

From the cooking I smelled methi, besan, oil.

I thought about the two brothers, so different. My second son is like a version of me projected into the future. He's industrious, always wanting to get ahead, without knowing where. He has his mother's softness, her intelligence.

There's something about us that neither of them has. But not every bit of material can be used.

C ome on, she said.
     Just a minute, I said. I checked again in the bag.
What now?
Did you bring the . . . But I couldn't come up with a word.
A towel? I said.

Her eyes, lighter than mine, golden almost, were intelligent, not quite pitying. I pulled up the zip. All right, I said. Wait – I paused, wondering if I needed to go. No, I said, it's all right. No, wait, I'll just be a minute.

In the bus she gazed out of the window, as though the road was telling a story. I looked across her: a stall selling neera, another bus stop, people waiting in their dhotis and a man in a cap; kids in a four-wheel drive; those new hotels springing up, all glass and signs. Everything depressed me.

What happened? I felt like asking Deepak when they met us at the bus stand.

Sujata is at home, he said, finishing lunch. The boys beamed. I thought of embracing my son, and didn't. I'd shrunk. Or had he grown taller? He was wearing a short-sleeved shirt, that material with holes in it. His moustache was neatly trimmed. His mother hugged him. She never looks out of place.

You can rest while you're here, Deepak said, as he opened the door. Relax, take it easy.

The flat was as I remembered: white floor tiles, fans in every room. Sohan, the littler one, gave me his hand.

Do you always use the fan? I asked.

He nodded, but looked as though he wasn't sure how to answer.

What if it's cold? I said.

Then we use a sheet or a blanket, Rohan said.

There were extra mattresses, rolled up, for them to sleep on because we were there.

Baba's put the geyser on, Rohan told me, in case you want a bath.

I said nothing. Geysers make me uneasy; I don't like objects that do things in an unseen way.

I shambled into the bathroom and caught sight of myself in the mirror, an intruder with white ear hair.

In the kitchen we sat around the table, which was covered with a shiny cloth, patterned with bright fruit: bananas, apples, tomatoes, purple plums. There were vade and tea.

You don't need to cook while you're here, Sujata told my wife. The bai comes in the morning.

My wife nodded. Then she said, Unless I make something for the boys when they come home?

Sabudana vada! said Sohan.

My daughter-in-law smiled tightly. They don't need to eat something big, she said. They normally have milk and biscuit.

Sohan squirmed onto my lap. I put an arm around him. My son looked at me, then more closely at his mother. She was flexing her knuckles, pushing at those of the left hand. Certain joints give her pain until they warm up. Her eyes, always so clear, are clouding slightly.

In the main room I read the newspaper. I like to see the children, and my son amid his life, which seems to fit him better than the one he had growing up. Then he was patient, watchful. But perhaps that had to do with my drinking.

It isn't that I love to be at home. But being there is no effort, so I can go anywhere. Often that means returning to my childhood. The things around me are less real, but the past is immediate. When I was young I was always aware of the future, like a road ahead. The road is still there; there's a journey to be made. But this will be the last journey, one without return.

Even the past is incomplete. My mother, for instance, comes back not as an image but a collection of sensations. The hard, warm palm of her hand against my shoulder. The smell of her neck as she bent over me; smoky like a wood fire, maybe from cooking, but also her sweat. A little sweet, like a water flower. When she was angry her voice rang out like a clay pot that's struck – a note of metal. The rhythms of her speech were an ongoing complaint, a river without variation.

Not that she was always complaining. That's just how it sounded. My father's sister was more theatrical. She laughed loudly, sat with her legs loosely crossed and chewed supari. Even the things she did just for herself, like sneezing, or breathing, were amplified. She wore thick toe-rings and heavy silver anklets. In her presence I was delighted, reduced to nothing.

My father was a big man, with a big voice. He didn't speak much, unlike my aunt, but around her he became more talkative, more smiling. I dreamed of him the other day. He was standing in near darkness on the road, holding one chappal. He looked confused when he saw me.

Where are you off to? I said.

I'm going home, he said. But – where's your brother?

I felt the usual disappointment.

Is he all right? he asked. His face was full of anxiety. Better you don't tell anyone you saw me, he said, and hurried away.

When I was drinking the world became a crazy circus, entertaining and hilarious, or annoying and to be battled.

How often I saw my room, the bed, the calendar, the blue wall, the cupboard swim around me. I was extremely mobile, enamoured of my agility.

If I could just be alone. I'd think about it while I was working, hands busy, but mind elsewhere. While I was eating, or standing outside watching my sons run around, I thought of the future, a time when they would be older, there'd be a little more money, and I'd be free, to do something I still hadn't thought of.

One afternoon I went to the workshop to drop off some finished pairs. It was the same as usual, the radio on; around the corner I saw the cracked feet of old Kadam who always took a nap after lunch.

Pawar! said a short fellow near the door. Borkar is a little younger than I but he was already bald. He looks foolish, which offsets that sly cast to his eyes, so that he resembles a slightly cunning baby.

We never see you, he said.

I'm there to be seen, I said, but suddenly I wasn't so sure.

Come out some evening, he said.

Out? I said.

Satpute sat a couple of places from Borkar. He had hair then, thinning but crow-black, a wizened face. He was thin except for a slackness at the stomach, a weak but enduring sort of man. He put down his needle and made a tipping gesture towards his mouth.

Oh, I said. The truth is I was at a loose end. I hadn't thought of myself as having spare time, before my affair with Ratna. My world had been hermetic: the family, and work. But I'd made time for those excursions and now the seal was broken. I felt a little expectant all the time, a little disappointed. Maybe, I said. When?

Tonight, Satpute said.

Tonight, Borkar agreed. At sunset. We'll meet here.

There is a sort of chowk, outside the workshop, just before the area where most of these people live. Our house isn't far but is off the main road. We are a little separate.

Sunset? I said. We normally ate just after then.

They nodded.

In the evening I told my wife I'd be going out.

Now? she said.

I have work, I said. You all go ahead and eat. I'll eat later. I left. I was annoyed with her for making me feel awkward. Had I no freedom? Things had come to a pretty pass. I shrugged it off and got to the workshop. There was no one there but a pale pi-dog outside. I loitered next to the dog. Pages of an old calendar blew about. It was dusk, summer, and still very warm.

After a time, feeling let down, I squatted near the dog. I was hungry. I'd go home soon. I imagined our room as though I were looking in, saw under the electric light my wife and sons sitting down, my wife giving them rice and dal and maybe some mutton.

The dog sighed, and licked his balls. I got up.

Borkar and Satpute sidled down the road. Where have you been? I wanted to ask, but I'd lost confidence.

Come, we'll go to the bottle shop, Satpute said. You have money?
Obviously, I said. I felt the notes in my pocket.

Three Santra, he said at the liquor shop. He nodded at me.

We take turns, Borkar said at my other side.

I paid, and felt a pain in my stomach. When did I ever hand over money in this way? Every week I gave my wife the money for groceries, and otherwise we kept it in a tin in the cupboard. Sometimes there was a bit spare, but often there was something coming up – school books, shoes, expenses. I was a working man, I reasoned. I could spend my money as I saw fit.

Borkar reached out a hand for the paper bag. We walked off.

Where are we going? I asked.

We know a good place, quiet, Satpute said.

There were no lights around the old godown. Under the tree, near the tiny Datta temple, I felt as though I was back in Miraj. The air smelled like fields. I heard crickets.

Borkar had a bag with him. He took out three tumblers. The first bottle was opened. I'd drunk alcohol as a young man, but only a taste. I hadn't enjoyed it. I swigged as much as the others, and my stomach began to burn. The orange flavour was intense, like cheap perfume. I thought of Ratna and felt mild nostalgia, as a man of many experiences.

Borkar said, This is better than sitting at home.

Satpute agreed. I looked at his drawn yellow face and thought, I am just seeing what this is like, I won't do it regularly.

A warm breeze sighed in the leaves of the banyan tree and tickled my neck. I relaxed. Perhaps I'd spent too much time alone.

What are you chewing over? Borkar said. There was an insensitivity about him, but a humanity too, a warmth. I made these assessments as my father would have, my father who was it seemed so upright. I never saw any doubt or uncertainty in him.

It's new to me to be among other men, I said. Not since I was much younger, before I was married almost.

Don't you get bored, at home? Satpute said.

SHOES

Bored, I said. I don't know. I felt the instinct to defend my family. And was it boredom, or fear – the fear of being responsible, day after day, but with no idea how to go about things?

Leave him alone, Borkar said. He waved a fat paw at me.

There's no need to be uncomfortable, Satpute said. He smiled and showed his browning teeth.

What about that woman of yours? Borkar said.

I started, but it was Satpute who shrugged. It's going on, he said. Sometimes.

He too? It was confusing. The remaining light was orange, that orange dusk. Bats wheeled about the godown and the tree.

It's eerie here, I said, a little ghostly. This light.

They laughed. Pawar is a sensitive soul, Satpute said.

I laughed too, uneasily. A friend of my grandfather's told us a story when I was younger, I said. A man was walking home along a dark road near a forest.

Where was this? Satpute interrupted.

Bengal, I said, picking the name out of the air.

Bengal? How would you know a story from Bengal?

I drank some more. Are you going to let me tell the story or not? I said.

He gave a dry laugh. Tell, tell, he said.

He had no light and was afraid of ghosts. But a fellow traveller with a lantern came along and kept him company. The first man felt relieved.

Of course, Borkar said.

Satpute laughed. Were you there too, in Bengal?

Satpute, don't be an idiot. Who wants to walk alone near a forest?

I said, They talked and got to know each other. After a while the first man told the man with the lantern that when they met on the road he'd been afraid in case the other man was a ghost.

Oho! said Borkar, pouring more Santra for all of us. I took my tumbler and put it against my foot so I'd know where it was. It was nearly dark now. Even the bats were hardly visible, sudden cinders against the darkness. It was silent. The city lights seemed far. I thought of the field temple I used to walk to as a boy, its blunt found idols of Narsoba and his wives. I must be tipsy; I felt detached from the physical world, sliding away at some oblique angle.

Then what happened? Satpute said. He was a rough voice, a few feet away in the darkness.

Oh. Then the first man said he remembered it was all right because ghosts who take human form have feet that point backwards.

Ah, of course, Borkar said, as though this was well known.

I paused. Then the man carrying the lantern laughed, pointed it at his feet and disappeared, I said.

Ah! So he was a ghost? Borkar said.

What do you think? I said. In the silence I heard the crickets.

We should have had boiled peanuts, Satpute said. Something.

I was hungry too. Next time I'll bring something savoury, I said. My wife makes good chivda.

Chivda! We should have meat. Kebabs.

A confusion of acid moved in my stomach. My head began to float.

At first I enjoyed the uselessness of these evenings. We were like children, smutty children, it's true, but there was an innocence to it. I enjoyed being drunk, I discovered, the way things would loom closer, suddenly, and then swim back. It was like the way you get to know someone, as getting to know Ratna had been, those overwhelming moments of too much proximity, then retreating into distance.

Chaturthi was on a Sunday, and after we went to the temple with the children to see the idol, which I didn't care about at all, the rest of our stay was quiet. Mukta bai came in the morning to cook. The house smelled of phenyl for hours after she'd cleaned. At lunch my wife would make the bhakris. Then she'd watch television, and I'd rest. I'm not used to sleeping in the afternoon, but in the city it's possible to feel tired without doing much.

Two days before we were leaving I lay on Sohan's bed and felt myself slipping into unconsciousness. I stayed there a long time it seemed, on the boundary between two worlds. Here in this house, and my near-dream state, the furniture of my life fell away. My things at home – the cupboard, the bed, Tuka with his orange fur and green eyes, the cracked bucket – seemed to be part of an old dream. Like scraps of leather, oddly shaped, things from life, people and sayings and objects, found themselves spliced together. My father walking past me, holding one chappal. My brother, stolid, next to me outside the old house. In the dream he and I were talking about his daughter. He wants to get her married this winter. She's nineteen, a bright, calm girl.

She's studied enough, he said.

But she's intelligent, I said. If she trained for something. She could work in the city, in a call centre.

Her husband will want her to help him. That's the main thing.

Yes, I said.

I woke up and went to the bathroom. Amid the white tiles I began without incident, but couldn't complete. I started again, a trickle. Then stopped, before I felt I'd stopped. Head still heavy, bladder still irritated, I went to the kitchen for tea.

We'll take a walk, she said, before the boys come home? I want to make sabudana vada for them.

Groggy, I sat at the table, reassembling the world, which wasn't mine. Tablecloth with pictures of fruit, ceiling fan, salt shaker. Photographs on a board behind the table. Pictures of the children, round-faced, serious in Rohan's case, smiling in Sohan's. None of it real. Did I have to go? Yes – no, I wasn't sure. Perhaps not yet.

We walked up the lane and turned right up another lane. We looked different from other people around, she in her nine-yard sari, I in my shirt and dhoti. Or perhaps it wasn't what I was wearing. There aren't many people of our age in this area, and few people around in the daytime at all. Everyone's working or at school. She smiled at a watchman we've passed before, and at a man selling sukha bhel.

How do you know all these people when we've just been here a few days? I grumbled.

I don't walk around pretending the world doesn't exist, she said.

Sometimes I think I'm the one who doesn't exist, I said. My penis twinged. I couldn't need to go again.

Oh, you exist, she said drily.

Sanjay wants to marry off Sangita, I said. Why, he should let her study a bit longer, let her work.

Work as what?

Something. She said she might want to train, work in a beauty parlour. What's the point of just marrying her off? I said. Half my mind was on my dream, half on the probably misleading urgency I was experiencing.

A koel screeched in a tree we passed.

Quiet! I said.

She started laughing.

The koel screamed louder and louder.

These city birds are deranged, I said.

You don't think she should be married? she said.

What's the hurry? I said. Of course she should. But why now? She'll just be an add-on to her husband's life. What's the value of it, what's the point?

I was sure now: I did need to go. Let's go back, I said.

She stopped. It seemed to me suddenly that she was trembling. But I don't want to go back yet, she said.

Come on, I urged. I need to get back. Don't delay.

She stood irresolute.

Or take your time, if you want. Give me the key, I said. I hurried back, past the screaming koels. When I got to the bathroom, I leaked a few hot drops. She had returned too, but when I went to the kitchen where she was frying the vada, she didn't look at me.

I keep thinking about death, as though death were the answer to life, an answer that removes the uncertainty. Perhaps simply being answered is consoling.

She knows this, and when she is angriest with me she says nothing. The timing is confusing. It's not straight after I've done something

I shouldn't. For example, nothing happened after the episode with Ratna, though my wife didn't, I think, know about it, but she might have, for superstitiously I find it hard to believe she doesn't know everything I do and think and then, by moments, when I realize I can pass unnoticed, get away with things, I become callous to my fear, and think I don't need her approval. That's when she stops paying me attention, and I suffocate. It's not even that she stops talking to me, or stops cooking, nothing obvious. She doesn't sound angry or depressed. I just stop existing.

It's a living death. She is still there, but the invisible current that irritates me, the thread between me and her, is not only gone but it's as though it never had been.

The first time it happened, after Ratna, I watched myself, as though I were my own ghost; I pitied my lumpy existence as I shambled from my room to the kitchen. This poor fool, this clod of matter – truck horns outside, noisy in their indifference. What could he do? He had just enough spark of consciousness to suffer from the hostility of everything that was not him.

Even now, I did what I could to irritate her, to get a reaction. I made a noise when getting up that night. I banged the bathroom door, I dropped the toothpaste, I talked to myself.

What's the matter? I said loudly the next afternoon when she was sitting silently, in front of the television, which wasn't on, the newspaper next to her, not reading it.

She looked at me absolutely without anger.

What's the matter with you? I approached her, put my face close to hers, felt her forehead roughly. You seem ill, I'm worried about you! I said. I peered into her face. What's wrong?

After we had been home a day she relented. I knew it was nothing to do with my manoeuvres. I didn't care. All that mattered was that she relented. It's not that she is unable to maintain her solitude, or that she gets angry – that would be a victory.

I think what happens is that her belief in her rightness wavers. She isn't sure whether she should, after all, feel sorry for me. Her compunction, her being a good person, or is it weakness, I don't care, it gives her doubt, it creates a chink. After all, I saw her consider – the fair part of her, which is enormous, which has shaped all our lives – after all, perhaps I should come back. Perhaps he needs me.

In this way she never gets whatever it is that she needs; she is always brought back to earth, to the ugly world of truck horns and the plastic bucket with the rusty handle and the crack; to the groove in the latrine floor that never looks clean; to our pots and pans that are blackened and wearing out; to my inadequacies, which never come to a final crisis, but simply limp on. I do it to her every time. And then I breathe again, and am comforted, and insensitive, as before. ∎

ANOTHER WAY OF SEEING

Gauri Gill & Rajesh Vangad

Only a four-hour drive from Mumbai but a world away from the metropolis, Ganjad is a small farming village nestled in the hills of northern Maharashtra's coastal region. It's a modest, vulnerable community with intermittent electricity, and you have to climb a hill to get phone reception. The population are Warli, an indigenous, or Adivasi, people, who speak an unwritten language and are known for their folk paintings. Traditionally these were painted by women, using a paste made from flour and applied to dung walls inside their homes. Symbolic illustrations in stark white on an ochre background, they would commemorate special occasions such as weddings and harvests.

Warli paintings are no longer purely made for local village life; there is a mural by Rajesh Vangad, a celebrated Warli artist, at Mumbai airport. It was in Vangad's family home that the photographer Gauri Gill stayed when she came to Ganjad early in 2013 to work with the local primary school. The family has lived there for generations, and Vangad is intimate with the place and its history. He knows the stories of the violent political mobs and underhanded land-grabs, and what the fields are like at haymaking time, and how the forest looks under a full moon. The more Gill understood Vangad's bond with the place, the more she could sense aspects of his life in particular locations. Her landscape photographs alone couldn't convey what Vangad would see and recall in these places. So she placed him in her landscape photographs, composing them as settings for his reminiscences, and to give expression to these she asked him to draw over the prints, projecting his memories onto the pictures. ∎

Michael Collins

3

4.

6.

More ways to read Granta

As a subscriber, you can now read everything from this issue on our

< **brand new** >

website and *Granta* app.

PRINT SUBSCRIPTION FROM £32	DIGITAL-ONLY SUBSCRIPTION FROM £12
New! Includes digital access	*Special launch price*

Visit granta.com, call + 44(0) 208 955 7011
or complete the form overleaf

GRANTA.COM

GRANTA

THE MAGAZINE OF NEW WRITING

PRINT SUBSCRIPTION REPLY FORM FOR UK, EUROPE AND REST OF THE WORLD
(includes digital access). For digital-only subscriptions, please visit granta.com

GUARANTEE: If I am ever dissatisfied with my *Granta* subscription, I will simply notify you, and you will send me a complete refund or credit my credit card, as applicable, for all un-mailed issues.

YOUR DETAILS

TITLE ....
NAME ....
ADDRESS ....
POSTCODE ....
EMAIL ....

☐ Please tick this box if you do not wish to receive special offers from *Granta*
☐ Please tick this box if you do not wish to receive offers from organizations selected by *Granta*

YOUR PAYMENT DETAILS

1) ☐ Pay £32 (saving £20) by Direct Debit
   To pay by Direct Debit please complete the mandate and return to the address shown below.

2) Pay by cheque or credit/debit card. Please complete below:

   1 year subscription: ☐ UK: £36   ☐ Europe: £42   ☐ Rest of World: £46

   3 year subscription: ☐ UK: £99   ☐ Europe: £108   ☐ Rest of World: £126

   I wish to pay by ☐ CHEQUE ☐ CREDIT/DEBIT CARD

   Cheque enclosed for £_____ made payable to *Granta*.

   Please charge £ _____ to my: ☐ Visa ☐ MasterCard ☐ Amex ☐ Switch/Maestro

   Card No. ☐☐☐☐☐☐☐☐☐☐☐☐☐☐☐☐

   Valid from *(if applicable)* ☐☐ / ☐☐   Expiry Date ☐☐ / ☐☐   Issue No. ☐☐

   Security No. ☐☐☐

SIGNATURE .... DATE ....

Instructions to your Bank or Building Society to pay by Direct Debit

BANK NAME ....
BANK ADDRESS ....
POSTCODE ....
ACCOUNT IN THE NAMES(S) OF: ....
SIGNED .... DATE ....

DIRECT Debit

Instructions to your Bank or Building Society: Please pay Granta Publications direct debits from the account detailed on this instruction subject to the safeguards assured by the direct debit guarantee. I understand that this instruction may remain with Granta and, if so, details will be passed electronically to my bank/building society. Banks and building societies may not accept direct debit instructions from some types of account.

Bank/building society account number
☐☐☐☐☐☐☐☐

Sort Code
☐☐ ☐☐ ☐☐

Originator's Identification
9 1 3 1 3 3

Please mail this order form with payment instructions to:

Granta Publications
12 Addison Avenue
London, W11 4QR
Or call +44(0)208 955 7011
Or visit GRANTA.COM for details

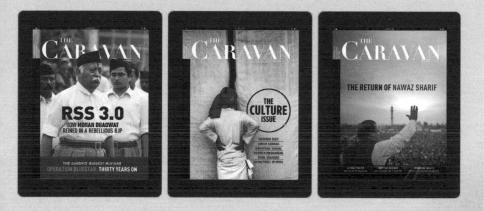

ENGLISH SUMMER

Amit Chaudhuri

July 1985

He got up at around nine o'clock with the usual feeling of dread. He threw off the duvet. Still unused to being vertical, he pounded the pillow and the sheet to ensure he'd dislodged strands of hair as well as the microorganisms that subsisted on such surfaces but were invisible to the naked eye. He straightened the duvet, tugging at it till it was symmetrical on each side. He smoothed the sheet, patting it but skimming the starchy bit – a shiny patch of dried semen, already quite old – on the right flank of where he'd lain.

The anger inside him hadn't gone – from the aftermath of the concert. He'd watched it six days ago on TV: Africa, London and Philadelphia conjoined by satellite. He switched it off after three-quarters of an hour. By the time the Boomtown Rats came on, and the sea of dancing people in Wembley Stadium was being intercut with Ethiopian children with innocent eyes and bulbous heads, a phrase had arisen in his consciousness: 'dance of death'. Didn't the exulting crowds in Wembley and in Philadelphia see their heroes' and their own complicity in the famine? But surely this line of thought was absurd, maybe malicious, and to interpret in such terms an event of messianic goodwill, meant to bring joy and food to Ethiopia, nothing but perverse? So what if it brings a bit of joy to Londoners as well? Is that what you're resenting? He'd discussed it with Mark while having lunch in the student union building; Mark, in the incredibly tolerant way of one who's brushed aside death (he was a cancer survivor; his lower left leg was amputated), and who saw his friend's madness for what it was, said with self-deprecating reasonableness: 'I think *any* kind of effort that brings relief to Africa is all right.'

'Can one make an aesthetic objection, though, however awful that might sound?' Ananda had insisted. 'Can an aesthetic objection go beyond what might seem morally right? That all those people cheering and dancing in Wembley Stadium, all of them thinking that by dancing to the music they were doing those starving children a good turn – that it made it quite wrong and macabre somehow, especially when you saw the faces of the children?'

Mark smiled a smile of understanding – and of one who knew death's proximity. As for Ananda: his own position on this matter underlined to him his isolation from the world – from London, for that matter.

That feeling had come to him at other times, when he'd seen the necessity for certain actions and yet couldn't participate in them – including the great march that took place a couple of years ago, soon after he'd arrived here as a student. He remembered his first awkward hour in the college – joining the other first years for the freshers' get-together in the common room on the second floor of Foster Court, ascending the stairs under a painting by Whistler and ending up informing a bespectacled girl with a Princess Di haircut that the Sanskrit *prem* meant both carnal desire and love, that there was no separation between the two in 'Indian culture'. The girl had smiled distantly. Only a week or two after his arrival, the news of the imminent cruise missiles had gathered force, leading finally to the march. He didn't want to die and he didn't want the world to blow up (as it seemed it any day would), but he couldn't spend too much time thinking of the shadow of death hanging over mankind. Yet he didn't quite admit this to himself. It was his uncle, who'd come to see him the next day in Warren Street, who'd said, while watching the Hyde Park-bound procession on TV with Monsignor Kent in the foreground (a touch of revolutionary glamour it gave to this man, the word 'Monsignor'): 'They're not getting to the root cause. They're concerned about the symptom.'

This was uttered in the droopy-eyed, amused way in which he spoke aphorisms containing a blindingly obvious truth ignored by everybody.

'Symptom?' said Ananda, challenging his uncle, but part of him chiming in.

'The nuclear bomb's only a symptom,' repeated his uncle, almost contemptuous. 'Getting rid of it won't solve anything. *Arey baba*, they have to look at the root cause.'

He pottered about for three or four minutes, making wasted journeys in the room, before parting the curtains and lifting the window a crack. In crumpled white kurta and pyjamas, he looked out on the street and on Tandoor Mahal opposite, unconcerned about being noticed by passers by below. It was striking how, with the window even marginally open – heavy wooden windows he had to heave up or claw down, and which he was unused to (they made him fear for his fingers) – sounds swam into the studio flat, making him feel paradoxically at home. His mind was elsewhere. He was aware that the house itself was very quiet. The only time there was a sound was when he walked about, and a floorboard groaned at the footfall.

Upstairs, they'd sleep till midday or later. He knew when they were awake because of the sporadic bangs and thuds that announced movement. It was as if the person who first woke up didn't just get on their feet, but stamped on the floor. The noise they made wasn't intentional – it was incidental. It wasn't directed against others because it bore no awareness of others. It was pure physical expression, made by those whose heads didn't carry too many thoughts – at least, not when they woke and became mobile again.

He hadn't slept well. This was the norm; partly, it was the recurrent hyperacidity, which had him prop up two pillows against the wall – that made it difficult to sleep too – and, cursing, reach in the dark for the slim packs of Double Action Rennie he kept at his bedside. The taste of the tablets – with associations of chalk powder and spearmint – stayed with him slightly longer than their palliative effects.

But mainly it was the neighbours. They hardly slept till 3 or 4 a.m. There were three people upstairs, but also, often, a fourth. Vivek Patel, who wore pleated trousers and was lavish with aftershave; he wore accessories too – chains around the wrist, fancy belts, et cetera. He had a lisp – or not a lisp, really, but a soft way of saying his t's that was both limpid and menacing. His girlfriend Cynthia stayed in the same room. She was Bengali, but from a family of Christian converts. Cynthia Roy. She was pretty and a little cheap-looking, with her bright red lipstick and simper and the thick outline of kohl, and with her sheep-like devotion to Vivek. Cynthia was a new kind of woman – a social aspirant, like her boyfriend – that Ananda couldn't really fathom, especially the mix of characteristics: newfangled but unintellectual, independent but content to be Vivek's follower. Anyway, Ananda barely existed for her. Someone had said she liked 'tough men'. Vivek wasn't taller than five feet seven or eight, but he was probably tough – because he was broad. In spite of his chains and aftershave, he had a swift abstracted hammerhead air. Ananda had overheard him say 'Fuck off, fuck off' to Walia, the landlord, after the payphone incident – uttering the admonishment in his calm, musical manner ('Fukko, fukko') to which Walia clearly had no answer. Walia had nevertheless reclaimed the payphone coin box and carried it downstairs and out of 16 Warren Street. But in all other ways he was toothless before Vivek Patel because Vivek's father, an East African businessman, was an old contact of Walia's. Patel senior lived in Tanzania. From there, he'd sent forth two sons, Vivek and Shashank (who stayed in the single room next to his older brother) to study at the American Management School in London. Shashank looked like

Vivek in a narrow mirror: he was slightly taller, paler and a bit nicer. He spoke with the same lisp – which could have been a hallmark of Tanzanian Gujaratis. On his lips, it sounded guileless and reassuring. He'd told Ananda in the solemn way of one gripped and won over by a fiction that the American Management School offered genuine American degrees. This was the first time they'd discussed education and pretended to be high-minded students of a similar kind – to have different aims that somehow nobly overlapped and converged in this location, despite the signals to the contrary. *No wonder they don't have to study. Besides, who comes to London to do management?*

The dull pulse-like beat started at eleven o'clock at night. It was a new kind of music called 'rap'. It baffled Ananda even more than disco. He had puzzled and puzzled over why people would want to listen and even move their bodies to an angry, insistent onrush of words – words that rhymed, apparently, but had no echo or afterlife. It was as if they were an extension of the body: never had words sounded so alarmingly physical, and pure physicality lacks empathy; it's machine-like. So it seemed from his prejudiced overhearings. But down here he couldn't hear the words – only the beat and the bass note. It wasn't loud, but it was profound, and had a way of sinking through the ceiling into his body below. Each time it started, his TV was still on, and he'd allow himself to think, *It's OK, it's not so bad really, I don't know why I let it bother me. I can ignore it.* This gave him great reassurance for a few minutes. But the very faintness of the pulse, and the way it caused the remotest of tremors – so remote he might be imagining it – was threatening.

He could cope with it while the lights were on; he could see it in perspective (how do you see a sound?) as one among other things. When he switched off the bedside lamp, the faraway boom became ominous. Its presence was absolute, interior and continuous, erasing other noises. In a darkness outlined by the perpetual yellow light coming in through the curtains, he waited for sleep. But more than sleep, he waited for the next sound. That vigil subsumed questions that came to him intermittently, and which lacked the immediacy of *When will they turn down the music?* – questions like, What am I doing in London? And what'll I do once I'm back in India? What do I do if I don't get a first; will a 2:1 suffice? Of course I won't get a first – no one does. When will the *Poetry Review* send me a reply? I've read the stuff they publish – chatty verses are the norm – and they should be struck (he thought of some lonely editor tired of sifting through dry, knowing poems by English poets) by my anguish and music. Such thoughts occurred to him during the day but were now set aside in the interests of following – in addition to the bass beat – the movements upstairs. These were abrupt and powerful, as they were when the Patels first woke up at midday, and separated by typical longueurs of silence – and immobility. The gaps were excruciating, because it was then that Ananda concentrated hardest, avidly trying to decide if activity had ended for the night. By now the music would be so faint that he'd have to strain to hear the dull electronic heartbeat. But strain is what he wanted to do; to devote, eyes shut, his whole imagination to this exercise.

I t was odd. He hadn't realized till he moved to this flat that floorboards could be so porous; and that this perviousness was an established feature of English coexistence. 'But we were colonized by them,' he thought. 'How is it that our cities are so different? How come I'm so little prepared for here?' He briefly sought but couldn't find a connection between London and Bombay – except, of course, the red double-decker buses and postboxes. It made him ill at ease – over and above having to swallow the insult of having been ruled by this nation! A nation now in turmoil, with Arthur Scargill browbeating television presenters, and the indomitable grocer's daughter unleashing policemen on horses on the miners. Ananda himself was barely aware that it was all over, that the red-faced Scargill's time was up, and that his refrain, 'At the end of the day', had caught up with him sooner than you'd have guessed two years ago. Ananda was disengaged from Indian politics but dilettantishly addicted to British politicians – the debates; the mock outrage; the amazing menu of accents; the warmth of Tony Benn's s's and his inexorable fireside eloquence; the way he cradled his pipe; the wiry trade-union leaders, blown into the void by Mrs Thatcher's booming, unbudging rebuttals. It was a great spectacle, British politics – and the actual participants and the obligatory ways in which they expressed disagreement ('That is the most ridiculous tosh I've ever heard'; 'Excuse me, but I belong to a family that's been working class for generations') was even more entertaining than the moist nonsense that their counterparts regularly sputtered on *Spitting Image.*

Class! He'd hardly been aware of it before coming to England – which was not so much an indication that it didn't exist in India as of the fact that the privileged were hardly conscious of it, as they were barely conscious of history, because they didn't dream they were inhabiting it, so much did they take it for granted. History was what had happened; class was something you read about in a book. Living in London, he was becoming steadily conscious of it, and not only of race, which was often uppermost in his mind. Who had spoken of the 'conscience of my race'? He couldn't remember. It sounded like a bogus formulation – probably some British orator, some old fart, maybe Winston Churchill. Then again, maybe not. Could it be a poet? Poets said the oddest things – odd for poets, that is. He'd discovered that the words he'd ascribed to some populist sloganeer and even, unconsciously, to Marx actually belonged to 'A Defence of Poetry'; there, Shelley had proclaimed: 'The rich have become richer, the poor have become poorer; and the vessel of the state is driven between the Scylla and Charybdis of anarchy and despotism.' How astute of Shelley to have noticed, and to have made that throwaway observation well before Marx made his advent into London! Marx had come here in 1846, and Shelley's 'Defence' was published in 1840, belatedly, nineteen years after it was composed; had the bearded one noticed it, picked it up, investigated – did Marx read poetry? Did he like poets? Certainly, it appeared to Ananda that, in England now, the rich had suddenly become richer – but he could be wrong; he was no good at economics; his sights were set on the Olympian, the Parnassian: especially getting published in *Poetry Review*. He had a notion that the poor were becoming poorer, though he didn't connect this with the pit closures. His uncle had been made redundant. Serves him right. Poor man. But, if you thought about it, there was money about and people were celebrating it, the pubs in central London near his studio flat looked less despondent and ruffianly, they'd become smarter, even the curry as a consequence of this new financial self-confidence was in ascendancy, not the old spicy beef curry and rice he'd tasted when he'd first visited London as a child, nor even the home-made Indian food that left smells in hallways which white-skinned neighbours complained of, but a smart new acceptable curry, integer of the city's recent commercial success and boom. Even before he'd journeyed to England this time, to start out as a student, he'd heard that money was flowing in from North Sea oil. Lucky bastards. Lucky for Thatcher – like a gift to her from Poseidon, or whoever the appropriate god was (he was poor in Greek mythology). Poseidon had also given her a hand in the Falklands, a war the British should have lost if only because they were British – he was angry about that. Lucky island, with more than its fair share of windfalls, rewards and fortune. In his own land, all three million square kilometres of it, they'd dug and drilled but couldn't find a single vein of oil there, nor in the oceans surrounding its deceptively plump finger-like promontory from which Sri Lanka seemed to trickle off like a drop of water. This happy breed of men, this little world. This precious stone set in the silver sea. They were doing all right.

He didn't feel prosperous. That's because he wasn't. His father was going bankrupt paying for this studio flat – and for his tuition fees which (since he was an Indian) were a few thousand pounds while domestic students paid nothing. Thatcher was responsible, but he bore her no personal ill will – he was prepared to overlook some of her shortcomings for being so integral to the great British show. When he marvelled at her emphatic delivery, sitting in front of the TV, it was her performance he was concerned with and not her words – nor did he connect her directly with the murderous fees his father was paying.

Carrying more than five hundred dollars when you were abroad violated FERA, the Foreign Exchange Regulation Act; so his father had devised the following method around it. Ananda's uncle disbursed monthly largesse among relatives living in Shillong and Calcutta – mainly in Shillong, with straggly families displaced during partition – the principal sum going to an older brother. This made Radhesh (his uncle) feel kingly, and succumb to the tribulations of being a king on whom many were dependent. He could never forget the irony that the family – including this older brother – had dealt with him in his childhood largely with remonstrances, seen him as a bit of a loafer, and that he, buoyed up by the British pound (even if he'd recently been made redundant), was now helping them. 'The reason I didn't marry,' he claimed in one of his monologues, 'was because I' – he patted his frail chest lightly – 'wanted to be there for my family.' *That's not entirely true. You are, and always have been, afraid of women.* Now Ananda's father made all those payments to those remote towns in the hills; the equivalent amount was transferred monthly from Ananda's uncle's National Westminster account to Ananda's. In this manner, FERA was subverted but not exactly flouted, and Ananda's low-key, apparently purposeless education was made possible. It was an arrangement that both satisfied and exacerbated his uncle. His aristocratic urge to preside and dispense – trapped within his slight five-foot-eight-inch frame – was appeased, but his precious need for privacy (he was a bachelor, after all) was compromised.

Because of the paucity of money at any given time, Ananda had to ration his recurrent expenditure on lunch, dinner, books and pornographic magazines. The last comprised all he knew, at this moment, of coitus. They were a let-down. He anyway suffered from a suspicion that the women were only pretending to enjoy sex, and this consciousness was a wedge between him and his own enjoyment. He required pornography to be a communal joy, shared equally between photographer, participant and masturbator. But his suspicion was reinforced by Thatcher's repression of the hardcore. The men's penises, if you glimpsed them, were limp. There was hardly anything more innately biological and morosely unsightly than a limp penis. Meanwhile, the women's mouths were open as they lay back in their artificial rapture. Nevertheless, he pursued his climax doggedly and came on the bed sheet.

Last night, he'd brought home the first of his two customary Chinese dinner options – mixed fried rice and Singapore noodles – from the restaurant on Euston Road. The other side of that road was so still and dark (notwithstanding the sabre-like hiss of passing cars) that it might have been the sea out there for all he knew. By day, an unfriendly glass-fronted building reflected the rays of the English sun; neighbouring it was a post office. Whenever he was in the Chinese restaurant for his fried rice or Singapore noodles in the evening it was as if these were a figment of his imaginings – until he'd seen them both the next day when he crossed the road to Euston Square. The restaurant last night had been almost empty, and the staff were as distant as ever and didn't let on that they were familiar by now with him and his order (both the Singapore noodles and the fried rice were one pound fifty) and with his timorous aloneness. They hardly made any attempt at conversation; presumably because their vocabulary was so austerely functional. England and its tongue refused to rub off on the staff of London's Chinese restaurants, Ananda had noticed; they continued to be defined by a dour but virginal Chineseness. Their taciturn nature was a kind of solace. Thus, silence characterized the time of waiting during which a man rushed ingredients into a wok, producing a hiss and a piercing, galvanizing aroma that Ananda relished as he ate in solitude, watching *Question Time*. Having a small amount of money in his wallet meant he had to choose from an exceptionally narrow range of orders; but he didn't mind, because he mostly lacked appetite. The walk from Warren Street to the unexpected moonscape of Euston Road and back again, by when the Patels were stirring in expectation of the night, was so full of loneliness that it couldn't even be softened by self-pity. During the day, he sometimes forgot lunchtime, delaying eating since it was a boring duty, as sleeping and occasionally waking were. *What exactly should I do today? It's going to be my final year,* the hunger came and then passed, it had disappeared even from his memory, he saw it was an entirely dispensable thing he could cast aside with impunity if he ignored its birth pangs, and at half past three he bit into a green apple. For this reason, he'd grown – to his own abetting approval – very thin (poets were seldom plump) and more and more reliant upon Double Action Rennie, the acidity habitually returning to him at night-time with its stabbing pain. Still, none of these compared, in their undermining, with the stripping of his identity itself. None of the things that defined him – that he was a modern Bengali and Indian, with a cursory but proud knowledge of Bengali literature; that he wrote in English, and had spoken it much of his life; that he used to be served lettuce sandwiches as a teatime snack as a child; that in his early teenage years he'd subsisted on a diet of Agatha Christie and Erle Stanley Gardner; that he'd developed a taste for corduroys over jeans recently – almost none of this counted for anything in London, since everyone here spoke English, ate sandwiches and wore jeans or corduroys. In this way, his identity had been taken away from him; and he'd become conscious, in England, of class. Class was what formed you, but didn't travel to other cultures – it became invisible abroad. In foreign places, you were singled out by religion and race, but not by class, which was more indecipherable than any mother tongue.

A sunny day! Again! One end of his white kurta fluttered in the mild breeze that was coming through the crack he'd created by pushing up the window. Almost directly opposite was Tandoor Mahal, with its unprepossessing plastic sign. Its day had begun too, though its real day would start at half past twelve, when the board on the door would be flipped on its back to say OPEN. He looked at it. Sunlit, like all else in the world. Lace curtains drawn, cheap red curtains tied on the sides with a sash, the menu card showing.

Traffic into the restaurant began before it opened; the owner's two daughters, the older one in her teens, quite pretty but a bit bent, wearing jeans, the younger brother who must be nine or ten – they'd either linger on the pavement or walk (the older one leading) towards the Underground. At random moments of their choosing, the family went in and out of the restaurant, as if it were an annexe to their house: they lived next door. The children didn't know Ananda, but he knew their father, the round-faced man with big expressive eyes – like Vivekananda's, but *sans* the penetrating quality – that contained love and life in their gaze; hope, too, since it was possible that business might suddenly pick up. As behoves an owner, he was at all hours of the day in a suit, except he forgot his jacket half the time and so it was the white shirt and grey trousers you mainly saw him in. The principal traffic into the restaurant, it had become clear, comprised the family – though Ananda had never seen the wife – stepping out of the house next door and stepping into Tandoor Mahal. There were very few customers who were tempted to enter the door from Warren Street; there had to be a few who walked in through the Euston Road entrance.

If the place had at least rustled up a decent tandoori chicken, Ananda might have ordered a half chicken and naan sometimes as a takeaway and come back home with it in half a minute rather than rely repeatedly on Chinese mixed fried rice or go to Walia's Diwan-i-Am for an Indian takeaway. He quite liked the scored and singed flesh of tandoori chicken – his eyes feasted on the red lacquering – but the Tandoor Mahal bird was less than ordinary. He'd gone in there earlier this year with his uncle. By then, the oozing proprietor, Alam, was somehow aware they were of Sylheti ancestry, and addressed his uncle in that tongue, '*Aain, aain,*' a dialect his uncle abhorred – almost embracing them in his eagerness. Then, in this familial vein, he'd given them, as fellow Sylhetis, reluctant though they were, a tour of the kitchen in the basement, where the cook's helper, unmotivated and unhurried, was frying poppadom in a pan of frothy orange oil. It was early evening, they were the only customers and Ananda's uncle and he were pampered like honoured guests. Sylhetis behaved thus –

these people, who'd single-handedly recreated this menu, this cuisine, and invented these restaurants – they distributed nourishment to the English in general (tandoori tikka masala, tarka dal, vindaloo, poppadoms), but to long-sundered kin from their own land (that is, to Hindus) they extended a hand of familiarity and kindness. In their own land, Ananda's uncle and Alam's kind had been as strangers are; then they'd contested the referendum and his uncle, his parents and their ilk had found themselves outnumbered and had to depart their homes altogether. But here, in these restaurants, that bitterness was forgotten, and the Sylhetis unfailingly gave them – once they discovered his uncle hailed from Bejura in Habiganj district – a chicken jalfrezi on the house, or unobtrusively omitted the gulab jamun from the bill. Often there'd be an extra mint chocolate on the platter. The old wars were set aside; there was only compassion, transmuted from memory. The Sylhetis were great Samaritans – especially to a displaced member of the race who was now without a real home in London; or so Ananda felt, instinctively, in the interiors of these restaurants. Still, the slivers of onion, the poppadom and mango chutney, the chicken tikka that Mr Alam had served them had – it was undeniable – a stale aftertaste; his uncle and he made the extra effort as they lied to Mr Alam about the food, but that was their last visit.

*S*hall I compare thee
Shall I compare thee to

Although the lines were incomplete, they kept ending on a question mark. He felt his inner voice rising docilely at the end. Confronting the day in Warren Street with the mug of tea in one hand, a breeze beneath the now one-quarter-raised window flicking his weightless kurta ends, he reflected again – as he had only recently – on the beauty and particularity of the word 'summer'. It wasn't a word that had previously interested him. In India, it was a dead word, spoken almost without reference to its meaning, and all its mutations and locations – 'summery', 'a midsummer night's dream' – were ready clichés that locked up experience. What summer itself was in India, or in its different regions, was still untapped, unaddressed in this colonial language. Only after coming to England had he discovered the beauty of the word. On reading the poem itself in Bombay in his school textbook, he'd decided it was stupid; silly, even. And who, in India, would compare someone to a summer's day – except to insult the addressee? A near-imbecilic line.

Shall I compare thee to a summer's day?

But, no; it was beautiful. He'd reread the sonnet, for his preparations for the Renaissance paper, and then, after reacting against it through its earlier associations, read it once again, allowing himself to understand it. The lines had begun to repeat themselves in his head, like a jingle in a commercial. The poet – what was he up to? He'd meant to extol his beloved – not by saying she was as good as a summer's day, but better! Letting the wooden frame nestle his chin, Ananda daydreamed, studying Tandoor Mahal and its curtains.

Thou art more lovely and more temperate.

More lovely, *more* temperate! So the poet was dissing the summer's day, then, in order to praise his beloved. Yet what apposite terms for this summer, as a season, or in its incarnation as a single day: 'lovely', with its suggestion of innocence and newborn qualities; 'temperate', indicating calm, modesty and fortuitously echoing 'temporal', with its hint of the short-lived. 'Lovely' carried in it the sense of the short-lived too; the loveliness of 'lovely' was contingent on it not being eternal. And so the summer's day was transient in comparison to the poet's beloved, who'd continue to prosper and grow to 'eternal lines' in the effing sonnet. To emphasize this, Shakespeare must diss the English spring and summer in the third and fourth lines again:

Rough winds do shake the darling buds of May,
And summer's lease hath all too short a date.

It was the fragility and the undependability of the English summer that Shakespeare was drawing the reader's attention to – hoping, thereby, that the contrast would aggrandize his lover's qualities. But, for Ananda, it was summer – by being contingent – that came to brief life on his rediscovery of the poem in London, and not the beloved, immobile and fixed in eternity; because the imagination is drawn – not by sympathy, but some perverse definition of delight – to the fragile, the animated and the short-lived. In this unlikely manner, the near-imbecilic sonnet had been returning to him in the last four days.

A butterfly had settled on the upper window. It had closed its wings, simulating a leaf, or engendering a geometric angle, perfect as a shadow, but was now wavering and bending to one side – not out of any obedience to the breeze, but according to a whim. Almost nothing – but for this pane with faint blotches of mildew – separated it in its world outside (Warren Street) from the studio flat within, from where Ananda measured it, intrigued. All insects made him apprehensive. Where had this rarity come from? The principal danger of summer, he'd found, was bees. Almost every day one came in without invitation. He had to pretend he was unmoved by its floating, persistent exploration of the room, until, unable to cohabit with it an instant longer, his nerves already on edge, he'd have to, with an almost superhuman effort, quickly push the window up halfway, causing the house to tremble to its foundations, and then rally to chase it out with something appropriate – usually a copy of *The Times* or the *Times Literary Supplement*. The comedy and even the undeniable magic of that chase became clear to him the moment the bee had escaped, the room was empty but for him and – like someone in a storm – he grappled with lowering the window again.

He saw now, suddenly, that the butterfly was gone – the street's voyager; undertaking short, unsteady bursts of flight. ∎

Mahatma Gandhi (bottom row right) with members of the London Vegetarian Society, 1890

GANDHI
THE LONDONER

Sam Miller

July 1942. Sevagram Ashram, central India

DAILY EXPRESS REPORTER: Mr Gandhi, you have been in London yourself. Have you no comment to make on the heavy bombings which the British people have sustained?

MAHATMA GANDHI: Oh yes. I know every nook and corner of London where I lived for three years, so many years ago, and somewhat of Oxford and of Cambridge and Manchester too; but it is London I specially feel for. I used to read in the Inner Temple Library, and would often attend Dr Parker's sermons in the Temple Church. My heart goes out to the people, and when I heard that the Temple Church was bombed, I bled.

On 29 September 1888, an Indian teenager with a mild case of ringworm and a fine head of hair sailed into the Thames Estuary. He was wearing a white flannel suit that would soon become a cause of enduring shame. As the estuary narrowed after Canvey Island, the SS *Clyde* was forced sharply south, before heading west again, towards London – and the flat muddy shorelines of Kent, on the left, and Essex, on the right, were now visible. The busy Kentish town of Gravesend, with its cast-iron river piers and its Pocahontas church (the 'Indian' princess was buried there), soon hove into view. But the *Clyde* and the teenager were bound for more modest Tilbury on the Essex shore – and for the new port that had just been built to relieve pressure on London's more proximate docklands.

In the late 1880s, Tilbury became London's most important passenger terminal. The *Windrush* and its Jamaican migrants would dock here in 1948, and it was where many other migrants, such as the 'Ten Pound Poms', would leave Britain for Australia. Today, apart from the occasional cruise ship, passengers are unseen at Tilbury. And the only easy way to approach Tilbury by boat these days is the oldest: the foot ferry from Gravesend that has existed since at least the seventeenth century.

'Single or return?' asked the flat-voiced man sitting at a small desk in the ferry's only cabin.

'Single.'

'Single is three pounds fifty. Return is three pounds.'

'Single.' I wasn't really listening.

'Are you sure?'

And then I realized.

'OK. Return, then. That's a bit odd.'

He gave me an old-fashioned look.

'I don't make the rules, do I?'

I grinned and looked around. Another passenger tittered. I sat down beside her and her shopping bags. She asked me where I was going.

'Tilbury.' I giggled. We were all going to Tilbury.

'Yes, Tilbury.' I continued. 'A long time ago Mahatma Gandhi went to Tilbury by boat.'

'From Gravesend?'

'No. From India.'

She was silent, and thoughtful.

'He'd have been a bit chilly. In that loincloth thing.'

'Actually, he was wearing a white flannel suit.'

'Oh. Then it wouldn't have been so bad.'

I went on deck and was able to make out the three-domed Sikh gurdwara (completed in 2010), punching its way clear of the old Gravesend skyline. On the Tilbury side, the ferry slid past a coastal fort (completed in the 1680s), with a curved masonry gateway rearing out of the marshes. I wondered if Gandhi noticed the gateway, so similar to those in early colonial settlements in Gujarat or Bombay, or was he already preoccupied with his blessed suit, or with finding the railway station that would take him to London? And then we gently struck the landing jetty, and I was brought back to earth.

Ahead of me was the old railway station, abandoned in 1992, the main building still standing – the platforms now an unused car park, its pristine emptiness protected by harpoon-like palisades and coils of razor wire. I would have to walk to the main station in Tilbury town. The old railway siding, further inland, was now stacked high with shipping containers and, closer to the estuary, I could see the modern port, with huge blue cranes, a great mountain of shiny twisted scrap metal – and three spinning wind turbines.

I pushed on into Tilbury, along Calcutta Road, and peered inside an 'Indian' restaurant near the station, Le Raj. The waiter, from Bangladesh, couldn't tell me why it had that name, but said the 'le' should be pronounced 'lay'. I bit my tongue and smiled.

'Not many Asians around here,' he said. 'Mainly blacks and whites.'

He showed no interest in the fact that Gandhi had passed through Tilbury. I was beginning to lose interest myself. So I told him the story. How Gandhi wore a white flannel suit on the advice of his Bombay friends, and was mortified on arrival in England to find that no one else was dressed in a similar manner. He talked of 'the shame of being the only person in white clothes', and then, even worse, how he couldn't get his luggage delivered because it was the weekend, and so he had to remain in his embarrassing flannel suit for two more days.

'What is flannel?' the waiter asked, as he washed some beer glasses.
'Like cricket clothes, a bit.'
'Oh. Did he play cricket?'
'No, he didn't. Can I order some food?'
'No, it's a Tuesday. We're closed.'
'Oh, OK.'

I left, walked across Dock Road and, like Gandhi, an eighth of a
millennium earlier, took the train to London.

Mohandas Gandhi, the youngest son of the former prime minister
of a small princely state, had come to England to study law,
in the belief that a London legal qualification would improve his
career prospects in India. And he was wildly excited, despite several
embarrassing incidents, including the white flannel suit episode, to
be in the largest city in the world, the city he would describe as 'dear
London' and 'the centre of civilization'. He had taken a considerable risk
in coming to London, defying his caste elders and borrowing money to
finance his stay. He was leaving behind his wife (Gandhi and Kasturba
were married as thirteen-year-olds) and their baby son. His father had
died two years earlier, and he would never see his mother, Putlibai,
again. She had made him swear, before he left India, that he would not
touch meat, alcohol or women. And so far, despite temptations on all
three fronts during the journey from Bombay to Tilbury, he had kept
that vow. There would be further such temptations.

Gandhi's London years have often been skated over, or
deliberately ignored. They are entirely missing from the celluloid,
Richard Attenborough version of his life, a film that sadly seems
to provide the modern world with its canonical depiction of the
Mahatma. Some of his hagiographers seem a little uncomfortable
with Gandhi's antics in London, that he showed so little interest
in Indian nationalism, or in politics in general – and that he took
dancing and violin lessons, that he professed a desire to be 'an English
gentleman', that he flirted with young women. But not Gandhi
himself, who was always keen to reveal to the world his mistakes

and his peccadilloes. And most important it was in London, of all places, that two key strands of Gandhi's ideas developed, ones that would later be more closely associated with the land of his birth: he became a proselytizing vegetarian, and first showed interest in Hindu religious philosophy. The catalysts in both cases were English friends whom he had met in London.

Gandhi wrote at length of his time in the city in his autobiography, in what were his first forays into journalism (for the *Vegetarian*) and in a guide that he wrote, but never published, for Indian visitors to London. There is also a diary fragment, and sparse recollections from people who knew Gandhi at this time. He was studying to be a barrister at the Inner Temple for most of his London sojourn, but it was also a period of intense experimentation and change for a young man who would later subtitle his autobiography *The Story of My Experiments with Truth*, and who continued with those experiments throughout his life. And his tales of London, taken together, remain an entertaining and illuminating read, revealing of both the man and the city.

Gandhi is not always a reliable witness. When he came to write his autobiography in 1925, he had forgotten all about Tilbury, and seemed to believe that he had disembarked at Southampton. But he had forgotten none of his embarrassments – and remembered the white flannels, in particular. V.S. Naipaul, who seems to have read only the autobiography and not the other sources, compounds the Tilbury error, and embarrasses himself, by lambasting Gandhi in *India. A Wounded Civilization* for writing nothing about his impressions of Southampton. Typical Gandhi 'self-absorption', he declares, pressing on to point out with military imprecision that 'Southampton is lost in that embarrassment (and rage) about the white flannels'. From this exposed salient, Naipaul mounts a full-scale attack on Indians, in general, for whom 'the outer world matters only in so far as it affects the inner'. Naipaul is right to suggest that Gandhi was self-absorbed, but so, perhaps, are all the best autobiographers, and we might just as easily use the word self-aware, and come away thinking better of the man, and less well of his critics.

Our impressionable teenager, then, dressed in white flannels, and in the company of two other passengers from India, travelled by train from Tilbury to Fenchurch Street station. They took a horse-drawn cab to the Victoria Hotel, now an undistinguished hall of residence for LSE students on Northumberland Avenue near Trafalgar Square. 'I was quite dazzled by the splendour of the hotel,' he wrote in his diary. 'I had never in my life seen such pomp . . . There were electric lights all over.' He was taken into what he believed to be a waiting room, but which was in fact a lift. He describes how the doorman pressed a button, and it was a matter of 'great surprise' when he arrived at the second floor. And his room? 'When I first saw my room in the Victoria Hotel, I thought I could pass a lifetime in that room.'

A family friend from India, practising as a doctor in London, came over that evening and, Gandhi recorded many years later, smiled to see him in flannels. Gandhi picked up the doctor's top hat and stroked it against the grain, as it were, and 'disturbed the fur'. The doctor responded 'somewhat angrily'. This, Gandhi later wrote, was his 'first lesson in European etiquette'. The doctor explained that in England he should not, as he might in India, touch people's possessions, or talk loudly, or ask questions of a new acquaintance. The doctor then prescribed him acetic acid for ringworm (Gandhi would remember the burning pain of the acid almost forty years later) and suggested he move out of the hotel immediately, and into an English home.

Gandhi's early months were largely dedicated to his attempts at, in the words of his own chapter title, 'Playing the English Gentleman'. He began to dress snappily, discarding his ready-knotted ties and his Bombay suits with their old-fashioned cut. Gandhi spent nineteen shillings on a 'chimney pot hat' and bought an evening suit 'made in Bond Street, the centre of fashionable life in London' for ten pounds. An Indian contemporary who encountered Gandhi near Piccadilly Circus described him later in some detail, in a way that suggested he had put the white flannels incident well behind him:

He was wearing a high silk top hat burnished bright, a Gladstonian collar, stiff and starched; a rather flashy tie displaying almost all the colours of the rainbow under which there was a fine striped silk shirt. He wore as his outer clothes a morning coat, a double-breasted vest, and dark striped trousers to match and not only patent leather boots but spats over them. He carried leather gloves and a silver-mounted stick, but wore no spectacles. He was, to use the contemporary slang, a nut, a masher, a blood – a student more interested in fashion and frivolities than in his studies.

Gandhi the 'masher' decided, as part of his attempts to become an English gentleman, to take lessons in dancing, elocution and French. He persisted with French, and added Latin – the latter to help him with the law. But he soon dropped elocution, and the dancing was a disaster – he took six lessons in three weeks and gave up, because he was unable 'to achieve anything like rhythmic motion'. (How could the director of *Gandhi* have omitted this wonderfully Chaplinesque scene from the film?) Gandhi bought a violin for three pounds, and acquired a female violin teacher. The violin was soon sold off, with a bit of assistance from the teacher, who didn't encourage him to keep playing. Gandhi would later recall how his 'infatuation' with becoming a gentleman lasted only three months, but that his 'punctiliousness in dress continued for years'. He continued to wear well-tailored Western clothes until 1913.

By 1890, Gandhi's profligate days in London were over, and he took to counting his pennies, balancing his accounts every evening before bed. This was partly born of necessity, since his family in India could not support him in the style to which he had become accustomed – but it soon became a discipline, almost a way of life. He became obsessed with saving money, one of several emerging obsessions. He moved to cheaper and cheaper accommodation – though he would refer, admiringly, to those who could make do with even less than him by living in London slums – which is practically his only reference to the poor of London. Gandhi lodged in several parts of west London that he termed 'respectable', including Barons Court, Bayswater and Westbourne Park, and had short stays in Bloomsbury, Covent Garden and Richmond.

His guide to Indian students coming to London goes into meticulous detail on the subject of saving money. Gandhi boasts that he eventually learned to get by on just one pound a week – seven shillings for rent, nine shillings for food and four shillings for everything else. He began to walk everywhere, often ten miles a day, so as not to waste money on public transport (and to improve his health). He learned how to shave himself, pointing out to his spoiled fellow countrymen that 'even kings are not ashamed of doing so in Europe', and Gandhi thereby saved himself another two pence a day. He described how he used chalk for cleaning his teeth, which saved him a halfpenny each week. And three tumblers of hot water and a sponge were quite enough to clean his whole body, with the help of 'one cake of Pears soap [which] would last a month' and cost three and a half pennies. Sometimes he used his bare hands instead of a sponge. His parsimonious ablutions were backed up by a fortnightly or monthly visit to the public baths. He also records how he saved money on laundry by getting his underwear washed less frequently, or by not wearing any in the summer. Sometimes Gandhi provides his readers with too much information.

In the course of his London years, Gandhi became an evangelical vegetarian, and met fellow vegetarians who would have a profound influence on him. Previously in India, he had, for a while, regularly eaten goat meat, in the belief that it would help him become 'strong and daring'. And there's even a carnivorous twist to the struggle for independence as he records how he believed, in his mid-teens, that eating meat would make Indians better able to 'defeat the English and make India free'. In support of this position, Gandhi quotes the Gujarati poet Narmad:

Behold the mighty Englishman
He rules the Indian small
Because being a meat-eater
He is five cubits tall

But Gandhi was never a convinced carnivore. He described a recurring nightmare: of a live goat that was bleating inside his body. Eventually, he gave up meat, not so much because of his inner goat but because he could no longer bear lying to his parents. When the SS *Clyde* reached the Red Sea, an English passenger said that he would die in the cold climate of England if he did not eat meat, and predicted that by the time Gandhi reached the Bay of Biscay he would have changed his mind. As he neared Tilbury, Gandhi proudly procured a written certificate from his fellow passenger affirming that he had not eaten any meat.

In those early days in London, as he battled his first British winter, Gandhi's new friends counselled him to break his oath. London was not then an easy place for vegetarians, and there were no Indian restaurants. Gandhi lived almost entirely on porridge, bread and jam in those first few months, and he found boiled vegetables *à l'anglaise* insufferably bland. One of his despairing landladies told him that she had heard of a vegetarian restaurant in the City, and he wandered around trying to find it. Eventually, near Ludgate Circus, he chanced upon the Congregational Memorial Hall (built on the site of the old Fleet Prison) and inside was an eating house known as the Central Vegetarian Restaurant. As he was entering, he spotted a pamphlet called 'A Plea for Vegetarianism', written by Henry Salt, an old Etonian born in India. On that day, as well as having 'the first hearty meal since I arrived in England' (which he unfortunately fails to describe), Gandhi became, under Salt's influence, a vegetarian by choice and conviction, not because of a filial vow. The spread of vegetarianism became, he said, his 'mission'.

Gandhi bought himself an oil stove so he could cook simple Indian food – such as dal, rice, vegetables and chapattis – and found more vegetarian restaurants, including one called the Porridge Bowl on High Holborn. His guide for Indian students in London is full of culinary advice about rather un-Indian (but still vegetarian) foodstuffs that can be found in the city, including Gorgonzola, Brussels sprouts, macaroni, tapioca pudding, blancmange and a wheat powder known as Florador that is best mixed with milk.

Gandhi's favourite restaurants (and Florador) are long gone. The Congregational Memorial Hall, the enormous Victorian Gothic building where Gandhi's vegetarian epiphany took place, became associated with the labour movement; it was both the site of the creation of the Labour Party in 1900 and the headquarters for the General Strike of 1926. This was not enough to stop it being demolished in 1969 and replaced by an office block. The site of the Porridge Bowl is now a Spanish tapas bar. Gandhi has not been entirely forgotten in this part of London. On Gray's Inn Road there's a restaurant, recently refurbished, that bears his name, possessively, as Gandhi's. But there are no images of the man, or any obvious connection; and meat and alcohol are served. The head waiter, a man of Bangladeshi origin, was unapologetic about the non-vegetarian menu, the bottles of alcohol on display and the name of the restaurant. 'He was a great man, that's why the owner chose the name. But you see, most of our customers are non-veg; they want a beer or a glass of wine with Indian food, and chicken or prawns. Chicken tikka is the most popular. And there are lots of vegetarian items on the menu: we do onion bhajis, aloo chaat, vegetable kebabs, stuffed parathas.' London has certainly become an easier place for vegetarians.

Gandhi soon became a member of the London Vegetarian Society, and by attending its meetings he found a new social milieu. It was largely white, male, middle class, non-conformist and fiercely argumentative. His new best friend was a young lawyer called Josiah Oldfield, who edited the *Vegetarian* newsletter. Both Oldfield and Dr Thomas Allinson (whose name has been immortalized in a variety of brown bread still available in Britain) would later claim to have converted Gandhi to vegetarianism. Gandhi's quarrelsome new acquaintances expected him to take a stand, and he was dragged into their political infighting. At one point, almost by accident, Gandhi found himself 'in the losing party'. There had been an attempt to throw Dr Allinson off the executive committee because of his support for modern methods of birth control. Gandhi voted in favour of Allinson, in spite of his own opposition to contraception, because he felt the issue had nothing to with the purpose of the society. Allinson, and Gandhi, lost the vote. And it was while Gandhi was on Vegetarian Society business that he came closest to breaking his vow not to have sex. He had travelled to a conference of vegetarians in Portsmouth, where the Society lodged him in a hostel full of women who, he says, 'were not very scrupulous about their morals'. There he played cards with a woman who 'moved me to lust'. But Gandhi ran away at the decisive moment, and shut himself up in his room, declaring later that he 'passed the night sleeplessly, all kind of thoughts assailing me'. The following day he fled the conference and Portsmouth.

For a while, Gandhi shared a Bayswater flat with Josiah Oldfield – the first of several European men with whom he would develop a very close relationship. They held parties at the flat, serving rice and lentils to their guests. And they appeared as a double act at public meetings trying to convince Londoners to adopt a healthier lifestyle. Together they set up the Bayswater branch of the London Vegetarian Society, with Gandhi as secretary and Oldfield as president. As vice president they co-opted Sir Edwin Arnold, one of the best-known writers of the day and the author of a freewheeling translation of the Hindu philosophical and religious text, the Bhagavad Gita. Gandhi would later describe the Gita as his 'spiritual dictionary', but he admitted, slightly embarrassed, that he had first encountered the Gita not in India, nor in an Indian language, but in London, and in Arnold's translation. He also read Arnold's *The Light of Asia,* an epic poem about the life of Buddha, and was captivated by Christ's Sermon on the Mount 'which went straight to my heart'. He attempted to create a syncretic philosophy of his own: 'My young mind tried to unify the teachings of the Gita, *The Light of Asia* and the Sermon on the Mount.' Gandhi had begun to find his calling, his later spiritual direction, from these stories of renunciation, of turning the other cheek, but he gives no sense of there being a political dimension to his new philosophy. That would come later, in South Africa and India.

Gandhi also fell easily into the company of a number of slightly eccentric, religious freethinkers and psychomancers. He met the theosophists Annie Besant and Madame Blavatsky in London, and Blavatsky's often opaque writing 'cured' Gandhi of 'the notion fostered by missionaries that Hinduism was rife with superstition'. Gandhi used to visit the City Temple, a newly constructed neoclassical church on Holborn (and not the Temple Church that he confused it with more than fifty years later in the *Daily Express* interview) to hear the celebrated Congregationalist minister Joseph Parker, famous for his vigorously theatrical sermons. And these were interests that would continue after Gandhi left London. A few years later, in South Africa in the mid 1890s, Gandhi would become the local agent of the Esoteric Christian Union, an occult group of English mystics who had broken away from theosophy, and whose theology was based on revelations that came to its co-founder, Anna Kingsford, while she was dreaming or in a trance.

Gandhi the 'masher' of 1889 had, by 1891, as he neared the end of his time in London, become Gandhi the 'faddist', a word he used to describe how others saw him and his group of friends. As well as vegetarianism and religious philosophy, Gandhi had begun to take a great interest in self-medication, in experimenting with his body by denying himself particular foods, by bathing in a certain manner. 'Constipation,' he declared in a way that would foreshadow a later obsession with enemas, 'is the father of many diseases.' His London pre-enema solution was to eat as much fruit as possible. Gandhi would lament later that he should have studied medicine. He even later toyed with switching from law like his friend Josiah Oldfield, who became a doctor at a fruitarian hospital in Kent – and who remained a friend of Gandhi's even though they would later disagree about Indian independence. Gandhi's obsession with natural treatments would be lifelong – an obsession that again can be traced to London, not India.

Looking back on Gandhi's years in London, it is striking just how uninterested he was in those who weren't part of his small, esoteric, nonconformist, middle-class world. In his writings he does not speak of the lives of the rich or the poor, or indeed the very large number of foreigners, mainly Europeans, living in London. He does not mention socialism, nor the major politicians of the day, nor the Irish Home Rule movement. He refers to the great Dock Strike of 1889, but only in passing. He did meet Dadabhai Naoroji, then a Liberal parliamentary candidate, and already London's most famous Indian. But he fails to mention the great rumpus that was caused, while he was in London, by the prime minister, Lord Salisbury, who referred to Naoroji as 'a black man', whom no right-thinking English voter would elect as an MP. Salisbury was wrong, of course, and in 1892, the year after Gandhi left London, Naoroji was elected as MP for Finsbury Central, by a margin of just five votes, almost certainly helped to victory by the negative reaction to Salisbury's comments.

What is perhaps most significant is that there is not the slightest sense on Gandhi's part that he, or any other Indian, faced any racial discrimination while in London. And this is very important, given what ensued. On his return to India and during his subsequent time in South Africa, he did feel discriminated against, and his autobiography describes this in some detail. In 1892, the year after he left London, he was ejected from the office of a British official in India, with whom he hoped, as a London-qualified lawyer, to be able to talk on equal terms. The official got his peon to take Gandhi by the shoulder and throw him out of the room. The following year in South Africa, there was the famous Pietermaritzburg station incident, when Gandhi was thrown off a train by a railway official when a white passenger objected to Gandhi's presence in a first-class carriage. In retrospect, London must have seemed like a colour-blind utopia.

Gandhi never lost his affection for London – even though he came to despair both of urban life and of British imperial rule. He visited the city four more times. During the period covered by the first three of those trips (in 1906, 1909 and 1914) he gradually emerged as a public figure – as South Africa's most prominent Indian politician of the Edwardian era. Gandhi's first biographer, writing in 1909, quotes him as saying, 'Even now, next to India, I would rather live in London than in any other place in the world.'

In 1931, on his final visit, Gandhi was a celebrity, a superstar of sorts, followed everywhere by journalists and admirers. He was officially in London to take part in the Second Round Table Conference on the future of India, but he was much in demand socially. Charlie Chaplin asked to be introduced to him; he visited the prime minister in Downing Street, and the King-Emperor at Buckingham Place. He also found time to address the London Vegetarian Society, and to meet Maria Montessori, George Bernard Shaw and the Archbishop of Canterbury.

This time, Gandhi chose to stay in a part of London that he did not know from his previous trips: the East End. He said he wished to live among the poor, and so he ended up sleeping in a small rooftop room in a newly built community centre in Bow. The centre, known as Kingsley Hall, was run by Muriel Lester, a middle-aged English Baptist who had visited Gandhi's ashram in India. Most mornings before dawn, Lester and Gandhi, and others from his entourage, would head off on long walks. Muriel Lester called these the 'sewer walks', because their favoured routes were along fetid canals and, in particular, a covered sewer, now prettified as the Greenway. 'I love the East End,' Gandhi declared, 'particularly the little urchins in the streets.' But the poverty was, he said, 'nothing' compared to India. He pointed out how much things had improved in the forty years since he had lived in London as a student, and remarked on how he would see 'outside each house a bottle of milk, and inside the door there is a strip of carpet, perhaps a piano in the sitting room'.

Kingsley Hall has survived, against the odds. Many surrounding buildings were destroyed during the Blitz. In the 1960s, the building became briefly famous all over again as the place where the psychiatrist R.D. Laing experimented, in a way that would have intrigued Gandhi, by living with some of his more disturbed patients. Kingsley Hall was then abandoned. In the 1980s, when Richard Attenborough wanted to film key scenes from the 1931 visit at the real Kingsley Hall, he found it derelict, but he was still able to use the tall brick facade of the building. The area, once solidly white working class, is now just as solidly Bangladeshi. Kingsley Hall has been restored, and is once again officially a community centre, with a circular blue plaque on the wall marking Gandhi's visit: the only one of Gandhi's many London residences to be marked in this way. The building was closed when I visited.

'It's always closed,' said a passing Bangladeshi woman with a shopping trolley and a small boy.

'Gandhi stayed there,' I said, pointing at the plaque.

'I know,' she responded unenthusiastically, and then she screamed in Bengali at the small boy, who was clinging to her left leg. She raised her hand as if to hit him, but held back at the last moment. He cowered, and let go of her leg. They moved on, and so did I.

I found a passageway around the side of the building, and a locked door. There was an intercom and a small label next to a button on which were written the words GANDHI FOUNDATION. A plummy English male voice answered, and invited me up onto the terrace. 'You're lucky to find me here, I'm only part-time,' said the smart young man, who went by the name of William. 'Just two days a week. The Gandhi Foundation is not very big, you see.' He showed me the small room, six foot by eight, where Gandhi stayed in 1931, with a thin mattress and a suspiciously modern portable spinning wheel, with a label saying that it had been used by Gandhi.

'Are you sure?' I asked, pointing at the spinning wheel.

'No, we don't know for sure.'

We looked at the view from the terrace. Trees and new housing developments to the south and west.

'None of this would have been here in 1931,' I said gloomily.

'But there are a few old houses left. Come and look on the other side.'

William pointed out the Bryant & May factory, famous for the matchgirls' strike of 1888, which was over just before Gandhi turned up at Tilbury. And to the east was the twisted steel tower, constructed for the Olympics, designed by an Indian artist, and manufactured from Indian steel.

'Britain's tallest sculpture,' William said.

'Gandhi wouldn't have approved. He hated the Eiffel Tower.'

William told me about the Gandhi Foundation, how it was set up after the film came out in the early eighties – and that the founder president was Richard Attenborough.

'We try to promote knowledge about the life and teaching of Gandhi.'

'Are you a follower of Gandhi?'

'Yes, I am. *And* I'm a Christian. Lots of us are Christians.' He showed me a leaflet for the annual summer school held in a medieval abbey. Lots of yoga, meditation and even some spinning. No meat and no alcohol. Gandhi would have approved.

'Do you get much interest in your work from the local community?'

'No, not really. Though we put on a play at the time of the Olympics. About Gandhi and Chaplin meeting in 1931. That was popular.'

I left bearing a large quantity of promotional literature and a peppermint-green T-shirt (for five pounds) bearing the likeness of Gandhi, and some words that he probably never said ('An eye for an eye only ends up making the whole world blind'). I traipsed downstairs and sat in the small park beside Kingsley Hall. No one was around so I stripped the top half of my body, ready to put on my Gandhi T-shirt – and then suddenly lots of young mothers, speaking a mix of Bengali and English came into the park. I quickly struggled back into my original shirt, ignored by the mothers, who may have mistaken me for a rough sleeper. A young boy, perhaps ten years old, circled me as I adjusted my clothing.

'Hello,' I said.

'Hello,' he responded.

'Do you know who Gandhi was?' I showed him the image of Gandhi on my T-shirt.

'Of course I do.'

'Who was he then?'

'He was an Indian. I saw a play about him.'

'And?'

'He came to London. He was a friend of Charlie Chaplin. He had no hair, and wore a white sheet, like a ghost. He was funny.' The boy scratched his ear, thoughtfully, and as he ran off he shouted back at me, 'He said we shouldn't fight each other.' ∎

Japanese Internment Camp, Purana Qila, Delhi, 1942–1943
Courtesy of the Estate of Fua Haripitak

THE GHOST
IN THE KIMONO

Raghu Karnad

It is possible to live in Delhi and not believe in ghosts, but that would be stubborn considering that they're everywhere. And some, more than others, have to be believed. A dead woman in a kimono visits the grounds of the Old Fort, the Mughal massif at the heart of modern Delhi. She is seen at dusk, especially in the winter, on the lawns or in the ramparts now pinched between the squealing stampede of the ring road and the gloomy cortège of the river. She is too strange to have been invented in mischief or fantasy; who here has even heard of a kimono? She must be real.

I heard about her from a friend, the lawyer Talish Ray, who had heard from the papad-wallah, who sold discs of crackling wafers out of a polythene sack as tall as he was. It was back in 2007, when Talish was younger, and not yet too sensible to walk about Delhi ruins alone, talking to men.

'*Lambe jhabley pehne bhooth,*' the papad-wallah told her. 'A ghost in long robes.'

'Really,' said Talish. 'And who is she, Princess Draupadi?'

'Oh no,' the papad-wallah said. 'It's a Japanese ghost. A Japanese dress. And she roams around asking for food for her children.'

Talish absorbed this in silence.

'Chow mein chow mein!' he suddenly added. 'That's what she

says.' The one fanciful detail apart, the papad-wallah could say no more about the ghost. Others said even less.

The staff of the Archaeological Survey rule out the possibility of there ever having been any Japanese there. 'Japanese?' snapped one official. 'Where is the proof?'

It wasn't a question.

'People will say anything that comes in their head. There is no evidence of it, no reference to it and no truth in it.'

Still we persevere. A ghost like that, in a place like that, is a pale bookmark remaining even after its page is gone. Where she meant to lead us, probably, was not across the darkening lawn, but into the dense volume of Delhi's history; there, in the very endnotes, is the remarkable, untold story of the Japanese in the Old Fort. They were tenants for one bewildering year, 1942, when Britain was losing a war against Japan, and the fort was an internment camp for enemy civilians brought here from across its Asian empire. Their story is not a ghost story, but one as factual, as technical and as burdened with consequence as any sceptic could desire.

The problem is there's too much history here already. Like the ghosts, it is everywhere in Delhi, and as with the ghosts some of it should be believed. The walls of the Old Fort, called the Purana Qila in Urdu, are not the oldest in Delhi, not by many centuries. Underneath them, however, the past runs deepest. Here is some of the most saturated archaeological terrain in India, cluttered with ceramics, stone, bone and crystal, toys, dice, gods and potsherds, mineral memoranda from every human age. They form an aquifer of fluid pasts, to be left sunken or pumped up according to modern convenience.

The official history of the Old Fort has acquired a symmetry that would please the kings who built it. Its walls and interior monuments were raised by the second Mughal emperor, Humayun, and his antagonist, the Afghan Sher Shah Suri. Its ruins were inherited by the British Raj, which built a new capital around them. Britain chose to restore the Mughals from contempt into glory – the better to inherit that glory from them – and the avenues of Delhi were named after Muslim kings, and a great promenade rolled out from the high-mounted Viceroy's House towards the Old Fort: a physical line connecting the gilded future to what was a noble past. Archaeologists improved the device by excavating, inside the Fort, ceramics dated to the Guptas and the Mauryas, kingdoms preceding the arrival of Islam in India.

Soon enough, the fort shivered off these appointed meanings. In 1947, the Viceroy's House became the home of the president, figurehead of a free republic, while at the Old Fort newer governments began to excavate deeper, seeking their reflection in further antiquity. From the 1950s onward, the Old Fort was appointed as the site of fabled Indraprastha, the dream-palace of the Pandavas, heroes of the Sanskrit epic Mahabharata. The city's new architects prepared to 'welcome the Pandavas back to the Purana Qila', and from being sixth of Delhi's Seven Cities, it was slyly promoted to first. Now the Old Fort could be grasped by modern Hindu rulers, who wielded myth where the Britons had made do with history.

As the useful, symbolic pasts piled up, it's no wonder that the incongruous fact of the Japanese in the Old Fort was allowed to vanish beneath them. What were we supposed to make of finding them there in '42, hidden in the crease between one empire and its successor? Nothing, so we remember nothing, except when they come back from the dead to surprise us.

I wonder if the ghost is Okiku, whose full name I haven't learned. She must have worn a kimono. And she was no stranger to captivity, which could account for her captive state in death, if indeed it is she. I learned about Okiku from the writer Mariko Nagai, who is fascinated by the lives of the *karayuki-san*, foreign-bound women who left Japan for the archipelagos to the south, or in other words, prostitutes. Mariko had just written a verse novella about a girl arriving at an internment camp in Idaho. She'd never heard of the camp in Delhi, but she'd found a book by Noboru Ooba, titled

Karayuki-san Okiku no Shōgai, or *The Life of Okiku, Japanese Overseas Prostitute,* from which she translated and sent me the following story.

Okiku was born at the turn of the century, in a thatch-roofed hamlet in Hiroshima prefecture. Her family belonged to the *hisabetsu buraku,* an ostracized caste of tanners and undertakers who handled the unclean and the dead. When Okiku turned seventeen, she was indentured to traffickers who took her to Penang in British Malaya. It took her three years to pay off her pimp and her brothel, after which she escaped, a free woman and a freelancer, to Singapore. There she met a fellow migrant, a Tamil named Kosaravan, whom she married. A photograph exists of Okiku and her beau, he in a snowy white shirt and pressed *mundu,* and she in a pinned and awkwardly pleated sari, smiling and clutching a purse.

Those were happy days, by her own account, and the couple had moved back to Kuala Lumpur when, at the end of 1941, Okiku's countrymen stormed the British port of Kota Bharu, inducting British Asia into the world war. The resistance, offered by Indian and Australian soldiers, was a shambles, and as the beleaguered sepoys fell back across the peninsula to Singapore, Japanese nationals were arrested and carried away in the same direction.

In *Marē Senki* (Mariko told me), a chronicle of the war in Malaya, the journalist Torakichi Sakai describes a scene of a boy begging a British soldier, 'Don't arrest my mother! She's married to an Indian!' The wives of Britons and Indians stood some chance of retaining their freedom, but Okiku, like the woman in Sakai's book, would not. Her group of internees, whom she called the *intānī,* were marshalled at Port Swettenham, where Okiku had first arrived in Malaya. They were tagged at the wrist and then transported onward to Singapore, to become the first wartime inmates of Changi Prison.

At Changi, Okiku shared facilities with numerous Japanese who would not, under normal circumstances, have anything in common with a *buraku* prostitute. One of them was Kichijiro Omori, a graduate of the Tokyo College of Commerce, and an agent of the Senda Trading Company in Singapore. Omori knew precisely the value of Malaya's rubber, tin, coal and iron ore. He read the Tokyo dailies, had heard the drums and, unlike Okiku, had been preparing for a war. Senda's top executives had already quit the colony, leaving Omori in charge of the company rubber estate at Renggam across the strait. He was still working to place it in the custody of the Anglo-Thai Corporation, which owned neighbouring plantations, when a state of emergency was declared in Singapore. There was a police list, he knew, and his name was near the top of it.

In 1993, Omori was interviewed about his experience by the Singapore National Archives. On the morning that he woke, he recalled, to the thunderclaps of bombs falling near the coast, he knew he had missed his chance to leave. '*Kuso!*' he thought. 'The war has begun.' Within hours, he was arrested in his mansion flat by an enormously tall Sikh constable, who permitted him only to pack a small case and take a last shot of whisky with his subordinates around the house shrine. Then he was taken to the Orchard Road police station, and on by boat to Port Swettenham, where he spent some days at a foul quarantine station built for Tamil coolies, before being shipped right back. At Changi, he and his cellmates climbed onto one another's shoulders each morning to watch the bombardment of the city. Omori, whose only previous concern had been how an invasion would affect business, now cheered the Mitsubishis as they droned by overhead.

The advance from the north was relentless. At the start of 1942, though it was still inconceivable that Singapore might fall, the internees at Changi learned they would be drawn back even further, right to the breast of the Empire. They were taken to the wharf by the prison, to be evacuated to India – a privilege that local Indians, not least Okiku's husband, would never receive. The voyage onboard the steamer *Ethiopia* lasted two weeks, passing west through the straits where Britain's fleet was keeling over on every side, and then north across the Bay of Bengal to Calcutta. From there it was a thousand miles further to Delhi's Nizamuddin station, where they were disembarked to walk the final mile.

The dazed procession passed through thick scrub and native hovels, and watched the beacon-white dome of Humayun's tomb, nearly equal to the Taj, rotate against the sky behind them. After a further stretch of jungle, they turned to behold it: the red gateway arch, sky-high, all covered with rosettes and six-pointed stars, bands of white marble and fields of blue tile. It was flanked by two burly bastions that led off onto the fort walls, baring openly their stone-meal of grey quartzite, red sandstone and mortar, and topped with fat crenels like giants' tongues. A peacock wailed and launched like a jewelled boat over Okiku's head. Then they were inside, crossing more scrub and sharp gravel towards a wide field of tents; their new, alien and awesome address.

The Old Fort, the first great palace of the Mughals in Delhi, had new occupants. Besides Okiku and Omori, who were they? Britain's grasp of history, its consistent virtue, may have failed them, but bureaucratic paperwork – a complementary vice – would not. The National Archives in Delhi index a series of files among the proceedings of the Home Department in 1942, more than thirty relating to the Purana Qila camp. Thirty requisition slips I filled, and each was returned with a scrawl in the corner: *Not traceable*, or *Brittle*, or *Not received from Ministry*. The natural process of attrition at Indian archives seemed to have been hurried, in this special case, by some invisible, guilty hand. It was only in the National Archives of the UK, at Kew, that I laid hands on the powdery pages of the file 'Welfare of Japanese in India: General questions'.

Here were detailed the names and vocations of the 725 Japanese women, 1,718 men and 246 children brought to the Old Fort at the start of 1942. Among them were consular staff and family members, the editors of the *Singapore Herald* and the *Singapore Nippo*, the presidents of the Japan Societies in Burma and Johor Bahru, the manager of the Fujiya Hotel, and proprietors of banks and trading firms. Yet the majority of the *intānī* were not agents of the Rising Sun, but a motley of workers and petty tradesmen. Among the women were midwives, masseuses, dressmakers and a press photographer; the men were mostly planters or fishermen, but also clerks, compositors, dentists and monks. Most had been born in Japan, but many were natives of Formosa, an early piece of Japan's rampant empire; 143 were residents of India, seventy-three of Burma and one of Iran.

Last to arrive, after their government was suborned into declaring war on Britain, was a small group of Thais, many of them art students from Rabindranath Tagore's university in Shantiniketan, Bengal. Taken all together, their only polity was as a republic of flotsam. Like Elizabeth Yamane, about whom all that is recorded is that she was born in Tiflis in the Russian Caucasus and had been living for years as a housewife in Chhapra, Bihar. She must have been astonished to be suddenly, and forcibly, rechristened a subject of the emperor.

Where they found themselves now was no Gulag, nor even a lifeless corral in the desert like the ones then receiving the Japanese of California. Rather it was a citadel in the centre of the new capital of India, which was itself the centre of the British Empire, keystone of an arch stretching from the Cape of Good Hope to the isles of Tasmania. They were, too, already at the centre of anxious consular solicitations between Tokyo, London, Delhi and their neutral intermediaries.

On 21 February, a delegation from the Red Cross visited the camp, and departed mostly satisfied. The report by Charles Huber, which survives in the archives of the Red Cross in Geneva, allows us to spy on the routines of life in the Old Fort that spring. Though bewildered by the eerie surroundings and the extreme dislocation from their civilian lives, the internees were not uncomfortable. (At the news of the fall of Singapore, just a week before, they had scraped together a celebratory feast.) The men were housed in narrow, military-pattern tents, the kind used by Indian sepoys, with brick paths running between them. Women and children lived in curtained chambers in the arcades along the fort wall. They slept separately but were not kept apart in the daytime.

February in Delhi is cool with clear, pale skies, and in most respects it was a better place to be than those places, encroached by horror, from which the *intānī* had been snatched. One Ms Oda, a clerk from the Japanese consulate in Rangoon, asked to be exempted from repatriation – available to her as a diplomatic privilege – and to remain instead with her brother in the Old Fort. Authorities had provided a roofed common kitchen and a screened area to wash. A hospital was active in one of the fort's galleries, and the internees had elected a council and raised a police patrol from their own numbers to ensure discipline.

So the children explored the fort, right up to the delicate pavilions that clustered over the farther gates; the men conferred; the women worked. They learned the timeless Delhi ways of living together within ruins; learned where among the buttresses to dry clothes, hide turds or make love. And at night Okiku must have lain down in the twitching light of whatever lamp she had, and looked up at the pale webs and trellises of stars, flowers, vine leaves and arabesques, the living capillaries of stone moulded by the Mughals into the low ceiling.

What could they have made of it? Strange envoys of a new empire threatening India, trapped in the ruined grandeur of empires gone before. Were they proud, and in their hearts did they plant the flag of their emperor here? Of all the people in the camp, Okiku said, the *karayuki-san* were happiest, and also most patriotic: the first because they had known captivity, maybe, and the second because they'd known exile. Twice a day they led the prayer to the east, towards their celestial Emperor Hirohito. Perhaps they thought that if the circumference of his realm grew large enough, they would find themselves at home again.

Or maybe they just knew what it was like to be at the mercy of too many aroused men, and were glad to be far away from it. Okiku might have prayed for the emperor, but secretly she demurred. 'Even if Japan wins,' she thought, 'it's not going to help us. It'll do nothing for us. It doesn't matter to me if Japan wins.'

For now, between them and their emperor was the advancing havoc of the war. While Rangoon and Mandalay collapsed in cinders, the main complaint in the Old Fort was about the rations, described by the Red Cross as '*juste suffisantes, elles sont conformes aux menus asiatiques*'; by Okiku, to herself, as 'sand-filled rice and soup that stinks of rotten onions'. The internees' council made a request for a more generous provision of fish. A few hundred internees, accustomed to Western living, put it on record that they'd be quite happy to receive the scale prescribed for Europeans.

It was still presumed that the two empires would deal with each other on matters like civilian internees – and it was certainly expected that civilians would be well treated. Upon receiving the Red Cross report, Tokyo began to draft a protest. The disparity between the '*menus asiatiques*' and the rations given to Germans and Italians was reprised in the matter of cash allowance – five rupees a month for Asians; for Europeans, twenty – and the fact that Europeans lived in stone-walled dormitories, while Japanese men slept six or eight to a tent, at the standard of Indian sepoys. These tents were a touchy matter: Britain had protested when its own nationals were held in tented camps by the Fascist powers. 'These camps are temporary, however,' the Red Cross reported. 'Once the new barracks are completed, all internees will be transferred.'

On 8 April, even as the Nagumo carrier group completed its raids on naval bases down the Indian and Ceylonese coast, Delhi received a fresh entreaty. Five Japanese consuls held at the hill station of Mussoorie, guessing that their welcome in India would soon be over, asked to visit their wards in the Old Fort one last time. 'It will prove to mutual benefit,' they wrote, 'as we are sure that after our return to the FO in Tokyo we will have a great deal to do with the internment business of British subjects and thus will be in a position to contribute much towards fair and just comparisons and adjustments.' With the verbose grace of obvious winners, they concluded: 'We wish to take this opportunity to express to you our sincere appreciation of all the kindness and consideration you are showing in taking care of so many Japanese internees in India.'

An internal memo pinned to their letter says: *The Japanese officials are indeed optimists.* Their request was denied. Still, Tokyo had conveyed that it was watching the treatment of its subjects in India, and could reciprocate on British subjects. By then Japan held tens of thousands of British and Commonwealth prisoners, among them the former ruling class of the colonies and the British governor of Singapore, who may well have lain perspiring in Okiku's or Omori's old cell at Changi. At the end of April 1942, apart from the civilians at the Old Fort, Britain held exactly one Japanese officer and four conscripts as prisoners of war.

The Home Department of India grew anxious to find new arrangements for the internees. Even in a country of India's size, it was not easy: the war to the east had put intense pressure on lodging of every kind. In Delhi, US airmen were arriving by the hundreds to begin the airlift to China. In fact, the demand for bare bivouacs was so great that Delhi's Chief Commissioner, A.V. Askwith, far from providing room for the Japanese, insisted they be cleared out so he could use the Old Fort himself.

A file in the Delhi State Archives spells out his intention in its title: 'Use of the Purana Qila to accommodate persons in Delhi whose homes might be destroyed in air raids'. On 17 April, Askwith wrote to the head of India's Internment Office, E. Conran-Smith, about a meeting he had convened to discuss the looming crisis. 'It was the unanimous opinion of the conference that the Purana Qila was one of the first places which should be used,' he wrote, and added that 'the non-officials present in the meeting were strong on the point . . . that it would be something of an outrage if Delhi residents bombed out of their homes had to be content with inferior accommodation, while the Purana Qila was reserved for internees or refugees from other places'.

Conran-Smith replied within the week, apologetic, saying he was 'quite as anxious as you are to remove the Japanese internees from the Purana Qila camp'. He had plans to move them to Deoli, on the edge of the north-western desert, to a camp which presently held Germans shipped in from Sumatra. But a fire at Deoli had burned down some of the dormitories and made it necessary to postpone the move. The Japanese remained in the Old Fort, and so their ordeal began.

THE GHOST IN THE KIMONO

The summer sky heated to incandescent. A terrible, total sun burned above the Old Fort and the temperature in the tents rose to nearly fifty degrees. Heat filled everything. On Sher Shah's mosque, the sparks of pink and white, as delicate as any work in Delhi, must have swum into motion before Japanese eyes; the upright grand library must have seemed a trembling hallucination. One man died of heatstroke. In response, camp officials did no more than raise some sunscreens.

Then the monsoon gusted in, and the monuments and the far gates withdrew behind curtains of rain. It grew cool, but in only a few days the basin of the fort was a swamp, slopping over the tents' brick floors. In the camp kitchen, which had felt airtight and stifling only a month before, dirty water streamed down the inner walls. The *intānī* waited miserably to be moved.

Outside the camp, the only progress was in arranging the repatriation of important internees, whose return had been expressly negotiated by Tokyo. Its concern extended to consuls and chancellors, editors, managers and executives, which of course included Kichijiro Omori. He sailed from Bombay on 22 July, aboard the *City of Paris*, to be traded into freedom at Lourenço Marques, capital of Mozambique, then ruled by neutral Portugal. The *Kamakura Maru* then delivered Omori to Singapore's Keppel Bay, and straight into the hands of the Kempeitai, the military's secret police, who were waiting to interrogate the returning exiles. It was a cold welcome. The repatriates – the most privileged of the *intānī*, who had felt the ordeal most keenly – gave the most damning account of it, all noted by the Kempeitai.

From this point, the Kew papers about the 'Welfare of Japanese in India' are concerned only with the diplomatic argument over them, rather than with their actual welfare. On 28 September, a new protest was lodged by the Japanese legation at Berne: aboard the *City of Paris*, six repatriates had succumbed to the strain of their internment and died before they got home. The survivors, and other 'sources worthy of faith', had told Tokyo all about the afflictions of those still in Delhi:

anaemia all around, and dysentery spreading from soil to mouth. Once again Tokyo admonished Delhi to see that conditions in the fort were humane.

And this from the Japanese! scribbled the memo writer. Affronted but increasingly nervous, the Indian government made pledges and refutations, insisting that the 'complaints are highly exaggerated' and 'fresh inspections unnecessary'. R.N. Gilchrist, a civil servant in Delhi, wrote to Sir H.R. Satow at the Foreign Office, explaining that the repatriates had not been ill when they left Delhi – and if those who remained were ill now, it was because it was monsoon, when anyone domiciled in India must make peace with some risk of dysentery.

Unsaid, because it did not bear saying, was that the government of the Raj was in tough straits itself. It was grappling with the largest civil uprising in its history, the Quit India Movement, which occupied fifty battalions: more than the number then facing the Japanese on India's doorstep. Native rebels and foreign enemy might soon be fighting side by side, if Japan chose to invade once the monsoon was over. Elsewhere at Kew is a document called 'Defence of India', prepared by the Joint Planning Staff and a Joint Intelligence Committee. It records that 'the direction of the next Japanese drive cannot yet be established, but there is no reason why she should not stage a full scale attack on India'. In this event, 'her object will be the effective control of the whole country, and she will aim at reaching the West Coast at an early stage, either by a direct landing or a rapid advance from the East to the South'. Pity the government of India, which had to contemplate the full evacuation of the eastern provinces, billets further west for thousands of whites and camps for millions of wretched Bengalis: it could hardly be concerned with a handful of damp Japanese.

Still, communiqués and ciphers flew between Delhi, Whitehall and Tokyo, bounced off the neutral Swiss and Swedes. On 6 November, Tokyo issued a statement to the US, Canada and Britain: 'The fact that the Japanese Government has been extending very fair and humane treatment to Prisoners of War, civilian internees and other enemy nationals . . . is clear in the light of various reports of representatives of the ICRC [International Committee of the Red Cross], as well as by broadcasts and communications of enemy nationals themselves.' And yet 'the compulsory removal of Japanese residing on the [US] Pacific Coast to the interior' is 'severe and inhumane' and the 'treatment of our nationals in British India has also been extremely inhumane, and therefore cannot be left unrectified'.

The following day, a letter from Tokyo to London, conveyed through Berne, quoted the accounts of the repatriated internees: their food, 'of inferior quality and lacking in variety . . . insufficient in seasoning necessary for Japanese taste'; the facilities, with 'neither a proper bathroom nor a laundry, only concrete walls screening a place purporting to serve both purposes'; the hope of improvements dismal. 'They promised long ago to transfer internees to permanent buildings but delayed carrying their promise into practice on some excuse or other.'

Sir H.R. Satow, by ciphered telegraph, on 23 November: 'That the Japs lodge protests against the Allied treatment of Japse [sic] nationals seems the strangest inversion possible. But I am not certain that our own house is in as good order as it ought to be . . .'

New Delhi on 6 December: 'Even Japanese Govt should realize that we would not endanger the health of New Delhi by retaining a large insanitary camp in our midst . . .'

London, by ciphered telegraph, on 8 December: 'The Allegations are part of Japanese propaganda, nevertheless they are being used as a pretext for reprisals against Allied nationals in their hands.'

Behind the stern clatter of keys and rustle of official carbon papers, one letter arrived that expressed what was really at stake, a humble note much diverted and long delayed. It reached London in November, after passing through the Red Cross Commissioner for India and the Officer in Charge of the Japanese Prisoners of War Intelligence Bureau. It had been written five months earlier, by Ian MacRae, commandant of British civilians held in the camps at Singapore.

'I have often to be in contact with the Nipponese supervisor of our camp,' wrote MacRae, 'and recently an opportunity had occurred of raising the subject of Red Cross matters, more particularly as affecting the welfare and conditions of Nipponese civilian internees in India. This is naturally a matter of concern to the authorities here, and is closely connected with my Camp's welfare . . . If you will be so good as to write to me and give as full details as possible of particulars as to the welfare and conditions of internment of Nipponese civilians in India, I shall be grateful.'

To this, the memo writer says: *Doubtful whether India is the best place to go for details of the treatment of Japse* [sic] *civilian internees as a standard on which our civilians in Singapore should be treated. But copy to India Office.*

It was winter in Delhi by now, the season best loved there by those who live indoors, and most lethal to those trying to live outside. A watery orb slipped through the sky, barely opening the envelope of chill mist enveloping the Old Fort. Inside, *intānī* were dying. On the camp roster at Kew, a thick red pencil had passed over one name after another, until 106 were struck out. In the hot months, the odd casualty had been a victim of dysentery or burns – or in the monsoon, malaria – but by November, as the anniversary of their captivity approached, the toll began to multiply, and the red pencil to repeat in its margin: *beriberi*.

Among its victims, the soles of the feet would start to burn, as if a current ran through them. Bellies and thighs swelled with oedemas, and arms withered to the bone; a limping gait gave way to partial paraplegia. Lips cracked, bled at the corners and then spoke no more. Beriberi was well known in the colonies as a disease that snuffed out the most neglected: coolies and convicts. It was also known, by then, that what caused it was no raging tropical microbe, but simple malnutrition. Even the men at the India Office, who would overlook a vast famine the following year, were 'shocked' that blameless civilians, in their government's care, had died of beriberi. Too many did, and with them died the faint chance of clemency for their counterparts in

Japanese hands. After that, the Kew files suggest, all correspondence ended.

Might happier reports from the Old Fort have saved Allied captives, or at least postponed their torments? A cloud of counterfactuals whirls over the question. What if the propaganda war in Asia had not descended, as it did, to both sides portraying the enemy race in bestial caricature? What if Japan's fortunes had turned sooner, before their armed forces were reduced to general famine and crazed measures? Surely Tokyo's protests had been disingenuous, if not outright and adroit hypocrisy. Yet in the sole English-language reference I have found to the Purana Qila camp, the historian C.A. Bayly writes (in *Forgotten Armies: The Fall of British Asia*) that 'the British believed, with some justification, that the ill-treatment of Allied prisoners of war was a reprisal' for the fate of the Japanese in India.

In the first year of the war, as Bayly notes, only twenty-nine Europeans had died in Changi Prison. In the years that followed, Changi became a word to conjure the whole cruel circus, the death marches and famine camps, all of what the Japanese did to enemy nationals in their power. There could be ghosts at Changi now, at Bataan and a thousand other places; one spectre may float above each sleeper down the length of the Thai–Burmese railroad. But if acts of memory disperse them, they should be gone. Those enormities are well remembered in the winners' history; these were the crimes for which Japan was convicted and sentenced to the Bomb.

A ghost in a kimono remains at the Old Fort. She will have no name. I confess I don't think she is Okiku after all, because Okiku lived through that morbid winter, and the next summer moved to Deoli, at last. The whitewashed buildings had been vacated by the Germans, who had been moved up into the hills of Dehradun. A new Red Cross delegation led by Jean-Alfred Rikli visited Deoli at the end of 1943, and his report praised the camp 'with its many gardens, large playgrounds, and a pretty lake nearby where the internees can fish'. From this visit there are photographs: women at their washing, men sitting at mah-jong, two boys in white caps poised at a ping-pong table.

In the winter they were visited by Siberian cranes, and the year after, they were joined by other *karayuki-san* and *sensen fujin*, 'battlefront women' freed from sex slavery in Burma. In the homeland, their native towns were sucked one by one into the firestorms of American bombing, but in Deoli they tended a miniature garden, complete with tiny walls and monuments of their own devising.

There was an art competition, of which both first and second prizes went to Fua Haripitak, one of the young Thai art students from Shantiniketan. His paintings, of tempera on paper, were in a geometric style that he was then attempting. Haripitak would come to be recognized as a pioneer of Thai modernism, and the painting that won first prize would be hailed, in a 2005 catalogue from Tokyo's National Museum of Modern Art, as 'one of the earliest examples of Asian cubism'. For all that, it was only from the daughter-in-law of the late Haripitak, in Bangkok, that I could obtain an image of the artwork and learn its authentic title.

The painting is called *Japanese Internment Camp, Purana Qila*. Rendered in its arcs and chords are women in kimonos, bowed over children and utensils, and a familiar, lofty silhouette of a gateway between pavilions. I don't hold out hope of ever seeing the ghost in the kimono, but I did believe, when I saw that image, that I saw her likeness painted from life.

As for Okiku, she lived to see Japan lose, to contemplate her emperor's surrender, to be shunted further west to Karachi, then back east to Singapore, to be released to Kosarawan in May of 1946 and, years later, to cremate Kosarawan's body. She returned to Japan, alone and aged seventy-four. There she found the reporters waiting, and enjoyed a brief celebrity while she settled back into her home town. Okiku liked to say that people like her were doomed to be forgotten – a quote naturally cherished by Noboru Ooba, who wrote her biography, which was later adapted into a documentary film. Okiku was not forgotten; she was picked, somehow, while her fellows were rejected in the shell-game of history. Her ghost abides in movie reels, not in the Old Fort.

As for the Old Fort, after the internees' removal, Commissioner Askwith changed his mind about ever housing anyone there again. Its air was deemed malarial, and medical brass declared that 'the entire reverain sector . . . east of Muttra Road, in which Purana Qila lies, is entirely unsuitable for residential purposes'. Askwith recommended that the fort be released from Defence of India Rules and returned to the care of the Archaeological Survey; that the main gates be reopened to the faithful, so they could pray at Sher Shah's mosque, facing west.

New consequences of the war washed over the Old Fort only two years after the surrender, when it became a squalid harbour for refugees from partitioned Punjab – Muslims escaping the valedictory blood-fest in Delhi, then Sikhs and Hindus arriving to shelter in the same arcades. They must have trampled any artefacts of the earlier camp. Here, as nearly everywhere, India's role in the war was effaced by the requirements of its independence. Soon it was convenient to forget the war entirely, forget our final duty to the British Empire – or at least that we fought *for* the Empire, while also fighting to be free of it. The idea that Delhi once steeled itself against Japanese bombardment seems a fantasy. In our dim, concussed recollection, we hold a single clear image: the Indian National Army, the turncoat heroes under Subhas Bose, marching with the Japanese to make us free.

It might seem that in Japan, at least, they have reason to remember the Old Fort and pay tributes there, but they too averted their eyes. Seventy years on, when I came enquiring, the Purana Qila camp was unknown to Japanese scholars of the war based in Singapore, Tokyo, Nagasaki and Hiroshima. According to Yuki Tanaka of Hiroshima University, it's unlikely any Japanese has ever researched it. Since the 1960s, their historical inquiry about the war has been bound by the parameters of *sensō sekinin*, war guilt. It remains a conscious stance of their scholars to ignore Allied treatment of their nationals in recognition of Japan's own, much greater crimes. When renegade historians try to publicize the secret sufferings, they're seen as revisionists or revanchists; unfortunately, they usually are. Japan's discretion is a mirror to India's discretion, reflecting two opposite expressions of guilt. Everywhere, the reasons to forget overwhelmed the reasons to remember. As Ian Buruma writes in *The Wages of Guilt*, his survey of the war's legacy in Germany and Japan, 'When society has become sufficiently open and free to look back from the point of view neither of the victim nor of the criminal, but of the critic, only then will the ghosts be laid to rest.'

The Old Fort is tidy now, wearing a calm expression of lawns, grilles and locked doors that's almost a sign of guilt in itself. Its outskirts, below the southern wall, accommodate the Delhi Zoo, where a diverse and colourful menagerie slouch about in the shade and pass the time, mainly by looking at the animals. Inside the walls, the Archaeological Survey is at work, and they are as skilled at burial as they are at excavation. After uprooting the last refugees of Punjab, they planted grass and signboards for an optimum view of the history. The stone plaques constantly invoke Indraprastha, as if they were intended to sink underground and re-emerge as sudden, conclusive proof of the mythic city.

The past of this place has been rendered in a glossy and symmetrical design: Mughal and monarch, bounded by ancient and future Hindu reigns. On this tapestry the *intānī* would be a speck of grit, and need to be rubbed out. I thought of the archaeologist in his office, in one of the same vaulted rooms that had housed the women whose existence he ruled out. 'There is no evidence of it,' he had said. 'No reference to it, and no truth in it.' As he spoke, I thought I felt an offended shiver in the ether, though it may just have been the kick of the air conditioner cooling the room. ∎

Sanjay Nagar Blues

The oldest building's from 1962
and proud of it too. The tailor says
everything depends on the price of petrol.

At midnight motorcyclists like to howl
and dogs drop bulging bags of garbage
from their mouths when they see other dogs
they want to mount.

A guy died once crossing the road but I couldn't
imagine the exact spot. A legless man guards the
slippers of the slippered outside the house of God.

It's hard to say if the loungers by
the police station are more sinned against
than sinning or the other way around.

A bar to magnify the night, but I don't want
bald businessmen in my hair, I don't want
Baileys Irish Cream and Sula wine and lights
that go from magenta to orange to clinical white.

You give me three nice shirts
for the price of two but it's still quite hard
to love you.

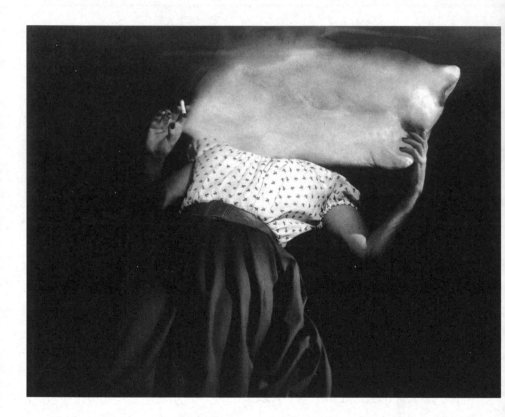

© NOÉ SENDAS
Crystal Girl no 80, 2010
Courtesy of Michael Hoppen Gallery, London

OTHELLO SUCKS

Upamanyu Chatterjee

This being at some moments a piece of non-fiction, at others a radio play and at yet others a comic strip in prose, Father, one of its four principal dramatis personae, feels that the title is incomplete without a colon. Othello Sucks, colon, and then an apposite phrase from Shakespeare's play.

The radio play starts with Younger Daughter at dinner spitting out the title without looking up from reading her mobile phone. No one responds. *Othello sucks* does not even register with either Mother or Elder Daughter.

Chomp chomp slurp slurp gas. Father is in four minds. He does not want to be distracted from his khichuri with meatballs or his meditations on his indigestion or his plans on what to take in his tiffin tomorrow. Yet not to respond to a cry for help would be churlish; Younger Daughter would then flounce back to her room and slam the door shut so hard on her family that it would once more bring down plaster from the ceiling; in a chain reaction, the trembling of the entire building would in turn trigger the frenzied barking of the three Great Danes in the apartment two floors above.

Thus Father, airily: Well, who doesn't, in this world?

Prompting from Younger Daughter a torrent: Well, if it's English, no one in class can follow it. 'Ay you did wish that I would make her turn. / Sir, she can turn, and turn, and yet go on / And turn again; and she can weep, sir, weep; / And she's obedient; as you say, obedient, / Very obedient –' The lines sound like gobbledegook so you read the notes and learn that 'turn' also means 'pursue sexual encounters' and 'obedient' also means 'sexually pliant'. So then the lines make sense but big deal it simply isn't worth the effort! And the boys go around saying, 'Miss Miss make me your obedient servant.' You dig deep for all that meaning and all you come up with is a potato and I have a class test tomorrow on it and I'll fail and I won't get an Excellence Award this year!

Noises off of plaster falling while Mother, coldly: How competitive you've made them.

And Elder Daughter, in a daze, as though remembering 11 September: *I had The Merchant of Venice*. In not more than five hundred words, explain which of the gold, silver and lead caskets you find the most screamingly boring. Compared to that, a retarded black guy who sucks is a rock concert.

Whose bright idea is it to subject the children in this day and age and clime and country to Shakespeare? is an issue that Father has raised at several parent–teacher meetings. He'd thought that the school, being a good right-wing south Delhi Punjabi institution, would be receptive but it has turned out to be as deaf as the regulars around the dining table at home. But he has persevered: Shakespeare is not on the Central Board exam syllabus, then why the hell? I mean, do we want them as adults to speak in iambic pentameter when they apply for internships to CNN–IBN? No. Grammatically correct and lucid English, that's what we want. Think Rex Harrison in *My Fair Lady*.

Indefatigable Mrs Dasgupta the Language Skills Teacher in response suggests that he come and give a talk to the senior classes on 'Which English Do We Want to Learn? The Relevance of Shakespeare to India in the Twenty-First Century'.

She is renowned, says Elder Daughter, for roping in parents to lessen her own work. She sucks.

A t the thought of Father performing in front of her classmates, Younger Daughter stops going to school. No one notices. She also begins to be markedly absent from the dining table. Her three-hour karaoke sessions in the bathroom, however, continue. Father begins reading up for his lecture and is soon an irritable wreck.

For beneath his own babble, he is actually shocked by how dull and dim-witted he finds Othello the personality to be. And pompous. Pompous and dull and dim-witted, because he is black. That is what Shakespeare has made him out to be. How could any reader ignore that?

The bugger is as embarrassing, he tells the bathroom mirror while flossing, as Hurree Jamset Ram Singh. And about as funny. But one is black and the other brown. Same thing. Noble princes both, one beggar merely duskier than the other. Or is it me? Am I just rereading the play at the wrong time and is it meant for younger people of another country?

O thou dull Moor. Am I sure I know exactly what a Moor is? Abebe Bikila isn't a Moor is he? And Anwar Sadat but not Kenneth Kaunda is that it?

Berbers! Mauretanians! shrieks Younger Daughter in response over the music and through the shut doors of her bathroom *and* her bedroom. Including Mauritanians!

No one reacts. The cat continues to doze on the tea cosy at the centre of the dining table and Mother to inspect the screen of her laptop and curse the Internet service provider. After a moment, Elder Daughter elaborates with a smirk: There's a black guy in her class whom I think she has a crush on. That's how she knows the little that she knows.

Into the conversation at the dining table, enter Cheikh Luigi Fall.

He is seventeen, tall, dark and handsome, one half Mauritanian, a quarter Italian, a quarter Turk. He is perfectly bilingual in Italian and French and claims fluency in Arabic and English. He is popular among his classmates in part because his English is a rich source of amusement for them. They envy him because he is exempt from

Hindi and wanders off to the computer lab to surf while their heads ache and rock and reel over Tulsidas and Chhayavaad and Nirala. In a school – and nation – obsessed with cricket, he is terrific at football. To break the ice, the girls ask him what he's doing with them. He confusedly explains that he's there because they arrived at the wrong time of year and that after some months he hopes to move to the American school.

He is completely tranquil, as meditative as the Gandhara Buddha, during *Othello*. Leave alone Shakespeare, he can't follow a word of Mrs Dasgupta's English.

Younger Daughter in fact is bemused to learn that for a large, underprivileged section of the globe, Shakespeare is not the first thing that comes to mind on hearing the word Othello. Cheikh, for instance, on grasping that his class devotes one session per week to the play, is puzzled; his brow furrows – rather attractively, thinks Younger Daughter – as he asks: Verdi? Are we going to listen in class to Verdi?

Two days pass before Mother says: Enough is enough. Why have you stopped going to school?

Younger Daughter does not look up from her mobile phone but in the slouch of her shoulders can be detected the crouch of a cornered feline. Her elder sister, smirking out of nervousness, responds on her behalf: There's been a bit of an Incident.

Exactly how black is Othello, ma'am? Would he be darker than you? is what Lamborghini has asked Mrs Dasgupta right at the beginning of class.

Everyone shuts up. It was so silent, recounts Younger Daughter, that you could hear Lamborghini's Tag Heuer ticking.

Wow, says Father. I imagine that Bengal's sable daughter was not amused.

It was horrible, continues Younger Daughter happily. We are studying *Othello*, said Mrs Dasgupta, because our own society is one of the most racist and skin-conscious in the world. There were tears in her eyes.

He's horrible too, comments Mother, that Lamborghini. No one in our time would've *dared* to say that to a teacher even in his or her wildest imaginings.

Younger Daughter waves her mother's time and her imaginings into the chicken curry. She then looks down at her mobile phone for inspiration to compose a case for the defence. He's been overlooked for Head Boy and he's sure it's Mrs Dasgupta's fault. At the teachers' council meeting apparently it was she who said that there should be a Head Girl this year because we've had a Head Boy three years running.

Aha, exclaims Father, Hell hath no fury like a man overlooked. In fact, that's *exactly* what I'm going to say in my lecture. *Othello* is about Iago. He is unjustly overlooked for promotion and so something snaps in his head. He *has* to be surrounded by dullards so that he can work his revenge out in a couple of hours. The rest is . . . noise.

No one pays him any attention. The only thing nice about Lamborghini, muses Elder Daughter, is his wealth.

L amborghini drives one even though he is underage. His family has no Indian car other than a Maruti Esteem that the servants use to go to the market. Younger Daughter's parents do not know his real name. They don't care. They become aware that such a being walks and drives on the face of the earth when a huge scarlet head-turning thing scrunches to a stop one evening outside the gates of the house. Younger Daughter, who has the hearing of a canine for things that matter, registers the arrival of the car through the music and the two shut doors, and within eighteen seconds is gliding out through the front door when:

Just where, asks Mother, do you think you're going wearing those clothes?

Mumble mumble, says Younger Daughter.

Is he playing the chauffeur in a getaway car that he can't come in to say hello to us?

Embarrassed, scowling and in a foul mood, Younger Daughter

exits and re-enters some moments later accompanied by something large. Mumble mumble, says Lamborghini.

The worser welcome! says Father. I have charged thee not to haunt about my doors. In honest plainness thou has heard me say / My daughter is not for thee. And now, in madness, / Being full of supper and distemp'ring draughts, / Upon malicious knavery dost thou come / To start my quiet.

No one speaks. The family members look horrified and Lamborghini frightened. Plaster falls as Younger Daughter, softly moaning in shame at having the parents she has, rushes off to change into something less revealing.

Lamborghini, who at the age of seventeen has made a reservation, is taking Younger Daughter out to dinner at the Taj Machaan.

The nerve. She has to have dinner at home. The maid's cooked. Carrot and beetroot soup. Full of vitamins. You want to stay too?

Mumble mumble.

Do lunch. Why don't the two of you do lunch outdoors on a sunny day? Vitamins. Our daughters are petrified of the sun for fear they'll turn black. You too?

Lamborghini is more pale yellow than fair, a shade that would look rather nice, notes Father, on an expensive car. Mrs Dasgupta's complexion actually would look even nicer, like an advertisement for Belgian chocolate with 72 per cent cacao in it. Only Cheikh though is thinking of all the chocolate that he can't find in India as the class holds its collective breath while waiting for Mrs Dasgupta to throw Lamborghini out for saying what he has just said.

She doesn't have to. Without even mumbling anything, Lamborghini himself stumbles out of the room, down the stairs, across Assembly Quadrangle, out the gates and into the waiting Toyota Lexus. The guards at the gate stop their game of cards to stand up and salute his wealth. They don't do that for every student.

He hasn't been back in class since, concludes Younger Daughter impressively.

A nd so? What does *his* lack of breeding have to do with *your* truancy?

Younger Daughter waves her mother's question into the sprouted moong dal and garlic fry. But that is not the only one left unanswered. No one in school has replied for instance to Lamborghini's question either. Exactly how black is Othello, ma'am?

It is Cheikh who, surfing the web in the computer lab, returns with the responses of history's well-known men.

Pretty black, is the answer, and not particularly pretty, for it is not Othello's stupidity that disturbs Samuel Taylor Coleridge but his blackness. 'It would be something monstrous to conceive this beautiful Venetian girl falling in love with a veritable Negro.' Ditto Charles Lamb: there is 'something extremely revolting in the courtship and wedded caresses of Othello and Desdemona'. Neither critic is disturbed by the fundamental assumption of the play that Othello is dumb because he is black.

Nor is Elder Daughter. Desdemona is even dumber, she snorts. I mean, Desdemona *really* sucks. They're made for each other, so what's the problem? No one in fact is sorry to see her strangled. It does improve the play.

It is again Cheikh who points out in class that white audiences being disturbed by Othello's blackness was – is – will be – a global phenomenon. He quotes Stendhal recounting an incident that occurred in the August of 1822: 'Last year, the soldier standing guard at the interior of the theatre in Baltimore, seeing Othello who, in the fifth act of the tragedy of that name, was going to kill Desdemona, cried out: "It will never be said that in my presence a damned black would kill a white woman." At that moment the soldier fired his gun and broke the arm of the actor who played Othello.'

Playing Othello therefore has proved dangerous for some white actors even when they, for a protective shield, have painted themselves blacker than jet.

And exactly how black do *they* consider Othello to be? Here is Laurence Olivier in his autobiography dated 1986: 'Black all over my body, Max Factor 2880, then a lighter brown, then Negro No 2, a stronger brown. Brown on black to give a rich mahogany. Then the great trick: that glorious half yard of chiffon with which I polished myself all over until I shone . . . The lips blueberry, the tight curled wig, the white of the eyes whiter than ever, and the black, black sheen that covered my flesh and bones, glistening in the dressing-room lights . . . I am Othello.'

Or Enid Blyton's Mr Golly. A tragic golliwog given to histrionics and hyperbole, an old black ram, a Barbary horse who, gullible and garrulous, murders an innocent woman and then commits suicide. Well, why not? Even golliwogs have souls. Being black, a lot of soul.

M rs Dasgupta unfortunately is not impressed with that line of argument. The parents bump into her when they are summoned to school to discuss with the Principal Younger Daughter's means of transport between home and school and back again. Discussions around the dining table at home, round in shape, it may be added, have revealed that for the past two months, Younger Daughter has been dutifully waving to Father and boarding the school bus in the morning but hopping off it before the first teacher gets on at the next stop; she, however, arrives in school in the Lamborghini well before the bus. It is a comfortable and powerful car and she can unwind in it properly over her morning cigarette.

If she gets thrown out, says Mother, I'm packing up, getting a transfer and taking them with me away from this foul city.

Father doesn't argue. They prefer to bicker in front of the children, firmly believing that hearing the verbal duels of their parents helps in their mental development, giving them metaphors and turns of phrase that they would otherwise have taken a decade to make their own. Elder Daughter for instance, ever since her second term in nursery, has peppered her exchanges with 'bootlicker' and 'asshole'.

You want to go on ahead, asks Father, hoping against hope, and seduce the Principal while I chat to Madam Ma Kali about my views on the Moor of Venice?

Father is annoyed to learn that Mrs Dasgupta has practically forgotten her invitation to him to talk to the senior classes about Shakespeare.

Oh . . . I didn't know you were *that* keen . . . we'll have to see about a slot . . . Saturday seems possible but I can see the children *not* being enthused at having to come in on a holiday to listen to your radical views on Othello . . . They *love* the play, you know.

Oh.

Suddenly they are surrounded by a dozen noisy children, all at once overwhelmed by the youthfulness of youth. The students are all talking at the same time and squeaking excitedly about nothing of interest to anyone else. They turn out to be Younger Daughter's classmates on their way to an elocution class in the open air. Mother recognizes some of them. Good morning, Auntie! Hello, Uncle! The elders smile at their youth. It is infectious. One girl, with eyes more sparkling and a manner saucier than those of the others, asks Father: What happened at the Principal's, Uncle?

Father prepares to mumble a reply but is tongue-tied, suddenly, by how *old* he feels in their presence. The boys seem so lithe and . . . uncaring of their bodies and the girls so . . . so in bloom that he feels creaky, musty, disjointed, as fragile and yellowed as a page of an unopened classic.

They don't fortunately need an answer, for just then, the tall North African boy at the back, realizing whose parents they are, greets Mother and Father with: Good morning, Mrs _ and Good morning, Mr _ . His classmates, laughing and shrieking, pounce upon him with quotations from *Othello*: We don't say that here, you erring barbarian, we say Auntie and Uncle because all humanity is one hopelessly enormous Hindu joint family!

Villain, adds Father, half recovering, that was most heathenish and most gross.

What you know, you know, sir, responds Cheikh in an accent that – like those of the others – falls far short of that imaginary Shakespearean ideal; a European accent his is – unlike those of the others – of one who has grown up in a world wherein English barely appeared on his radar, who has experienced it *en passant* as the language of Hollywood and North America. From this time forth I never will speak word.

Amid the laughter, O dear, says Father to himself, for he notes that Cheikh is green-eyed.

In his talk to the students that Mrs Dasgupta has not found the time for, Father has planned to devote some space to the green-eyed monster. For decades he has known Act Three Scene Three – the great temptation scene – by heart, and has recited chunks of it to himself the way his contemporaries sing Kishore Kumar and Blind Faith in the shower. O beware, my lord, of jealousy! It is the green-eyed monster which doth mock / The meat it feeds on. To Father, the *Othello* music is more melodious than the most irrepressibly peppy Hindi film hit or any epochal rock anthem. But the intensity of his love for that euphony is secret because he has always felt it to be freaky, absurd, so out of place as to be an embarrassment. Shakespeare is white and his audience is white, and don't you forget it. For two centuries he has been used as a whitening agent for the colonial mind – bleaching powder, if you will; read him as white, for the poet of all humanity is fiction and does not exist; black Othello sucks because the Bard behind him is white.

The Principal is fair, affable, huge, hairy. Mother is annoyed that he and Father spend the first quarter-hour chatting about the good old days at St Stephen's College. That is *not* what she has taken half a day's leave from the office for. And then suddenly the googly: And is your daughter ha ha smoking your brand of cigarette? Wills Navy Cut, wasn't it?

Ha ha *ha*, responds Father, not ready to be outdone, I don't know, we haven't smoked together yet.

The issue is complicated. Younger Daughter is in the running for Head Girl but they cannot have a Head Girl who smokes.

The issue is simple, argues Father at the dining table. Puff away to death *after* you've left school, what's the problem?

She can't stop smoking, slips in Elder Daughter, because Lamborghini has just gifted her an entire carton of Silk Cut as a pre birthday present. When he kills her, he can then become Head Boy. It is much cooler though to smoke than to be Head Girl.

She doesn't want to waste the remaining two thousand cigarettes, adds Mother in a tone of ice. Those are *your* miserly genes.

In India, females who smoke are morally loose, you know that, returns Father to the attack. They smoke, they wear skirts and elope at midnight with some most unsuitable weirdo.

That's not me, counters Younger Daughter, shrieking, en route to slamming two doors and setting off once more the Great Danes in the building. That's Desdemona!

With whom all the girls of the class have a problem. They find Act One to be fun because here's this obviously kinky Venetian chick doing a moonlight flit with some old and ugly ram, some army type. I mean, how freaky is that? To them, the real tragedy of the play is twofold: one, how Desdemona so rapidly descends from kinky chick with a mind of her own to dumb dame, silly and passive and – oof! – so dull. And then secondly, it is simply dreadful how all those horrible males in the play continually refer to all the females as whores and Shakespeare does fuck all to dispel the impression that Venice has of women. I'faith and zounds, ma'am, but the Bard of *Othello* is an MCP.

To wind up then, a coda. Or in the words of Iago in Act Three Scene Three, Scan this thing no further, leave it to time.

And to wind up then, one by one the loose ends. Father gets so entangled in the Shakespeare industry, in the critical biographies, the scholarly monographs, textual variations, performance histories, the post-colonial discourses that he never finishes preparing his paper. At the dining table, he is appropriately embarrassed to learn from Younger Daughter that it has been two weeks since the class has finished *Othello* and moved on to *How to Win Friends and Influence*

People; not surprisingly, the class as one has begun to pine for sweet Desdemona, the blacker devil and honest, honest Iago.

The loose ends continued. Snigdha is chosen Head Girl. She is a horrendous tart, elaborates an outraged Elder Daughter. Younger Daughter smokes thirty cigarettes in two days and stops all other activities except for breathing. This can't go on forever, says Mother's SMS to her after two days.

Wait and see, responds Younger Daughter after another two days.

Nirbhaya Bhavah, advises Father, feeling multilingual. No one is sure whom the advice is for.

L eave it to time, says Iago. It is thus a week later that Father, in the car on the way back from work, hits upon the title for a paper that he will never deliver. Othello Sucks, colon, The Pity of It Iago for It Is Your Play. Father is delighted; Shakespeare, however, is obliterated from his head even before he has parked in front of the house. The lights in all the rooms are on and the music so loud that no passer-by fails to glance up at the windows. The Great Danes, more attuned to postmodern rock 'n' rap, frenziedly bark their disapproval like fans booing at a concert. Father has the impression that the mad woman who owns them has placed before their muzzles the microphone of a public address system.

He cannot immediately place the music. That is not saying very much. At the front door, with some of the wonder of Alexander Fleming examining his blue mould and its penicillin, he says to himself: But it's *opera*. He rings the doorbell fourteen times. He searches for his house keys. *Italian* opera.

Chi è là? Otello?

Father opens the door and is physically engulfed by sound. His eardrums hum and he can actually feel it tingling his skin. He is certain that Younger Daughter has hanged herself out of depression, her lack of vitamins and her love of bloody drama, and Verdi is her way of saying *arrivederci*. Mother in front of her laptop and Elder Daughter before her iPad are both at the dining table. Father is sure that they are asking Google what to do when a near and dear one hangs herself.

Elder Daughter sees him. She is beaming with joy and mischief. Communication is possible only by means of SMS, email or sign language. She SMSs Father: Guess who gifted her the Verdi CD?

He couldn't care less. He SMSs back: Frankly my dear I don't give a damn. How can we stop the music?

Reading his mind, Younger Daughter presses a button in the bathroom. The silence is shocking; it feels like kilos of winter clothing being shed all at once, clouds lifting, like freedom, as though one could stretch one's limbs again in the warm sun. The dogs, flummoxed, remain open-mouthed and dumb for a whole day.

She wants to know, says Mother, if she can go out for dinner. I've said yes but she has to ask you too.

Father feels the presence of Younger Daughter behind him. He turns. He hasn't seen her for a day and a half. Beneath her bandanna, her face is radiant, almost unrecognizable.

It suits you, that rag on your head.

Cheikh wants to take me out to dinner. We've made a reservation. Younger Daughter is blushing with joy.

The bandanna is Cheikh's first gift, a silk handkerchief, spotted with strawberries; the silk is from Egypt.

Oh, says Father, so what is the plot for the evening? You lose the handkerchief, he goes on and on and on about monumental alabaster and Promethean heat; when you can't take it any more, Heaven have mercy on me, you moan, then he strangles you?

Your daughter has made arrangements for any eventuality, says Mother in a voice so dry that the cat on the tea cosy twitches her right ear in appreciation.

At least he doesn't smoke, points out Elder Daughter. And if they have children, their skins will have more melanin to better absorb ultraviolet light.

Sure, go ahead, have fun, says Father. But who's 'we' in 'made a reservation'?

Lamborghini of course. A threesome. She just loves that car. ∎

Bom By Night 1

BREACH CANDY

Samanth Subramanian

If you climb onto the diving platform of the pool at the Breach Candy Club, and if you turn your back to the ocean expiring upon the rocks a few yards away, you look up into Mumbai. Or perhaps Mumbai looks down upon you, from its skyscraping fastnesses, the buildings rising higher and higher, pressing down upon the low, easy profile of the club, crowding it into the sea. To the left is the egg-white hulk of the Breach Candy Hospital; to the right, an apartment complex of similar height, painted a cheerful blue. In the distance hovers Antilia, the twenty-seven-floor, billion-dollar home of India's richest man. Much closer – right across the road from the club, in fact – is the stillborn residence of a slightly poorer tycoon, a textile baron. For years now, it has been shrouded in green netting because, rumour has it, Antilia's owner was so affronted by the thought of another luxury mansion sharing the skyline that he stalled the permits it required. At night, when the rest of the buildings burn with light, the textile baron's house stands dark and cold, like a big rotten tooth. There, further away, are the Imperial Towers, twin condominiums sixty floors high, the tallest buildings in India. On a Diwali night, a friend told me, he had attended a party on the twentieth floor of one Imperial Tower or the other, and from the balcony, amid the fireworks, the city looked like Fallujah during the Iraq war. Not that he had been to Fallujah during the Iraq war, but somehow Mumbai seems to prod you into reaching only for the most fevered comparisons. Yet another skyscraper is under construction, a crane perched atop its shell. And curiously, nearer to earth, are a gabled roof and a pointed, clay-coloured turret – a turret! – that belong to Windsor Villa, where Salman Rushdie lived as a boy during the 1950s, and from where, as he wrote in *Midnight's Children*, he could spot pink people 'cavorting in the map-shaped pool of the Breach Candy Club, from which we were, of course, barred'. This very pool, in other words, the one excavated in the outline of undivided India, such that Kashmir lies right below your feet as you stand atop the diving platform.

The minute I saw the pool, I realized that its designers had missed a trick. It should have been laid out, really, so that the western coast of Pool India was aligned with the western coast of Real India, given that the club perched so conveniently on the shore. That way, when the sun doused itself in the Arabian Sea every evening, both Indias would have slipped in clean parallel into night. Instead, Pool India has been rotated a quarter-turn counterclockwise, so that a large lawn stretches away to its west, near Pakistan, while a smaller lawn and cafe sit roughly in Myanmar. The restaurant and bar are in southern Afghanistan. Sri Lanka is the kiddies' pool.

In vivid contrast to the country, the pool is nearly always thinly populated. One March afternoon, when summer was already breathing down our necks, I had lunch at the club with a friend who had been a member there for two years. During a lull in the conversation, he stared at the pool as if he was seeing it for the first time. 'People don't swim much here, I've realized,' he said. 'They just sort of potter about, more than anything else.' At the time, the only person in the water was a bald man shaped like a Roman senator, stroking slow, diligent breadths across the pool. After he emerged, dried himself with a lilac towel and walked away, the pool lay empty for hours. I returned for dinner that same week, on a balmy evening, and still the pool was uninhabited; it remained that way until 10.45 p.m., when an attendant rang a bell to announce the pool's closure for the day. Nobody needed to pay the clangour any attention. The pool, floodlit and desolate, floated in the darkness like a pale blue amoeba.

By virtue of its outline, the pool is able to inject a charged symbolism into any consideration at all of the club's affairs. In building the pool during the Raj, for instance, the British were emphasizing their ownership of India, their iron control over its borders and its topography. After 1947, when India gained its independence, the club insisted that it would continue to restrict membership to Europeans only, not quite ready to hand India – the pool, the country – over to its people. In the late 1960s, when protesters picketed the entrance to the club, demanding that Indians be made members as well, they were trying to wrest India – the country, the pool – out of the persisting fug of colonialism.

And so to the present, to the events that began in 2012, when the erection of a wall next to the kiddies' park precipitated a schism within the club. Nominally, at least, the factions were tussling over the club's arch commandment: that while Indians can become 'ordinary' members, only Europeans can become trust members, therefore entitled to serve on the managing committee and steer its business. Once, this rule could safely be said to favour white Europeans and no one else; today, in theory, its ambit includes Indians with European passports, but white people still fill most of this upper tier of membership. This is a deliciously shocking situation, so fat with political incorrectness that a brawl seemed proper and justified. But then the matter took on broader contours. There was a legal battle. There were signs of an old elite rattled by, and ready to be contemptuous of, the brazenness of new money. There were rumbles of fraud and corruption, of a mania for land and of politicians flexing their muscles in the shadows, until we appeared to be talking not of the Breach Candy Club but of India herself, the country once again in perfect congruence with the pool.

The kiddies' park – as the members of the club uniformly call it, even in stodgy legal documentation – is a square of land, measuring just under an acre, lying to one side of the parking lot. The very presence of a park, in a city starved of open space, is a marker of a rarefied world. This park contains the expected facilities: a couple of see-saws, a jungle gym, a set of swings, a slide that shoots you straight to the ground and another that passes you through a couple of curls on your way down. A metal shelter must once have housed a merry-go-round, but it now stands vacant, and gusts of sea breeze rattle its roof. A security guard sits at a desk in one corner, watching over the children at play. Not that anybody expects grievous breaches of peace in a kiddies' park, but it is pro forma today in India to strew security guards thickly through any establishment, protecting nothing except the fancy that the premises are worth protecting.

In the early summer of 2012, the club's members noticed strange changes being made to the kiddies' park. More than a dozen old, sturdy trees around the park's periphery had already been chopped down some months previously. Now a ten-foot wall sprang up, separating the park from the rest of the club. The turf sustained fresh damage, as if it had been dug up. A new concrete road, wide enough to accommodate a truck, was laid from the gate to the park. A club gardener testified that at least some of this work had occurred under the cover of night, lending it all the rank scent of skulduggery.

Another rumour was in the air, and Gerry Shirley got a whiff of that too. In the annual general meeting scheduled for that August, he heard, the managing committee would do away with the two-tier system of memberships, so that Indians could be allowed onto the committee as well. He decided he would go to the meeting, his first in the decade that he had been a member of the club. 'All you do at one of these AGMs usually is just pass the club accounts. It's not exactly a popular pastime to go watch that,' he said. 'The previous year, I heard that only twelve people had attended.' But even the timing of that 2012 meeting – 11 a.m. on a Tuesday – had roused suspicions. 'What the fuck is that about? Most of us are supposed to be at work!'

Of the 3,500 or so members of the club, roughly five hundred were European trust members, and eligible to participate in the meeting. A hundred and thirty of them turned up that Tuesday morning in August, packing the room almost beyond capacity.

Shirley is a sixty-four-year-old Englishman, although he prefers to qualify his age in the following manner: 'Sixty-four, twenty-five, nineteen,' he'll say, pointing first to his head that is fast divesting itself of hair, then to his heart and finally to his crotch. He develops commercial real estate, which explains the well-preserved ticker: 'You walk up twenty-three flights of stairs on a building site that has no elevator, in this Mumbai weather, and see how much weight you lose.' Before he moved to India around the turn of this century, he lived in Hong Kong, and although he has ranged across the continent in the course of his career, he has not lost a sliver of his East End accent. It can make him sound highly indignant and righteous; when I met him last April, in a hotel lobby as hushed as a crypt, he appeared to be keeping his voice down only with a mighty effort. He felt strongly about the club. 'It was our little oasis,' Shirley said. 'It's a hundred metres from a very busy road, but you don't hear a single horn. You can sit there, on the lawn, with a nice, cold beer, watching the sun go down, and at that moment, all's well with the world.'

That annual general meeting was a bizarre and acrimonious affair. The seven members of the managing committee sat at the head table, having so confidently expected a fight that they brought along not just lawyers but bodyguards as well. For nearly three hours, club business dithered along, punctuated by angry demands for information from the audience; one member recalled shouts of: 'You cheating bastard! You're trying to sell the land in the kiddies' park!' Finally, Shirley stood up and asked of the club's secretary, Dipesh Mehta: 'You're not even European. How did you get onto the managing committee in the first place?'

Another member, a European woman, rose and shouted back at Shirley, he recalled. '"You're a racist! You're a racist!" she was saying. I took offence at that! I've worked in every country in the Asia Pacific. I don't have a racist bone in my body.'

Amid the din, Shirley persisted with his question to Mehta. Then, dramatically, Mehta gathered up his papers, addressed Shirley and said: 'Fuck you, I'll see you in court,' and stormed out. The accounts languished, unpassed.

In speaking about Mehta, Shirley lowered his voice, as if he was afraid of being overheard; at one point, he thought he spotted a fellow Breach Candy Club member on an upper floor of the hotel ('Fuck me, what's he doing here?'), and he refused to proceed until this man had passed safely out of eyeshot. Mehta was a lawyer of some standing in Mumbai, best known perhaps for representing a Bollywood star in a ghastly hit-and-run case but also plugged intimately into the highest, tightest networks of politics and corporations. He was a fixer, another lawyer told me. In India, such a description promises services of inordinate value. A fixer can hook up politicians and businessmen for mutual benefit; he can help companies wriggle out of niggling legal obligations or point them towards a bureaucrat on the make. The best fixers can, when presented with the wild thickets and tangles of India's business environment, tame them into disciplined topiaries.

In Shirley's eyes, Mehta was also the villain of this piece. Around the time that Shirley joined the club, Mehta became a legal adviser to the managing committee. Back then he had not been a member of the club at all, but in December 2004, he was folded into the committee wholesale, a barefaced breach of the constitution. This sequence of events, mystifyingly, went unnoticed by the club at large. 'We let it happen,' Shirley said, waggling his head with regret. 'It's our own fault.'

In the year following that heated AGM of 2012, Shirley and some of his similarly incensed colleagues thought they had found more reasons for Mehta to be ejected from the club. He had, they claimed, broken the rules a second time by inducting another Indian – a friend of his named Lalit Agarwal – onto the committee, and he had hoisted himself up into the chairman's seat. He had razed trees and built walls without approval. He had farmed out part of the club's legal work to his own law firm, paying himself handsomely in the process. He had hectically escalated the life membership fee, from the 20,000 rupees that Shirley had paid to a vertiginous 10 million rupees plus tax – more than £100,000. ('The London club White's, which was founded in 1693 and requires thirty-six other members to vouch for you when you apply, charges around £1,275; the Century Association in New York, which has counted as its members Franklin D. Roosevelt and Henry Kissinger, has an annual fee reported to hover around $2,000.) Under Mehta's stewardship, the committee grew about as transparent as a bomb shelter, refusing to release information when members asked for it.

Most of these complaints were listed in a circular that some distressed trust members drew up, calling for an extraordinary general meeting – a putsch, really, intended to topple Mehta and his committee. On the evening of 21 October 2013, forty-eight of these members convened in a college classroom, and this meeting brimmed with anger as well. 'There were thirty resolutions put forward! Thirty!' Shirley said, his voice squeaky with disbelief. The putschists elected a new committee-in-exile, with Shirley as chairman, and they decided that their lawyers would issue Mehta a notice, informing him that he had been dethroned by due process. Then, satisfied with an evening's work well done, they strolled down the road to their club for a drink.

Within a week, Mehta's committee suspended nine of the foremost rebels, including Shirley; in scolding letters to them, they cited 'instances of misbehaviour and misconduct' and acts that were 'per se anti-establishment'. When the husband of one of these suspended members once tried to enter the club, he was hustled out by brawny, black-suited bouncers who had been parked at the door specifically for this purpose. The gates slammed shut behind him. Shirley and his comrades found themselves exiled, suddenly and roughly, from their beloved Eden.

There are clubs like the Breach Candy Club all over the Indian subcontinent: relics of the Raj, institutions that were set up as bolt-holes for the British, where they could retreat to row or swim or play cricket or race horses. The activity, really, was secondary; foremost, these clubs were English corners of foreign fields, intended to keep the tumult of India at bay. Within their grounds, at least temporarily, the rituals of life could be enacted as they might have been in London or Shropshire or Edinburgh. To press home that illusion, Indians were originally not allowed as members and only rarely as guests; as liveried waiters or turbaned doormen, of course, they were welcome. The clubs carried their air of unmatched privilege even into the early twentieth century, when the rules of membership began to ease. 'You do not know what prestige it gives to an Indian to be a member of the European Club,' Dr Veraswami says in George Orwell's *Burmese Days*. 'In the Club, practically he *iss* a European. No calumny can touch him. A Club member iss sacrosanct.' Even Indians, it appeared, wished to be insulated from India.

The oldest functioning club in India is the Bengal Club, established in 1827, only three years after the Athenaeum in London. ('It is that kind of club,' the Bengal Club's website says with a straight face, 'where the flavours of fine life are to be savoured as in a brandy snifter.') The second oldest is the Madras Club, founded in 1832 and now located in splendid white buildings on a Chennai riverbank. I've been there on several occasions as a guest, and every time I was warned in advance, by the member who was hosting me, to remember the club's dress code: no sandals or shorts, no shirts without collars, no Indian clothing of any kind. Even these stiff regulations are a dilution of club policy that persisted well after the British left India. In the 1960s, a member of the Madras Club was turned away from a Sunday film show because he was wearing a white jacket and black tie; in the winter – which, in Chennai, runs to a frigid twenty-five degrees Celsius – a black jacket was mandatory at all times, he was informed. Through the shrewd deployment of such rules, the clubs have filtered the India that pressed against their gates. But the ardent aspirations of the Dr Veraswamis have also never ceased; in nearly all of these clubs, the waiting list for membership stretches to thousands of moneyed names. The gilded baton of privilege has been successfully handed off, from the British to the Indian elite.

The Breach Candy Club – or, to give it its formal name, the Breach Candy Swimming Bath Trust – was born out of the complications of pre-Suez travel. Before the canal was built, European travellers journeyed across the narrow Isthmus of Suez and waited at Aden to be collected by the next steamer bound for India. To lodge these passengers – the women, in particular – Bombay's Europeans raised funds and built a hostel in Aden. Once the Suez Canal opened, though, ships made directly for India, eliminating the need altogether for a transit in Aden. The hostel, having thus fallen into disuse, was sold for 7,300 rupees; when this take was pooled with another 2,000 rupees in custody of the British Resident at Aden, the caretakers of the steamer fund now had 9,300 rupees. Bombay's municipal commissioner suggested, in 1875, that the money be spent to spruce up a cemetery, but at a meeting of the city's Europeans that March, this idea was roundly rejected. Plumping for the joys of life rather than the prettification of death, the conclave decided instead to buy itself a new saltwater pool.

Accordingly, Benjamin Disraeli's Secretary of State for India marked out five acres on Bombay's shore and donated them to the swimming bath. 'It gave one an idea,' an Indian member of the Bombay Municipal Corporation would later grumble, 'that the Secretary of State for India . . . had been disposing of land as if it was his ancestral property.' The name 'Breach Candy' had already stuck to this segment of the coast; it was said to be an anglicised corruption of the Hindustani words *burj khadi*, which referred to the temple tower (or *burj*) and the creek (*khadi*) in the locality. I could find no record of the people who were living here at that time; the club's official history is confident that this neighbourhood of Bombay was 'a barren wilderness'. A tarred shed functioned as the first bathhouse. In 1927, a new indoor pool was sunk; the following year, work began upon the outdoor, India-shaped pool, which cost 13,600 rupees. Eight years later, in settling a lawsuit, the Bombay High Court prised the facilities out of the custodianship of the municipal authorities and handed them over to the newly constituted Breach Candy Swimming Bath Trust.

The Swedish writer Jan Myrdal claimed to have seen, in 1959, a placard outside the club that read: 'For Europeans and persons of European origin only. Dogs and Indians not allowed.' It's difficult to ascertain if such a sign was ever really in place, but a politer one – 'Breach Candy Swimming Bath and Foreshore reserved for Europeans only' – definitely was, back in the 1920s. The club's racial policies chafed even then. City officials bickered about them in council meetings. Eminent citizens wrote letters of protest. Club members of an independent bent of mind called out the hypocrisy of their colleagues. In a column published in the *Times of India* in 1935, an anonymous European woman scolded Breach Candy members who 'object to a lot of ayahs sitting around chewing their betel nut and making themselves objectionable in other ways. All I can say is that if the ayahs are good enough to look after our children they're good enough for the inside gardens as well as the outside ones.'

When admission continued to be restricted after India became independent in 1947, the resentment started to boil into anger. Once, infamously, Mihir Sen, India's champion long-distance swimmer, was refused entry into the pool, although the club probably behaved less brusquely than in Rushdie's dramatization of the episode: 'He holds a cake of Mysore sandalwood soap; draws himself up; marches through the gate . . . whereupon hired Pathans seize him, Indians save Europeans from an Indian mutiny as usual, and out he goes, struggling valiantly, frogmarched into Warden Road and flung into the dust.' A member of the Bombay Municipal Corporation moved a resolution arguing that the club's principles were 'repugnant to the Constitution of India', so in 1959 Indians began to be permitted into the club as guests of European members, every day save Sunday.

'Some of the old users of the pool might have been surprised to find,' a withering *Times of India* editorial remarked, 'that this change did not change the colour of the water.'

Then, five years later, a further blow was landed. In February of 1964, on a Friday, a dozen political workers stationed themselves outside the club's gates; one of them promised, to the *Times of India*, that their vigil would 'continue daily . . . till such time as racial discrimination in admission to the pool is ended'. They erected a tarpaulin against one of the club's walls and hunkered down under it during the afternoons, sheltering from the sun. Notices appeared, nailed to wooden staves and bearing slogans such as: 'Down with Colour-Bar Swimpool'. The protest gathered steam. George Fernandes, a union leader named after George V and such an enthusiastic rabble-rouser that he was a regular lodger in the city's prisons, threatened to lead two thousand volunteers and storm the club's grounds. The mayor of Bombay dropped by to show solidarity.

Pinned down in this manner, the trust had at least to pretend to yield. The officials of the managing committee huddled with the state's chief minister, who then announced the membership formula that prevails today: Europeans as trust members, nearly all of them long-time residents of the city; Indians as ordinary members; and applicants with other passports as temporary foreign members, bankers and executives and journalists and similar itinerants who could quell their vague discomfort with the rules by recalling that they were only passing through. But the revision went just so far: Indian applicants were screened with high rigour, and they could never ascend into the managing committee. When the newspaper columnist Bhaichand Patel visited the club in 1969, the Indian quota of 150 members was fully subscribed. 'Who, one may reasonably ask, are these valiant 150 hobnobbing with the 2,300 whites without qualms or moral nuances?' Patel wondered. He climbed to the top deck of the restaurant and looked down, upon the India-shaped pool and upon the bodies unfolded in repose upon its grassy banks. 'Something was rotten. The thought occurred to me that if tomorrow

Breach Candy were to sink emptily in the Arabian Sea, it would not be missed by the Indians.'

One afternoon, I went to meet Kunal Kapoor, who runs Prithvi, a theatre in the seaside suburb of Juhu, where old Bollywood has pitched its mansions. The ocean couldn't have been more than two hundred metres away; we sat in a pocket-sized courtyard outside the theatre, and I could smell the salt in the air and feel puffs of breeze hit the sweaty back of my shirt. The moist fabric would cool and dry for a moment, and that was heaven; then it would be dampened again by fresh perspiration. Kapoor didn't seem to feel the heat. His white shirt was unbuttoned until midway down his breastbone, and his brow remained unbeaded. He drank several cups of Sulaimani tea, and he smoked so constantly that it was possible to deduce how he had acquired his distinctive voice: hoarse and low, as if an attack of laryngitis had never entirely faded away. Sundry members of the city's theatrical community would pass us and wave to Kapoor. 'Hello! How're you doing?' he would growl with love.

Kapoor's parents had also been actors. His father Shashi, who started Prithvi and is still seen there on many evenings, sitting in the cafe draped in a soft white shawl, belonged to Bollywood's illustrious Kapoor clan; his English mother Jennifer, who died in 1984, was the daughter of Geoffrey Kendal, the impresario of a travelling repertory named Shakespeareana. They were married in 1958, and from the following year, Shashi could well have frequented the Breach Candy Club as a guest on his wife's membership. 'But Dad wouldn't go,' Kapoor said. 'He wouldn't go because Indians couldn't become members. Simple as that. When he was allowed to become a member, he became a member, and then we all went.'

Kapoor has spent half a century as a member of the Breach Candy Club, and he describes his childhood there as a sort of rambunctious idyll. Rush to the club after school, and swim laps up and down the indoor pool. Then, eyes still pink from the chlorine, pelt outside and into the saltwater pool, emerging only for a snack, or to mess about on the rocks, or to attempt foolhardy stunts such as jumping from one diving board to another and thence into the pool. 'My friend did that, missed a board and broke his leg. The number of times we've been carried across in our swimming togs by our parents, into the Breach Candy Hospital, with broken arms or cut heads or cut legs!' Climb the trees, and be shouted down by Mr Parks, the club manager, for doing so. Train hard to make it into the club's swim teams. A little later in life, sneak kisses with girls behind the stepladder of the small island embedded in the middle of the pool. It was a perfected ideal of boyhood, as lived in swimming togs.

For teenagers, the club threw a party every monsoon, with a live band and dancing and hectic flirtations; adults were absolutely barred, except for Mr Parks, who orbited the flock like a watchful sheepdog. On Christmas Eve, the children of the members trickled into the club late in the afternoon, sat around a gigantic tree, and lustily eyed the presents their parents had deposited earlier in the week. From across the pool, Santa Claus made his way towards them atop a floating sleigh, pulled by his reindeer – members of the swim teams, their heads adorned with antlers. Once the presents were distributed, there was a band with bagpipes, and stalls with coconut shies and cotton candy, all manned by the club's members.

It sounded wonderful, I said. Kapoor patted his moustache – brigand-like, twirling up at the ends – and drank more tea.

Part of the club's yesteryear charm lay in its reluctance to think of itself as a club at all; to Kapoor and other diehards of the time, it was a swimming pool with attached facilities. Its restaurant was so basic that the chips were the best thing on the menu; when Kapoor's mother heard another member complain about the food, she shot back: 'If you want to have a good meal, go to the Taj Hotel or the Oberoi. You come here to swim.' The European expatriates transiting through the club – diplomats, British bankers, Dutch employees of Philips, Eastern bloc academics – held on to their committee posts briefly, and they amicably named their own replacements before bowing out. There has never been any voting or any other democratic nonsense. 'If you look at the politics of elections and committee elections at other clubs, we've never had that,' Kapoor said. 'It's a nightmare. There'll be election posters going up, and mud-slinging.' The fees were kept low, even as they climbed into the millions at the Willingdon Club just down the road.

Most importantly, the pool stayed fixed at the heart of the club's life. Kapoor recalled a story, absurd but true, about the Royal Bombay Yacht Club, where a few years ago a member had tried to pass a resolution demanding that the club sell its boats. 'Because they were a drain on the budget!' Kapoor said, incredulous. The newer members of the Royal Bombay Yacht Club were rarely sailors, he complained; they were there for the bar and the gym and the hobnobbery. 'That's the problem with the Breach Candy Club too now. Nobody swims.' Instead, people sought membership purely because membership was difficult to secure; for them, the sole benefit of belonging to this elite club was belonging to this elite club.

It was on this tide that Dipesh Mehta had washed into the club. Kapoor didn't think that he had ever even seen Mehta around at Breach Candy, but he remembered him from another context. A decade or so ago, Mehta had applied to join the Amateur Riders' Club, which owns a bunch of horses, hutch-like changing rooms in a corner of the racecourse, and very little else. Kapoor was on the club's membership panel that year, when Mehta came up for his interview. 'He didn't even ride,' Kapoor said, marvelling. 'I still don't know why he wanted to join. This is another thing that happens in our society. People like to be members of clubs, and people like to be on committees. I've seen people who have on their visiting cards, "Ex-chairman of so-and-so club". They take it as some kind of social or professional stamp, being on a committee.'

Kapoor had no quarrel with most of the members of the Breach Candy Club's committee, except that they had fallen so completely in thrall to Mehta. I asked him if he'd ever met Vikram Malik, a British citizen and the committee's secretary, who was being blamed by the putschists for boosting Mehta. 'I've always had very pleasant interactions with him. He seemed to be a nice guy.' But Mehta was a man of unsavoury reputation, Kapoor had been warned. 'A friend told me: "He isn't the kind of guy who'll shoot you from the front. He'll shoot you from the back, or he'll shoot you in a way that the bullet ricochets into you."'

It sounded mystifying, these awesome, supervillain-like powers that were being ascribed to a lawyer. Then Kapoor articulated an even bigger puzzle. Why was he doing all this? Why did he persist in the face of so much opposition? 'Why not just back down gracefully and walk away? Why stick on in this manner?'

I called Vikram Malik. He had once been a captain in the army's Gorkha regiment, but now he was a realtor.

'Captain Malik?'

'That's right.' He had a lovely voice, gracious, deep and honeyed, as if he were about to introduce *La Traviata* on a classical music radio station.

'This is Samanth Subramanian. I'm a journalist, and I'm calling about the recent events at the Breach Candy Club.'

'Right.'

'I'm in Mumbai right now, and I was hoping I could get your perspective on what's been happening there.'

'Right.'

'Is there any time over the next few days when we could meet?'

There was a short silence. Then he hung up. He never answered my calls again.

I've never liked Mumbai. I lived there once, for six months in 2003, and fled, and when some of its residents talk to me about their fondness for the city, I think of them as hostages, victims of a classic case of Stockholm syndrome. Mumbai feels like some giant Malthusian experiment, its resources stretched thinner and thinner by its multiplying population, so that the city edges closer and closer to absolute collapse. It hasn't collapsed yet, Mumbai's admirers will point out. But lives within its periphery collapse every day, in brutal and tragic and unnecessary ways, severed from the kind of support and opportunity that a successful city should be able to offer them. Mumbai gears its resources unashamedly towards its wealthy. Its land and water go to them first, its best roads lead to their houses, and their lungs work most of the time in air conditioning, away from the smoggy outdoors. Everything can be grabbed by using money or influence, in a manner that is only a semantic shade away from outright theft.

This sensation was amplified during the weeks I spent haunting the Breach Candy Club. A national election was under way, and at the sordid heart of all debate was the issue of corruption – the easy pliancy of the state before mighty corporations and politicians. The incumbent government was trying to overcome a spate of corruption scandals; the challenger, from a disturbing party of the Hindu right, claimed that he could build an efficient, corruption-free administration. His hardened acolytes believed him wholly; many of the others craved his vaunted efficiency enough to vote for him, even though they suspected that he was corrupt himself. The country grew obsessed with venality. We started to expect power to be selfish and dysfunctional; we assumed that unvarnished greed was a mainstay of the human condition. Those were enervating, disheartening times.

The putschists of the Breach Candy Club – who, in classical vein, called themselves the Forum – invited me to one of their confabulations. I took a taxi to Malabar Hill, where a duplex apartment had recently sold for 9.5 million dollars and a sea-facing bungalow for 67 million dollars. Mahesh Jethmalani, a Breach Candy Club member who was acting as a legal adviser to the Forum, lived on the top floor of a building that sat on a bluff overlooking the bay. Across the water, in the accumulation of dusk, the buttery lights of Nariman Point, Mumbai's financial district, sparkled into life.

I arrived early, not entirely by accident, and so for the first hour

I sat on the periphery of the group, pretending hard that I wasn't eavesdropping. Kunal Kapoor was there, and Gerry Shirley, and a couple of other Europeans and many Indians; in the midst of the dozen-strong circle sat Jethmalani, who called himself Tony, and who was a leading light of the Bharatiya Janata Party. This was the party that was selling itself hard to India, asking to be voted into power, and Tony had been travelling ceaselessly on election work; on his only free evening in weeks, the Forum had commandeered his living room.

A lawsuit, filed against Dipesh Mehta by Shirley and his fellow exiles, was already marinating in the Bombay High Court, but it transpired that the Forum was also attempting back-channel negotiations, to persuade Mehta to see the error of his ways. He had agreed to a meeting, but he was being temperamental about whom he would and would not talk to, and a mild squabble broke out at Tony's apartment about the composition of the three-member delegation to be dispatched to Mehta. It wasn't a popular assignment. Kapoor, for instance, said: 'We know he's vindictive. I have a theatre to look after, which is a pain in the arse.' He was constantly dealing with municipal officials over whom Mehta, that consummate fixer, might have influence, Kapoor said. 'He can create havoc for me.' The others murmured in sympathy. They understood, they said.

The conversation drifted to what Mehta was demanding as a price for walking away: a redraft of the constitution, which allowed both Indians and Europeans onto the managing committee, abolishing the two-tier membership altogether. This proved divisive in an unexpected way. Most of the Indians preferred to leave the system in place, at best offering woolly criticisms of it: 'It's true, it's out of whack in today's environment,' or 'The right thing to do may be to move with the times.' But Suvir Malaney, a Forum elder, told me: 'What does it matter? We're living in a global economy. Mehta's just using racism as a way to get people to support him. It's divide and conquer.' Later, Kapoor admitted this to me: 'In the wrongness of the membership rule, there is a check.' The existence of this unfair

SAMANTH SUBRAMANIAN

regulation, he meant, had allowed the club's European management to run it cleanly and well; Indians would have only played messy politics and wrecked the serenity of the place. I recalled Rushdie's line, describing the Pathans bouncing the swimmer Mihir Sen out of the club: 'Indians save Europeans from an Indian mutiny as usual.'

One courageous voice piped up: 'As an Indian, I think that you can't do this any more. As an Indian, I should like to vote.'

He was squelched instantly. 'Patriotism is the last refuge of the scoundrel!' Tony pronounced. 'I don't care a damn about voting rights. I'm never even going to attend an AGM. It's all you guys who have nothing else to do who'll attend these AGMs.'

It was among the Europeans, oddly enough, that I sensed prickles of disquiet with the plan to keep Indians out of the committee. This was precarious terrain, they seemed to feel, and they could not holler their support of a policy so easily perceived as discriminatory. Only Shirley demurred, in an aggrieved tone that wondered why he alone was able to divine the future. In Mehta's renovated constitution, he said, every one of the club's members would be able to elect the trustees who served on the committee. 'Don't forget, out of three and a half thousand members, only about five hundred are Europeans,' he said. 'If we take away the two-tier membership, the minute the next AGM gets called –' and here he snapped his fingers – 'thank you very much. They'd vote him back in, and they'd shut us out.'

After the Forum had made its decisions for the evening, I was summoned into the circle. Tony, who was revelling in his abilities as both expansive host and legal luminary, asked me in a single breath: 'Would you like some coffee? What can we explain to you about the lawsuit?'

What I really wanted to know, I said, was why this rule of permitting only Europeans on the committee wasn't dropped years ago.

'Why? Right here in Mumbai, you have a Hindu Gymkhana, which allows only Hindus to join. You have a Parsi Gymkhana, which allows only Parsis to join,' Tony said. No Indian law explicitly forbids this sort of selectivity. 'There's nothing wrong with having a sectarian club.'

200

I had meant to ask about the rule's moral standing, not its legal one, and over the next hour I returned again and again to this question. But each time, I was offered the Hindu Gymkhana and the Parsi Gymkhana by way of an answer. Other clubs did it, and it wasn't strictly illegal; it was the sort of simple exoneration that children declaimed in schoolyards.

Another thing that puzzled me, I said, was how Mehta had insinuated himself and then his friend Lalit Agarwal into the committee, thumbing his nose so defiantly at the constitution. Didn't these changes have to be approved anywhere?

They did, it turned out – by the charity commissioner, a state official who oversees the operations of registered trusts. The Forum's faith in the government was frail. Officials could be bribed or squeezed, particularly by a fixer with outsized powers. In its lawsuit, the Forum claimed that Agarwal hadn't even been a member of the club when he entered the committee – that Mehta had fraudulently prepared a backdated membership application, featuring the name of a sponsor who was now conveniently dead as well as a Gmail contact address, even before that email service had properly launched.

All this sounded like too much trouble for what was essentially a migraine of a job, involving the scrutiny of swimming-pool maintenance contracts, the appeasement of whiny and entitled members or the balancing of the club budget. What was in it for Mehta? I wondered. Why did he want this position so much?

This set off a loud rustle of theories, the sound of brooding suspicion that has become ambient everywhere in India. Any post, even the chairmanship of a swimming-bath trust, can be massaged for personal gain. A contract, awarded to a favoured vendor, earns a plump little kickback; so does a nudge up the membership waiting list for a wealthy applicant into the club. The club's premises themselves, the stomping grounds of the city's rich and powerful, are invaluable to a fixer-lawyer, a man who relies on connections not only to secure new clients but to then hurry their work to a satisfactory finish. 'Today, if I have the right to offer someone a club membership – say the Ambanis – I'm doing a huge favour for them,' Archit Jayakar, one of the Forum's lawyers, said, referring to the first family of Indian industry. 'It's an IOU. And you can make IOUs with several hundred people.'

And then there was the land. Always at the heart of it all, in Mumbai, there's the land – precious, irreplaceable land that is in chronically short supply. Almost everywhere in India, the real estate market defies the boundaries of logic, but it is a particularly ridiculous animal in Mumbai. A city that once called like a siren to middle-class strivers now no longer wishes to offer them affordable homes. Instead, even though Mumbai's infrastructure is decaying, its skyline holds sheaves of luxury apartments – 'bespoke sky bungalows', as one developer described them – that can cost upwards of 20 million dollars apiece. These were outrageous prices, I thought, until Donald Trump, the maven of New York real estate, arrived in Mumbai in the summer, with plans to build a seventy-five-floor tower of four-bedroom apartments, each of which will sell for 80 million dollars. Land is prized and valued here as if in the lushness of a realtor's fever dream. A patch even an acre large – the size, say, of a kiddies' park in a swimming club in a ritzy Mumbai neighbourhood – can be leased long-term to a ravenous developer, making the club's management money on the side in return for its malleability.

This was the endgame, Jayakar said. Mehta was backed by two of Mumbai's most powerful politicians, so he could, if necessary, sidestep any regulations that prevented him building this condominium right in the front yard of the Breach Candy Club.

'But we don't have evidence of that,' Kapoor pointed out, carefully but glumly. Jayakar admitted this was true. Somebody had seen construction plans filed in the municipal office, he said vaguely, but the plans weren't there any more.

Shirley hadn't contributed to this discussion at all. 'It's all bloody conjecture. That's the bloody problem,' he told me, many days later. 'There are plenty of opportunities to make money – big money – at the club. But I understand that Mehta lives with his mum, and that he has a huge staff and is worth millions. So what does he want with kickbacks?'

'But then what is it?' I asked.

He leaned in towards me, so that I could see the mottles of a red spot on his chin, a razor nick that was slowly healing. 'I think he wants to go down in history by changing these rules. It can only be an ego thing. He wants to go out saying: "Fuck you, Europeans." He wants to be one of the people who beat down the old British Empire.'

Dipesh Mehta eluded me altogether. When I first called him, in March, he was faultlessly polite, said he'd love to talk about the club, and requested that I call him the following week, when he would be home from his travels. Over the next five months, I made roughly one hundred calls to his mobile phone, almost working it into my daily routine, slotting it in between breakfast and a shower or just before dinner; he didn't pick up. I also tried him from other people's phones. Mehta would answer, recognize my voice instantly, apologize for being so busy and suggest, with not a trace of guile, that he return my call as soon as he got out of the meeting he was in. Twice, I went without an appointment to his office, in the suburb of Bandra, but he wasn't in. 'Send me an email telling me what you want to talk about, dear,' he once said, when I had reached him from my mother's phone, 'and we'll definitely meet after that.' He called me 'dear' smoothly and happily, as if the dozens and dozens of calls he had ignored had forged an intimate bond between us. But Mehta, and his version of the truth, dangled in the shadows, out of reach.

This felt familiar. India has become a country where the powerful can feel confident of kneading the system to their benefit without overly worrying about public opinion. They have little need to talk to the people, through the media, and so they choose not to. The ensuing vacuum of information frustrates and confuses us; it invites us to spin delirious fears about the way India is really being run. On some days, everything can feel opaque; in fact, the existence of this wrap-around opacity is often the only transparent fact in sight.

By way of poor proxy, I listened to Mehta's lawyers. For two days, I occupied a corner of Court No 19 in the Bombay High Court, a Gothic Revival building from the 1870s, with high, raftered ceilings and bare walls and benches of hard wood worn smooth by anxiously shifting bottoms. The Forum turned out in force on both days. Shirley sat at the back, impassive and unhappy; in the lawsuit against Mehta, he was named as first petitioner. He remained alert even through the otherwise slackening texture of a day in court: the buzz of the first hour, then the settled keenness, the post-lunch torpor, the gradual straying of eyes to clocks, the dense energy of a system at work dissipating through the afternoon.

This was supposed to be a swift hearing – a hearing, in fact, to decide if a court could even sit in judgment upon this spat between Mehta and the Forum, or whether it was the sole preserve of the charity commissioner. But on the first day, after three other suits had been disposed of within fifteen minutes, Mehta's lawyer began by reading from a fat casebook marked with blue, pink and yellow fluorescent stickers. He had a voice that loped along without tiring, and an evident fondness for reciting the letter of the law in its ornate fullness.

'How long will this take?' Justice Roshan Dalvi asked after an hour. She was a tiny woman with salt-and-pepper hair, and since she was forced to bend forward to speak into the microphone, she chose not to use it at all. Instead, she leaned back and muttered so that only the lawyers in argument really heard her well.

'Between the two of us,' Mehta's lawyer said, 'I wouldn't be surprised if it took till the end of today.'

I may have been mistaken, but I thought I saw Justice Dalvi sigh. She turned to the bailiff and asked him to adjourn the twenty-five cases that remained on the day's schedule. 'Now continue,' she said.

The lawyers knew what they wanted. It was in the Forum's interests to convey, in the most ominous possible tones, the nature and magnitude of the fraud for which they held Mehta responsible, so that the court, shaken to its core, would insist on adjudicating this grievous lapse in justice. Mehta's lawyer, on the other hand, worked like a butcher stripping fat from a bone. Again and again, he sliced past these claims of fraud, tossing them aside to arrive at the fundament: that the law, properly interpreted, gave only the charity commissioner the powers to resolve club disputes. The court had no business here. This line of attack made sense: if Mehta could really co-opt or pay off the charity commissioner, as the Forum worried, then he would win through easily and gloriously. This single official, the charity commissioner, held the keys to the kingdom. But if Justice Dalvi thought her court should take on this case, Mehta's lawyer cautioned, 'it will be like opening Pandora's box, and 30,000 or 40,000 other similar cases will come your way'. He must have barely restrained himself from waggling a finger in warning.

For all of the first day, the arguments went back and forth; when the second day began, a member of the Forum's legal team assured the court that he needed only another twenty minutes, and yet we had staggered well past 1 p.m. when Justice Dalvi declared a recess. A couple of hours later, she announced that she was reserving judgment. Another two weeks would pass before she ruled in favour of the Forum and permitted the lawsuit to remain in the courts. The hearings about the actual allegations of fraud started later still. The suit became one among the 30 million cases making their slow, sticky way through the interminable entrails of the Indian judiciary.

Emerging from the court on the evening of that second day, I found that Mumbai had suddenly turned breezy and cool, with a smudge of rain cloud hanging above the city. I took a taxi to the Breach Candy Club, where a friend had signed me in for a swim before dinner. Lapping that enormous outdoor pool from tip to toe was too daunting, so I traversed its breadth instead, between Bengal and Gujarat on the map. The salt water desiccated my lips in minutes and crept past my goggles into my eyes, so that they were burning before I'd finished five laps. I spluttered through another ten with difficulty before stumbling out and finding my way to the changing rooms through a film of tears.

When I left the club later that night, after dinner, my eyes were still streaming. The insides of my glasses were speckled with teardrops. I looked up and down the road for a taxi, and everything swam before me in a watery haze, so that I seemed to be witnessing the absolute dissolution of the city. Only the very tops of the skyscrapers stood firm and bright above the murk, and in those moments without clarity, it was easy to assume that this was all there was to Mumbai, these forbidding towers and the privilege they contained. ■

ANNAWADI

Katherine Boo

In moments of intense reporting, I could be counted on to miss the incidentals: the nature of the light in the hospital ward, the presence or absence of bangles or teeth. To alleviate the strain of remembering, and the shame of getting stuff wrong, I began carrying a still camera, then a video camera, as I worked. My visual notes are mechanical by now, opportunistic, uncomposed: designed more to keep me from libel suits than to be looked at. The people I work with do better.

Between 2007 and 2011, I documented the lives of families in Annawadi, a small slum on Mumbai airport land, for a book called *Behind the Beautiful Forevers*. Dozens of Annawadi children also learned to use my cameras, making visual notes of their own.

The airport was being modernized in those years, and the slum increasingly confined by the fences of the airport authority, come-and-go concrete plants and neighbouring luxury hotels. Cameras in hand, the children of the slum respected the argument of those fences; the clangorous development all around them was rarely their documentary concern. Instead, they photographed home.

In the third photo here, Devo Kadam, then eleven, captures a sleepy afternoon on the rubbled maidan, just as the rain let up. This photo felt significant to him, historically. Had the maidan ever been so empty before? Devo's image of the water buffalo eating rubbish (photo 11) reflects an Annawadi private joke. The milk of the slum's water buffalo was sold as a health drink in more affluent neighbourhoods; Devo's single mother couldn't afford it. But he was one of many here who relished the idea that rich kids consumed a bit of Annawadi before heading off to their private schools.

In April 2008, when researcher Unnati Tripathi joined our documentary project, the slum gained a discerning new eye. Many of her photos here (4, 5, 9, 13, 14, 15, 16) are of the Husain family, who are featured in my book. The Husains buy and sell recyclable rubbish for a living, and the filth of this work had combined with tuberculosis to wreck the lungs of the patriarch, Karam (photo 5). In the ninth photo, Karam's youngest daughter Tabu tries to assume the work her father can't do as he bends over, coughing, outside the frame.

Annawadians didn't speak much of the physical cost of scrap work. Like the potential demolition of slums on airport land, it was a consistent and obvious threat, and thus a numb one. Sudden, uncalculated occurrences were a greater worry. In photo 13, Kehkashan Husain laughs with her mother and youngest siblings as manic boys with busted bicycle tubes try to ring the maidan's rusty flagpole. Two weeks later, Kehkashan, her father and eldest brother are falsely accused of setting a disabled woman named Fatima Shaikh on fire. In photo 14, a police van takes Kehkashan to prison – a moment her mother, watching her go, described as *Qayamat*, the end of the world.

But forgetting catastrophe is a large part of the art of perseverance. In photo 15, taken a few months later, Kehkashan's brother Abdul, awaiting trial on his own role in Fatima's death, inflates the lungs of a goat to amuse his little brothers. Beside Abdul, steadying the carcass, is Fatima's widowed husband. The couple's two children are underfoot. Mutual grievances have been set aside not just on this day, Bakri Eid, but on many days, because the exigencies of daily life demand it.

As with the garbage-eating buffalo or the girl sorting garbage for her fading father, many Annawadi images contain layers of uneasy implication. But in 2011, Unnati's husband Sudip Sengupta, a gifted cinematographer, visited Annawadi and captured its colour and light. In photo 7, the maidan has been paved by the Congress Party, freeing a girl to master a bike.

The final photo, by Vijay Gadge, is of his classmate Radha, whose parents were among a band of labourers brought from Karnataka to help build the new airport terminal. After years of inhaling construction debris, Radha's mother was gravely ill, but on this afternoon she sat up to direct her daughter's first portrait. Radha would pose beneath the family's prized plastic bag. ■

1. Two generations of scrap workers at the entrance to Annawadi

2. In a broken bucket seat from the airport terminal, a young scavenger waits for the rice t⟨
© SUDIP SENGUPTA

3. The maidan in monsoon
© DEVO KADAM

4. Mirchi Husain, tense as he waits for business
© UNNATI TRIPATHI

5. Karam Husain, sorting at home
© UNNATI TRIPATHI

6. Behind the fence, a lake of sewage is turned into an airport taxi stand; in front, a hut rises beside two *pucca* homes
© UNNATI TRIPATHI

7. The Congress Party woos residents by paving the maidan
© SUDIP SENGUPTA

8. Two young scavengers finish a day's work on airport grounds
© KATHERINE BOO

9. Tabu Husain, helping her father
© UNNATI TRIPATHI

10. At a game parlour, one rupee buys thirty minutes of play – an investment in fun taken seriously indeed
© SUDIP SENGUPTA

11. Rubbish with no recyclable value becomes the water buffalo's lunch
© DEVO KADAM

12. View from a scrap shop
© UNNATI TRIPATHI

13. Zehrunisa Husain and three of her children

14. A police van takes Kehkashan Husain to Byculla Women's Prison

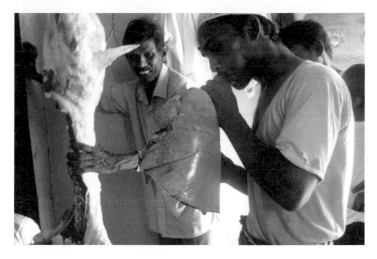

15. In a slum where Hindus predominate, Muslims stay inside to skin a goat on Bakri Eid
© UNNATI TRIPATHI

16. Zehrunisa and Kehkashan sew a quilt to replace one with which they covered their neighbour's bier
© UNNATI TRIPATHI

17. A pavement-dweller's clothes, airing out on a fence in Saki Naka
© KATHERINE BOO

18. Radha, looking at her mother
© VIJAY GADGE

GRANTA

THE MAGAZINE OF NEW WRITING

PRINT SUBSCRIPTION REPLY FORM FOR US, CANADA AND LATIN AMERICA
(includes digital access). For digital-only subscriptions, please visit granta.com

GUARANTEE: If I am ever dissatisfied with my *Granta* subscription, I will simply notify you, and
you will send me a complete refund or credit my credit card, as applicable, for all un-mailed issues.

YOUR DETAILS

TITLE ....

NAME ....

ADDRESS ....

....

CITY.. STATE ....

ZIP CODE .... COUNTRY.....................................

EMAIL ....

☐ Please check this box if you do not wish to receive special offers from *Granta*

☐ Please check this box if you do not wish to receive offers from organizations
    selected by *Granta*

YOUR PAYMENT DETAILS

1 year subscription: ☐ US: $48   ☐ Canada: $56   ☐ Latin America: $68

3 year subscription: ☐ US: $120   ☐ Canada: $144   ☐ Latin America: $180

Enclosed is my check for $ _____ made payable to *Granta*.

Please charge my: Visa   ☐ MasterCard   ☐ Amex

Card No. ☐☐☐☐☐☐☐☐☐☐☐☐☐☐☐☐

Expiry date ☐☐ / ☐☐

Security Code ☐☐☐☐

SIGNATURE ....   DATE ....

Please mail this order form with your payment instructions to:

Granta Publications
PO Box 359
Congers, NY 10920-0359

Or call 845-267-3031
Or visit GRANTA.COM for details

Source code: BUS130PM

Her
by Harriet Lane

Emma is a struggling mother who has put everything on hold. Nina is sophisticated and independent – entirely in control. When the pair meet, Nina generously draws Emma into her life. But this isn't the first time the women's paths have crossed. Nina remembers Emma and she remembers what Emma did. But what exactly does Nina want from her? And how far will she go in pursuit of it?

'Quality literary fiction meets psychological thriller' *Observer*

Weidenfeld & Nicolson | £7.99 | PB

The Alphabet of Birds
by S.J. Naudé

'Cool and intelligent, unsettling and deeply felt, Naudé's voice is something new in South African writing' Damon Galgut

'The arrival of a writer of great humanity and style' Patrick Flanery

'This collection is truly unmissable' André Brink

'This English translation will bring him the wider readership he deserves' Ivan Vladislavić

And Other Stories | £10 / $15.95 | PB with French flaps

The Tea-Garden Journal
by Somnath Hore, translated by Somnath Zutshi

The mid 1930s. The tea gardens of Bengal. A bitter struggle began that pitted unionists, organized by the Communist Party of India, against the British colonial tea-estate owners and their thugs. The Party sent young Somnath Hore, who'd later become one of India's foremost artists, to document this struggle. The result is this book – a fascinatingly illustrated document of a major socialist movement.

Seagull Books | £31.50 / $45 | PB

Art Rules! (And How to Break Them)
by Mel Gooding

A spectacular new box book from Redstone Press, *Art Rules!* offers a completely new key to enjoying and understanding contemporary art by showing how it is made. The box contains forty-two illustrated, interactive cards and an original book, *Modern Art: Inside Out*.

www.theredstoneshop.com

Redstone Press | £19.95 | Box book

This year too in the plains

This year too in the plains
There are no mountains.
For centuries the mountains have stayed in one place;
It's time they moved.
The Vindhyas, for instance, should come closer
To the bus stand and law courts
And the Satpuras go behind
The village school or farm.
The Himalayas seem unfair
To a place that doesn't have the Himalayas;
This maidan seems unfair
To a place that doesn't have a maidan;
Tatanagar seems unfair
To a place that is not Tatanagar.
This year let this level ground be displaced
Not to the Terai but the Himalayas
The ground's highest point rising like a Himalayan peak.
Let's have Bhopal this year
Near Bakal and Paniajob
Varanasi on the banks of the Mahanadi
Gariaband near the Ganga
Chandigarh near Sanchi
Nandgaon near Faridkot
And Madras next to Moradabad.
All places should be displaced
And brought near all other places
So that every place is near every other place
And not a single person is displaced
From the village this year.

This colourful picture

This colourful picture
Picked up in the bazaar
And hanging on the wall
Is of chubby pink-faced
Children – so unlike our own,
Who're neither as chubby,
Nor as pretty, nor wear
Such nice clothes.

These pictures sell a lot.
There's always someone in every family
Who'll feel as a father feels
And bring one home.

The truth is, though no one says it,
They're all worried about their children.

Translated from the Hindi by Arvind Krishna Mehrotra

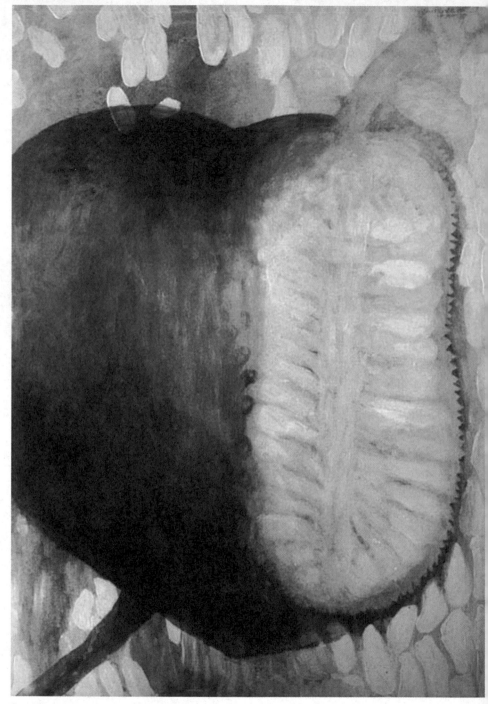

© KIRUSIYA RANI V.
Silence Speaks of Jackfruit, 2011

STICKY FINGERS

Arun Kolatkar

My father had always been hard of hearing. Nothing was wrong with the old man's ears, mind you – he could hear perfectly well when he wanted to – but he had this knack for going deaf at will. Whenever it suited him, as a matter of fact.

Like when I'd ask him, 'Baba, may I go have a cup of tea?' and he'd give no sign of having heard.

Ask him once. Ask him twice. Nothing. No reaction.

For it meant having to cough up money, you see. Not much, two paise could get you tea and biscuits those days. But it wasn't the amount involved that bothered him. It was the principle of the thing. It always upset him, the very thought, I mean, of giving money to anyone. And when it meant shelling it out to sonny boy, he positively hated it.

'Baba, it's been a while. Is it all right if I break for tea now?' I'd ask him one more time.

He'd sigh then, and turn, reluctantly, to look at me.

'What was that? You said something?'

'I was wondering whether I should just nip across for a quick cup of tea,' I'd mumble.

'Tea?' he'd say, 'It's teatime for you already, eh? How long has it been since you came here to the shop this morning?'

'A couple of hours.'

'But I mean we came here together, didn't we? You and I? Or were you here ahead of me?'

'We came here together.'

'Then how come you're dying for a cup of tea already? I'm not. And all this stuff lying around here the whole morning? Who the fuck's going to sell it?' he'd ask me, indicating with a wave of hand the masses of vegetables that surrounded him, the basketfuls of tomatoes, cabbages, eggplants, snake gourds, cauliflowers, capsicums and cucumbers.

I could always have told him what to do with all the stuff, if he really wanted to know, but I'd keep quiet.

One of the other shopkeepers would take pity on me then, and come to my rescue.

'Let him go, poor boy,' they'd say. 'All the other boys have had their tea break already.'

And it was only when others had pleaded on my behalf that my father would relent and part, magnanimously, with the two paise.

He was a big talker, though, my father.

Like, for instance, when people remarked on the poor state of my health and said, in worried tones, 'You got to do something about Balwant, you know; the kid's really in bad shape!' he'd say, 'The boy's hopeless! Go to the gym, I tell him, drink plenty of milk, eat lots of jalebis, lots of almonds. If I've told him once I've told him a hundred times; but he just won't listen. I'm completely fed up.'

Milk and almonds, indeed! Two paise went a long way in the good old days, but not that far, I can tell you that. Where was I going to get milk, jalebis and almonds at that price?

So, naturally, if I had to look after myself, I had to steal. You see that, don't you?

And steal I did; my father left me with no alternative.

It got so my hands itched, my body burned, I went hot and cold all over if I was anywhere near a till. My hand would be drawn to it, unable to resist. I had only to dip in and symptoms disappeared instantly; get my hands on a bit of nickel, copper or silver and my fever came down; everything was cool again, everything set to rights. My father had only to go for a pee, nod off or merely look away. It was enough; I got my chance.

A born thief. That's what I was I guess, a *chor*. And something of a child prodigy as well. My talent in that direction had found early expression, but it matured and truly began to blossom during my career as a helper in various shops at the Crawford Market.

This is as good a place as any for me to acknowledge the debt of gratitude I owe my father. For it was my stint in his shop that gave me the time and the opportunity to work out, test and perfect a nifty system, as simple as it was beautiful (and damn near foolproof at that), of spiriting away my ill-gotten gains.

I hid the loot inside a tomato or a bell pepper, and smuggled it out of the shop.

Small tomatoes, mind you. Nothing like what you're used to seeing nowadays. They seem to be getting bigger and bigger with every passing year. But even then they were large enough to accommodate a modest sum of two-anna or four-anna coins, which was good enough for a small-time thief like me, for although a true artist, I'm essentially a miniaturist.

Tomatoes. Oh I love 'em! Push it in edgewise, and a coin sinks into it; just disappears from sight! It's amazing.

And a bell pepper, or a capsicum, if that's what you call it, is all space. You can go on feeding coins to it and it still has room for more. Tempting. You can easily hide a small fortune in one of those things. But don't touch them. I certainly wouldn't recommend them to a novice. You need to exercise extreme caution while handling them. Trouble is, they make a lot of noise. You might as well take one in each hand and you have a pair of maracas like the ones that street singer, a Negro woman, used to play. Dicey business, bell peppers. By and large I left them alone.

Having deposited my money in a tomato, I set it down among the multitude of tomatoes in a basket, close to the edge, and covered it up artfully with a few others. I knew at all times where exactly that particular tomato was in the basket. I had to stand guard over it; take good care that it didn't get mixed up with the others and end up in a customer's shopping bag by mistake – which wasn't very difficult since it was part of my job to help a customer choose the vegetables, weigh them and drop them in his bag.

'You won't die if you miss your cup of tea for one day,' my father would say sneeringly, as I stood before him with a suitably contrite expression on my face, all the while looking down with intense concentration at one particular spot in that basket full of tomatoes waiting for him to relent, which eventually he would.

'OK. Here, take your two paise and bugger off. And don't forget: I want you back here in five minutes flat.'

I'd be off the moment I had my tea allowance in hand, stop just as suddenly after I'd taken no more than four or five steps, as if I'd just thought of something, turn round, come back, pick up the stuffed tomato, as if at random, show it to my father and say, 'Something to munch. May I take it?'

My dad would look at me, first disapprovingly, and then at the tomato in my hand critically, before deciding to be generous and letting me get away with it.

Selecting the right kind of a tomato was crucial for the scam to work. Do you think the old man would've let me walk away with a perfectly good tomato, ever? If there was even the slightest chance of selling it, he'd have snatched it out of my hand and tossed it back into the basket. A tomato had to be, well, you know, kind of poised between overripe and rotten, if not downright rotten, to have any hope of getting past my father's trained eyes.

Once my father had given the nod, I'd be in a hurry to get the hell out; I could barely wait until I was out of the market to rip open the tomato and get at the contents.

You don't think I ever actually ate the damn things, do you? Good God, no. Never. What do you take me for? I don't care for tomatoes, as tomatoes I mean, I never have, and wouldn't dream of eating one raw, ripe or rotten; it's what's inside a tomato that counts if you ask me. I did bring it up to my lips as I walked away from our shop, I even kissed it a couple of times, as long as I felt my father could still see me, but that's as far as it went. As soon as I stepped out on the road I took the substance and threw away the shadow.

My father suspected of course!

Just when I thought I was getting away with it – tomato in hand, song on my lips – he'd call out after me; I'd freeze in my tracks and the song would die on my lips.

'Balwant!'

Oh fuck, I'd say to myself.

'Come here!'

I'd go back then. Stand in front of him.

He'd look at me then with his piercing eyes and say, 'So! You've started smoking now, have you?'

'Smoking?' I'd say, 'No, Baba.'

'What's that box of matches doing in your pocket then?' he'd ask me.

'Matches? No, Baba!'

'Let me see,' he'd say, and start going through my pockets.

He didn't expect to find any matches, but it gave him an excuse to search me. Both my hands held high up in the air, I'd stand before him with a resigned expression and submit myself to the search. When the ruse didn't work, and he didn't find anything in my pocket, he'd frown and say, 'Hmmm, and what's that in your hand?'

'A tomato,' I'd tell him truthfully.

'And in the other one?'

'The two paise you gave me.'

'OK, OK,' he'd say then. 'But remember: don't let me ever catch you with a bidi, a cigarette or a match in your pocket. Understand?'

As soon as I had encashed my tomato I'd head straight for the nearest mithai shop and treat myself to a king-size helping of burfi, half a seer to be precise, which you got for just five paise in the good old days when burfi was two and a half annas a seer and twenty-eight tolas made a seer.

I gobbled it up as fast as I could and kept looking over my shoulders as I did so, alert, lest somebody should catch me in the act. It was only after I had polished it all off, and got rid of the wrapping paper as well, that I could afford to relax. I'd go down to Khandu's teashop then, to linger over my legitimate cup of tea and the two biscuits, dipping each one thoughtfully in the tea before eating it, and in no great hurry to get back to our shop.

Sometimes I'd be found out.

One of my father's buddies, for example, during the course of a chance conversation, would mention casually, 'I saw Balwant the other day.'

'Where?' my father would ask.

'Oh, he was standing in front of that mithai shop round the corner.'

'Yeah? And what was he doing?'

'Eating burfi, of course.'

Burfi?

Gotcha! My father would say to himself. That can only mean one thing: the bastard's been dipping into the till. How else would he get the money to buy burfi?

He never said anything to me though; never accused me.

Evidence. That's what he wanted. To confront me with hard evidence. And that's where I had him completely baffled. Every time he searched me under some silly pretext or other and found me clean he was obliged, however reluctantly, to let me go. But he couldn't get rid of the feeling that his pissant of a son was pulling a fast one on him, that somehow he was being made a sucker of.

And so, sometimes, more determined than ever, the old fox would jump off his perch in the shop after I'd gone and actually follow me – can you beat that? – to see for himself where I went and what I did. And do you know that, on one occasion, I had to throw away half a seer of perfectly good jalebi, untouched, on the road, because of him?

I had just barely managed to puzzle out the string tied around it and get the paper package open when I saw my father. Heedless of traffic, and with no thought to personal safety, he was crossing the street with the purposeful air of someone from the intelligence branch closing in on his quarry; he was heading straight for me. I dropped the package to the ground, sent it flying into the open gutter by the roadside with a smart sideways kick, folded my arms and stood nonchalantly looking up in the air, with a tilt to my head, trying to look casual while whistling (soundlessly, for I can't whistle to save my life) a song from the latest Marathi musical.

'Balwant! What are you doing here?'

'Doing? No, nothing. Just standing around.'

'I see,' he said disapprovingly, and shuffled off.

Look what you've done to my jalebis you cunt you arschole you shithead, I wanted to scream.

But you get the point.

If I hadn't stolen, I'd bloody nearly have starved.

All in all, I'd worked out a nice system, and it worked beautifully. Which is not say it was foolproof, though (what system is?); once, I really screwed it up and there was a balls-up of the first magnitude.

Like that time when I had stashed an eight-anna coin into a – no, not a tomato, not a bell pepper either, it was a mango this time – and a Pathan got it.

Although my father sold vegetables in the market most of the time, he also sold mangoes when they were in season, you see; and I'd found this beautiful mango with a dark patch on its golden skin.

A mango after my own heart, a defective. I had invested eight annas in it, buried it under three or four other unblemished mangoes in the basket, and I was sitting pretty.

There were hardly any customers about; it was nearly eleven, time to knock off; I was planning to take the mango out to lunch that day and I didn't foresee any problems with my father; since it was a damaged mango, my father was not likely to feel any wrench at the thought of parting with it, and in fact I was thinking about how I'd like to spend such a lot of money when this Pathan came to our shop. Don't ask me who he was and where he came from, I haven't the foggiest; all I know is suddenly he was there, standing before me, blocking most of my view and cutting off my light.

He started poking about in the basket, turning mangoes over, picking up one or two, sniffing at them and putting them down again. And the next thing I knew he had picked up the mango I'd sunk all my money into and he was examining it.

Before I could say anything, he grunted approvingly and asked, 'How much do you want for this one?'

I was in a panic. I didn't know what to do.

'It's not a good mango, boss,' I said. 'I'll find you a better one.' And I tried to take the mango away from him, or just made as if to, but he moved his hand away and said, 'This is the one I want. How much?'

There was no argument against that. But even then I gave it another try. I picked up another mango from the basket and said, 'Look, boss, just look at this one here. See how nice it is? A beauty.'

I should've known better. For he was a Pathan, after all. He didn't know what was so special about the mango he had picked, but once his mind was made up, he was not going to change it, the blockhead. And what's more, he was beginning to get annoyed.

He raised his voice a little and said, 'I want this one. You want to sell it or you don't want to sell it, hahn?'

I looked at him carefully. He was a giant of a man, tall even for a Pathan; a big burly brute of a frontiersman, a red-beard, with black mascaraed eyes and a scar on his face. The crisp fan-tailed turban that crested him further increased the impression of height. And I, who was certainly no taller then than I am now, was like a midget before him.

'How much for this one? Speak up,' he said in a gruff voice, 'or I'm going.'

I had no choice then. There wasn't another mango like it in the whole world, and I was the only one who knew its real worth. But I had to do it, and it broke my heart to sell that mango for all of two annas. The Pathan didn't even bargain with me. He tossed a two-anna coin at me and walked away with it. It was daylight robbery, plain and simple. It hurt, but there was no use thinking about it.

But do you know what that Pathan did next? Any other man, a well-bred man I mean, a civilized person like you and me, would've waited until he reached home; he'd have washed it first, put it on a plate, cut it into small pieces and then settled down to eat the mango.

Not this Pathan, though; that was not his way.

That boorish man walked towards the fountain which was just ten steps away from our shop, settled himself down comfortably on the low wall that surrounded the fountain, produced a large, vicious-looking clasp-knife from one of the innumerable pockets of his embroidered waistcoat, made two swift cuts down the whole length of the unwashed mango, lifted the piece he had carved out thus in his dirty fingers and pushed it into his ugly mouth as I watched him tensely. He smacked his lips with evident pleasure as he ate the piece – and did not even leave out the skin, can you imagine!

It was when he made another cut and picked up another piece that his mouth fell open; his eyes filled with an almost childlike wonder; and he stared as the lustrous eight-anna bit embedded in the flesh of the half-cut mango revealed itself to him.

He looked up then, lifting his eyes heavenwards, and said, 'Ya Allah,' in a voice choked with emotion.

Is Allah really so stupid as to put his money inside a mango? I ask you. I mean, doesn't he have an account in a bank somewhere like everybody else?

What are you looking up there for, you idiot? I felt like asking him.

Your Allah is not up there among the pigeons swirling under that shitty roof, I wanted to tell him.

Look this way, you fool; look at me. Your Allah is sitting right here in this shop at this very moment, working in his mysterious ways, one hand in the till. ∎

NOTE ON THE TEXT: Arun Kolatkar (1931–2004), one of India's finest modern poets, wrote in English as well as in his native Marathi, creating two separate bodies of work of equal distinction. However, those who have read it or heard him read from it believe that Kolatkar was also a supreme prose stylist, whose unpublished work of more than 1,200 pages in Marathi called *Balwant Bua*, written in the mid 1980s, may come to overshadow his reputation as a poet. Kolatkar came in contact with the eponymous eighty-four-year-old bhajan singer and raconteur in 1974. They met regularly after that, about once a week, until Balwant Bua's death in 1991. 'He didn't talk about the great events of this century; the two wars, for example, seem to have just passed him by,' Kolatkar wrote of their 'talk sessions', some of which lasted up to six hours. 'Mostly, he talked about micro-events, or non-events that make up his life – miniature comedies, adventures, misadventures, people he knew, the women in his life – with a sharp eye for the absurdities inherent in situations and the contradictions in human behaviour, looking at the world around him from street level, with his unique sense of humour which equips him with a sort of X-ray vision.'

'Sticky Fingers' is one of only six *Balwant Bua* stories Kolatkar wrote in English.

Arvind Krishna Mehrotra

Rain at Three

Rain at three splits the bed in half,
cracks at windows like horsemen blistering
through a century of hibernation.
The washing's on the line.
There are pillows in the grass.
All the weeds we pulled up yesterday
lie in clotted heaps, dying slowly.
We sleep with pumiced, wooden
bodies – mud-caked, mud brown,
listening to the fan-whir sea-heave
of our muscled Tamil Nadu nights.
We turn inwards
announce how patiently
we've waited for this uprooting.
Now that damaged petals of hibiscus
drown the terrace stones,
we must kneel together and gather.
This is how desire works:
splintering first, then joining.

© RIDDHI SHAH
Untitled, 2014
Courtesy of Exhibit320 Gallery, New Delhi

THE WRONG SQUARE

Neel Mukherjee

While trying to check the bill before settling at the reception desk – just an old habit, inculcated by his father, of giving any bill a once-over to see that he had not been overcharged – he realized that he had lost the ability to perform the simple function of adding up the individual items and the tax that together made up the grand total. He tried again and again. Then he took out his wallet and tried to count the rupee and US dollar notes nestled inside; he failed. Something as fundamental to intelligence as counting was eluding him. In the peripheries of his vision he could see a small crowd gathering to look at him; discreetly, nonchalantly, they thought. The news had spread. It was then that he broke down and wept for his son.

He hesitated about taking the boy to Fatehpur Sikri right after their lunchtime tour of the Taj Mahal; two major Mughal monuments in one afternoon could be considered excessive. But it was less than an hour's drive away, he reasoned, and to fit the two sites into one day was the generally accepted practice. They could be back at their hotel in Agra by early evening and after an early night with the television and room service they could leave for Delhi, refreshed, the following morning. The reasoning prevailed.

When he mentioned part of this plan to the driver of his hired car, the young man, all longish hair and golden chain around his neck and golden wristlet and chunky watch, took it as a veiled order to go about the business in record time. He revelled in the opportunity to drive through the dusty, cratered slip road to Fatehpur Sikri at organ-jostling speed, punctuated by abrupt jerking into rest when impeded and then launching as suddenly into motion again. They passed a string of dingy roadside eateries, teashops, cigarette-and-snack shacks. The bigger ones boasted signboards and names. There were the predictable 'Akbar', 'Shahjahan', 'Shahenshah', a 'Jodha Bai', even a 'Tansen', which was '100% VAGETARIAN'. There had been a speed-warning sign earlier, while leaving Agra: 'Batter late than never.' Not for the first time he wondered, in a country given over to a dizzying plenitude of signs, how unsettled their orthography was. A Coca-Cola hoarding adorned the top of one small shop, the brand name and shout line written in Hindi script.

'Coca-Cola,' the boy said, able to read that trademark universal wave even though he couldn't read the language.

'We can have one after we've done our tour,' he said, his mind occupied by trying to work out if another order to the driver to slow down to prevent their incipient motion sickness would be taken as wilfully contradictory; he worried about these things.

The boy seemed subdued; he didn't move from the bare identification of the familiar brand to wanting it. Ordinarily, he would have been compulsively rattling off the names written in English on shopfronts and billboards. While he was grateful for his son's uncharacteristic placidity, he wondered if he hadn't imposed too much on a six-year-old, dragging him from one historical monument to another. He now read a kind of polite forbearance in the boy's quietness, a way of letting him know that this kind of tourism was wholly outside his sphere of interest but he was going to tolerate his father's indulging in it. After a few questions at the Taj Mahal which began as enthusiastic then quickly burned out into perfunctory – 'Baba, what is a mau-so-le-um?', 'Is Moom-taz under this building?', 'Was she walking and moving and talking when

Shajjy-han built this over her?' – they had stopped altogether. Was it wonder that had silenced him or boredom? He had tried to keep the child interested by spinning stories that he thought would catch the boy's imagination: 'Do you see how white the building is? Do you know that the emperor who had it built, Shah Jahan, had banquets on the terrace on full-moon nights where everything was white? The moonlight, the clothes the courtiers and the guests wore, the flowers, the food – everything was white, to go with the white of the marble and the white light of the full moon.' The boy had nodded, seemingly absorbing the information, but had betrayed no further curiosity, had followed with no questions.

Now he wondered if his son had not found all this business of tombs and erecting memorials to the dead and immortal grief macabre, unsettling. His son was American, so he was not growing up, as he had, with the gift of ghost stories, first heard sitting on the laps of servants and aunts in his childhood home in Calcutta, then, when he was a little older, read in children's books. As a result, he did not understand quite what went on inside the child's head when novelties, such as the notion of an order of things created by the imagination residing under the visible world and as vivid as the real one, were introduced to him. He made a mental note to stick to historical facts only when they reached Fatehpur Sikri.

Or could it have been the terrible accident they had narrowly avoided witnessing yesterday at the moment of their arrival at the hotel? A huge multi-storey building was going up across the road, directly opposite their hotel, and a construction worker had apparently fallen to his death just as their car was getting into the slip lane for the hotel entrance. As they waited in the queue to get in, people had come running from all directions to congregate about twenty metres from where they were. Something about the urgency of the swarming and the indescribable sound that emanated from that swiftly engorging clot of people, a tense noise between buzzing and truculent murmuring, instantly transmitted the message that a disaster had occurred. Otherwise how else would the child have

NEEL MUKHERJEE

known to ask, 'Baba, people running, look. What's happening there?'
And how else could the driver have answered, mercifully in Hindi, 'A
man's just fallen from the top of that building under construction.
A labourer. Instant death, poor man.'

He had refused to translate, had tried to pull his son back from
craning his neck out, but as the queue of cars moved forward, through
a chance aperture in the hive of people around the death, he saw, for
the briefest of flashes, a patch of dusty earth stained the colour of old
scab from the blood it had thirstily drunk. Then the slit closed, the
car started advancing inch by inch and the vision ended. He saw his
son turning his head to continue to stare at the spot. But had he really
seen the earth welt like that, or had he just imagined it? There was
no way he could ask the boy to corroborate. As soon as he thought
that, all the worries came stampeding in: had the child seen it? Was he
going to be affected by it? How could he establish if he had without
planting the idea in the boy's head?

All of last night his mind had been a pincushion to these sharp
questions until he had fallen asleep. They returned again now,
summoned by the boy's unnatural quietness. By the time they got off
at Agra Gate, having shaved all of ten minutes from the journey, the
boy was looking decidedly peaky and he felt that his own lunch had
risen up to somewhere just behind his sternum in rebellion.

The driver grinned: there was just the right touch of the adversarial
in the gleam of self-satisfaction. More than twenty years of life in the
academic communities of the East Coast of the USA had defanged
him of the easy Indian ability to bark at people considered servants,
so he swallowed his irritation, even the intention to ask the driver to
take it more gently on the journey back in case he couldn't control the
tone and it was interpreted as a peremptory order. Instead, he said in
Hindi, 'We won't be more than an hour.'

The driver said, 'OK, sir,' nodding vigorously. 'I will be here.'

He checked the car to see if he had taken everything – a bottle of
water, his wallet and passport, the guidebook, his small backpack,
his phone, his son's little knapsack – then shut the car door and held

out his hand. The boy's meek silence bothered him. Where was the usual firework display of chatter and fidgety energy, the constant soundtrack of his aliveness?

He kneeled down to be on level with the boy and asked, tenderly, 'Are you tired? Do you want to go back to the hotel? We don't have to see this.'

The boy shook his head.

'Do you want a Parle's Orange Kream?' he asked, widening and rolling his eyes to simulate the representation of temptation in the advertisements.

The boy shook his head again. Behind him, on a grass verge, a hoopoe was flitting across. He said, 'Look!' and turned the boy around.

The boy looked dutifully but didn't ask what it was.

'It's a hoopoe. You won't see this bird in New York,' he supplied the answer gratuitously.

The boy asked, 'Is this a moss-o-moll-lom?'

'No, sweetheart,' his father laughed, 'it's not a mausoleum. It's a palace. You know what a palace is, don't you? A very good and powerful king lived here. His name was Akbar. I told you about him last night, remember?'

'That was Shajjy-han, who built a big big marble stone on his wife and she died and he was very sad and cried all the time.' The innocence of his American accent suddenly moved his father.

'No, this is different. Akbar was his grandfather. Come, we'll look at it. It's a different colour, see? All red and brown and orange, not the white that we saw earlier.'

They passed some ruined cloisters, then a triple-arched inner gateway, solidly restored, and, slightly further from it, a big domed building that was awaiting restoration work. Touts, who had noticed a man and a small boy get out of the car, descended on them.

'Guide, sir, guide? Good English, sir. Full history, you won't find in book.' Not from one voice but from an entire choir.

Beggars, crippled in various ways, materialized. From the simplest pleading, with a hand repeatedly brought up to the lips to signify hunger, to hideous displays of amputated and bandaged limbs, even an inert, entirely limbless, alive torso laid out flat on a board with wheels – this extreme end of the spectrum of human agony filled him with horror, shame, pity, embarrassment, repulsion, but, above all, a desire to protect his son from seeing them. How did all these other people drifting around him appear to be so sheathed in indifference and blindness? Or was the same churning going on inside them? Truth was, he felt he was no longer a proper Indian; making a life in the plush West had made him skinless like a good, sheltered First World liberal. He was now a tourist in his own country; no longer 'his own country', he corrected himself fastidiously. He suppressed the impulse to cover the boy's eyes with his hands and said impatiently, 'Sweetie, can we move a bit faster please.' It came out as a command, the interrogative missing.

Men came up with accordions of postcards, maps, guidebooks, magazines, photos, toys, current best-sellers in pirated editions, snacks, rattles, drinks, confectionery, tinsel, dolls, plastic replicas of historical buildings, books, whistles and flutes . . . He kept shaking his head stoically, a tight half-smile on his lips, and ushered his boy along.

The child, distracted one moment by a tray of carved soapstone figures, then another instant by a flashing, crudely copied replica of an inflatable Superman toy, kept stalling to stare.

'Baba, Baba, look!'

'Yes, I know. Let's keep moving.' He was so relieved – and grateful – that the cheap toys had diverted the child's attention away from the suppuration and misery that he almost broke step to buy one of those baubles.

That small manifestation of interest was enough. The loose, dispersed assembly of touts and pedlars now tightened into a purposeful circle.

'Babu, my child is hungry, hasn't eaten for four days.' The shrivelled girl with matted hair in the woman's arms looked like the living dead; she had no energy or will to swipe at the flies clustering on a sore at the corner of her mouth.

'Here, look, babu, babu-sa'ab, look.' A button was pressed and a toy came to mechanical life, emitting tinny games-arcade sounds of shooting guns as it teetered forward.

A man came up uncomfortably close and fanned open a deck of sepia prints of famous Indian historical buildings and temples with the dexterity of a seasoned card sharp. A picture of a naked woman appeared and disappeared so quickly that it could well have been the prestidigitator's illusion. He was shocked; didn't the man see that he had a small child with him? Or did he not care?

The surrounding gardens, well tended by Indian standards, shone in the white-gold light of the January afternoon, yet, looked at closely, all that riot of cannas and marigolds and manicured grass lawns could not really disguise their irredeemable municipal souls. There was the typical shoddiness – straggly borders; lines that could not keep straight; a certain patchiness to the planting, revealing the scalp of soil through the thinning hair of vegetation; the inevitable truculence of nature against the methodizing human hand – and underpinning all this amateurish attempt at imposing order and beauty he could feel, no, almost *see*, what a battle it was to keep the earth, wet and dark now, from reverting to red dust in the obliterating heat of the Northern Plains in the summer. He bought tickets and entered the great courtyard of the Diwan-i-Am. The world transformed – in the burnished gold of the winter-afternoon sun, the umber-red sandstone used for the whole complex at Fatehpur Sikri seemed like carved fire, something the sun had magicked out of the red soil in their combined image and likeness.

He looked at his son, expecting to see a reflection of his own wonder on the child's face, but all he could discern in that mostly unreadable expression was . . . was what? Boredom? Across another courtyard, all blazing copper in the light, lay the palace buildings. He backtracked to consult the map etched onto a stone block towards the entrance, but with no reference point to indicate YOU ARE HERE he felt confused.

While retrieving the camera and the guidebook from his backpack, he said to his son, 'Stay still for a moment, don't run off. We'll go to all those beautiful little palaces, do you see?' By the time he had slung the camera around his neck and opened the guidebook to the correct page, he could tell that the boy was itching to run across the courtyard. He tried to keep an eye on him while skimreading the relevant page. Yes, he had found it – this must be the Mahal-i-Khas, the private palaces of Akbar. His head bobbed back and forth, like a foraging bird's, from page to surrounding environment. When he had established beyond any doubt that the two-and-a-half-storeyed building on the left, which had a touch of incompleteness to it, was Akbar's private apartments, he caught hold of his son's hand and made to enter the building.

But he had been spotted leafing through the travel guide, his hesitation and momentary lostness read shrewdly. A man materialized behind him and began to speak as if he was in the middle of a lecture he had been giving. 'The recesses in the ground floor that you will see were meant for his books and papers and documents . . .'

He wheeled round. The sun caught his eyes and dazzled him. All he could make out was a dark, almost black, sharply pointed face, a human face on its way to becoming a fox's; or was it the other way round?

'If you go up to his sleeping chamber, the *khwabgah*, on the top floor,' the man continued, 'you will see fine stone latticework screens along the corridor leading to the women's quarters, the harem. These jalis protected the women from the public gaze as they went back and forth from the *khwabgah.*'

The man spoke with practised fluency. If he was trying to advertise his skills as a guide to get hired, then there was nothing in his manner or his speech that betrayed this purposive bent. If anything, the man seemed almost oblivious of his presence and his child's. The sun had blinded him so he turned his head away, both to face his son, whom he was afraid to let out of his field of vision for any duration, and to signal to the man that he was not going to be needing his services. The buildings that lay in the slanted shade were an earthen matt pink.

Elsewhere, the red sandstone that caught the sun burned a coppery gold. When he turned around to see if he had shaken off the tout, there was no one to be seen.

In the rooms on the ground floor of the emperor's private quarters he was held by the flaky painted decorations depicting flowers and foliage; these faded ghosts still managed to carry a fraction of their original life-spirit. They had been touched up, restored, but with a brutal mugger's hand. From the vantage point of the courtyard, the interior had looked poky and pitch dark and he had wondered about the smallness of the chambers and, correspondingly, the physical stature of those sixteenth-century people: did they have to huddle and stoop inside? Was it light enough to see things by in there during the daytime? Why were there no doors and windows? What did they do for privacy? And then, the crowning question: did he know just too little about the architectural and domestic history of the Mughals?

Now that they were inside, the idea that the rooms were cramped somewhat diminished, but the feeling that they were, or could be, dark remained. Was it something to do with his vision, or from having just come in from the brightness outside? He blinked several times. The interior seemed to shrink, expand and then shrink again, as if he were in the almost imperceptibly pulsating belly of a giant beast. In the pavilion at the top, where Akbar used to sleep, faded frescoes, nibbled away by time with a slow but tenacious voracity, covered the walls. But the fragments seemed to be under some kind of wash; a protective varnish, perhaps, but it had the effect of occluding them under a milky mist. A winged creature, holding an infant in front of a cave in a rock face, looked down at him from above a doorway. It looked as if it had been assembled from large flakes of once-coloured dandruff. His heart boiled against the cage of his chest.

'Baba, look, an angel!' the child said.

He closed his eyes, gripped his son's hand, turned his face away, then back again and opened his eyes. The angel continued to stare at him. There was intent in those eyes, and even the very first touch of a smile in those delicately upturned corners, as if Persian artists had brought forth a Chinese angel. He shut his eyes again; the face of the fox-guide, accompanied by shifting confetti-links of floaters, flickered across his retina.

Outside, the courtyard, large enough to be the central square in a city where the crowd inciting a revolution congregated, held widely scattered groups of colourfully clothed visitors. The spiky phalanx of red cannas blazed in their plots. A square stone platform, bordered by jalis, rose from the centre of a rectangular pool filled with stagnant water, virulent green with algae. Four raised narrow walkways, bisecting each side of the rectangle, led to the platform. The musical rigour that the Mughals brought to the quadrangular form struck him again; he riffled through his guidebook to read something illuminating about this pool, Anup Talao.

'Baba, can we go to the middle? There are lanes,' the boy said.

'I don't think we are allowed to,' he said, then tried to distract him by summarizing the few lines on the feature: 'Look, it says here that musicians used to sit in the centre there, on that platform, and perform concerts for the emperor and his court.' After a few beats of silence he added, 'Wasn't that interesting?', hearing his own need to keep the boy interested fraying with exhaustion.

'Why aren't we allowed to?'

'Well –' he thought for a second or two – 'if people were allowed in, we would see a lot of tourists here walking in and out, posing on the platform, taking pictures . . . but there's none of that, do you see?'

It was better outside in the sun – the relative darkness inside on a day like this had, oddly, unnerved him. But the pressure of tourism was relentless, bullying. Surely they hadn't come all this way to stand in the sun and look at pretty buildings from a distance, when they could be inside them, poring over the details, going into every room of every palace, absorbing what the guidebook had to say about each and then relooking, armed with new knowledge?

In the strange and beautiful five-storey Panch Mahal, each ascending floor diminishing in size – eighty-four, fifty-six, twenty, twelve and four columns on each level, respectively, his guidebook told him – until there was only a small kiosk surmounted by a dome on top, arches between columns took the place of walls and he was glad of the light and the breeze that came in unimpeded.

Outside once again, he noticed the squares marked on the courtyard, with a raised stone seat at the centre of the regular cross formed by the squares, and pointed them out to his son. 'Do you see the squares in the four directions, making the four arms of a big plus sign?' he asked, tapping a few with his feet and indicating the rest with his pointing hand. 'Here, and here, and this . . . do you see?'

The boy nodded.

'Show me the plus sign then,' he asked.

The child danced around, stamping on each square, repeating his father's 'Here . . . and here, and this one . . .'

'Good,' he said. 'Do you know what they are for?'

'This square has X on it, and this one,' the boy said, jumping on each of them.

'Yes, so they do. Do you know what these squares are doing here?' The boy shook his head and looked at him expectantly.

'This is a board game, like ludo or chess. It's called pachisi. Instead of having a small board at the centre, which is surrounded by a circle of a few players, they had a big one marked out permanently in this courtyard.'

His son stared silently, as if digesting the information.

'But do you know why it's so big? I mean, so much bigger than a ludo or a chess board?' He was hoping the child was not going to ask what ludo was: why should the ubiquitous board game of the endless afternoons and evenings of his Calcutta childhood mean anything to an American boy? That worn question of his son's disconnection with his father's culture reared its head again, but weakly. He pushed it down, easily enough, and offered the answer to the question he had asked by reading an excerpt from a nineteenth-century book quoted in his travel guide: '"The game of pachisi was played by Akbar in a truly regal manner. The Court itself, divided into red and white squares, being the board, and an enormous stone raised on four feet, representing the central point. It was here that Akbar and his courtiers played this game; sixteen young slaves from the harem wearing the players' colours, represented the pieces, and moved to the squares according to the throw of dice. It is said that the Emperor took such a fancy to playing the game on this grand scale that he had a court for pachisi constructed in all his palaces . . ."'

Again, that expression of wide-eyed nothingness on the boy's face. He explained the quotation slowly, in simple words, pointing to the squares and the stone seat, to spark some interest in the boy. The child's face lit up for an instant. He hopped from one square to another, then another, finally sat, cross-legged, on one of them and chirped, 'Am I a piece in this game?'

'You could be,' he laughed.

'What will happen when you throw the dice? Will my head be chopped off?'

Before he could answer, a voice behind him intervened sharply. 'Get that child out of that square!'

He wheeled round. It was the man with the face of a fox. His eyes glittered. The moustache looked animal too.

'Don't you know it's bad luck to have children sit in these squares? Do you know what happened here? Don't you know the stories?'

He was annoyed enough by the man's hectoring tone to protest, 'Show me a sign that says children are not allowed on this board. It's part of the courtyard, anyone can walk on it. And who are you, anyway?'

'Look around you – do you see any children?'

Almost involuntarily he turned around: to his right, the extraordinary symmetry of the detached building of the Diwan-i-Khas; behind him, the jewel box of the Turkish Sultana's House; and in the huge courtyard on which these structures stood not a single child to be spotted. All those colourfully dressed tourists he had seen earlier seemed to have vanished. There were one or two to be seen standing in the shapely arches of buildings or colonnaded walkways but there was no one in the courtyard and certainly no children.

Incredulous, he turned a full circle to be sure he had let his gaze take in everything. No, no children. The man too was gone. There was a sudden, brief vacuum in his chest; then the sensation left.

'D-did you see the . . . the man who was just here? Where did he go?' he asked his son.

The boy shook his head.

'But . . . but you saw him speaking to me, didn't you?' He was nearly shouting.

'Speaking? What?' the boy asked.

Of course, the child wouldn't have understood a word; the man had been speaking in Hindi.

'B-but . . . but . . .' he began, and then that futility was inside him again, making him feel weightless.

He extended his hand to his son and caught the warm little palm and fingers in his grip and wanted to hold on to it to moor himself and at the same time to scrunch it, so fierce was the wave of love and terror that suddenly threatened to unbalance him. He took the boy and ran into the Turkish Sultana's House but was blind to the ways craftsmen had made every available surface blossom into teeming life with dense carvings of gardens, trees, leaves, flowers, geometric patterns, birds, animals, abstract designs. At another time he would have been rooted to the spot, marvelling, but now his senses were disengaged and distant and all he saw was the frozen work of artisans and their tools. In one of the lower panels, the heads of the birds of paradise sitting in trees had been destroyed. An animal, crouching below, had been defaced too, making it look much like the lower half of a human child, decapitated in the act of squatting; it brought to mind ritual sacrifice. A small thrill of repulsion went through him. The mutilated carvings had the nature of fantastical creatures from Bosch's sick imagination; left untouched, they would have been simply beautiful. Then the dimness started to play havoc with his perception. Shapes and colours got unmoored and coalesced in different configurations. It was like discovering a camel smoking a pipe formed in clouds in the sky, then watching it shift and morph into a crawling baby held in the cradling trunk of an elephant, except there was no movement here, no external change of shape to warrant one thing becoming another.

He forced himself to read a few lines from the relevant section of his guidebook but they remained locked too; signs without meanings. He asked his son, 'Do you like what you see? Can you tell me what these are?' He couldn't make the words come out animated.

The boy shook his head.

'All right, let's go look at something else.' No amount of beauty could counter the permanent twilight of the interiors.

The baize-table lawns and the begonia bushes radiated light like a merciless weapon. A ripple passed through the blazing froth of shrubbery, as if the vegetation had sensed him and shuddered. Almost dragging his son along, he ran towards a small, perfectly formed building, standing in the flag of shade that it flung on the pied stones of the courtyard. Maryam-ki-Kothi, the guidebook said. It was the colour of something that had been sluiced indelibly in blood in its distant past. Under the stone awning three-quarters of the way up, the ventilation slots – surely they were too small to be windows? – looked like blinded eyes, yet the house gave the effect of looking watchful. It struck him then, suddenly, a feeling that the walls and stones and cupolas and courtyards were all, as one organism, watching him and his son.

And something was: another angel, this time above a doorway. Barely discernible through the slow, colourless disappearing act that time and the well-intentioned but wrong kind of preservative varnish had together enforced on it, it still managed, through some inexplicable resurrection, to fix him with its eye. It was like looking into the face of an ancient light transmitted back from the beginnings of time.

He took hold of his son's hand to return to the car, moving as fast as having a six-year-old physically attached to him would allow. The larger half of the site remained unvisited; he had had enough. The very air of the place seemed unsettled, as if it had slipped into some avenue where ordinary time and ordinary circumstance did not press against it. Then, with rising anxiety, he knew what was going to happen next, and it did. From the dark inside of a square building, the fox-man came out and stood under the domed canopy of a platform at one corner of the building. He could see the man so clearly, so close, that it was as if all the distance between them across the courtyard had been telescoped into nothing. Then the man retreated into the dark again. He had known the exact sequence of events beforehand, even known the bending of distance that would occur, known that the platform on which the man had stood was called the Astrologer's Seat even though he had not visited that section of the palace quadrangle. He felt himself pursued by the place as they ran out, retracing the route through which they had made their way into and through the palace complex.

While waiting for the car, he dared to look up: the sky was an immense canvas of orange and red, not from the setting sun, it seemed to him, but from the red sandstone that burned, without decaying, under it. Everything was ablaze.

On the road back, a huge, slow procession of shouting men, hundreds and hundreds of them, coming from the direction in which they were travelling, stalled all traffic. The car windows were rolled up instantly, the people were within touching distance. The vast, crawling snake seemed to be an election rally although he could not tell – the posters were all in Urdu, a language he couldn't read, and he couldn't make out a single word amid the shouting of slogans. They could have been in an utterly foreign country. The boy had his nose pressed to the window; he had never seen anything like this. There was no telling how far back it went, for how long the people would keep coming in an infinitely renewing stream.

'We just have to wait until it passes, right?' he asked the driver. A pointless question.

The driver shrugged. Time in this country flowed in a different way from the rest of the world. It was the flow that carried him a long time ago, when he was a boy, growing up in Calcutta, but now he could no longer step into it: it was an alien and treacherous stream.

The rally seemed endless. Occasionally, it stopped altogether. After forty minutes of sitting inside the car, the driver said, 'They're moving.'

A brave taxi up ahead had decided to cut through a narrow road on the left – a dust-and-straggling-dead-grass path, really – with the hope of rejoining the main one at a point further up where it would already have been traversed by the rally. Like mechanical sheep, cars started leaving the main route and entering this side lane. Their driver was quick – he manoeuvred the car sideways with manic energy and was into the path before the rush to get in there created a total gridlock. But he was still behind a few vehicles and the juddering stop-start stop-start stop-start movement down an unmetalled alley was the modern equivalent of running the gauntlet. Soon they came to a complete halt. The procession, well behind them, still seemed to be in full spate but at least they were now not in the stream of something volatile and unpredictable.

He must have dozed off. The next thing he knew was a shadow blooming inside the car at the same time as he heard a timid pattering on the window next to the boy. A bear, standing on its hind legs, was looking in, its muzzle almost pressed to the glass. There was an irregular patch of mist that changed shape in rhythm to the animal's breathing. Its pelt was a dark slate-grey shag-cushion of dust and tiny insects and bits of straw and grass. Up close, the hairs looked coarse and thick, somewhat like the quills of a hedgehog. Behind him, a man extended his arm forward and tapped on the glass with his black fingernails. The child pushed back on the heels of his palms and moved backwards, trying to burrow into his father's lap, but couldn't turn his fascinated head away. The man outside looked eerily familiar – he had the sharp, pointy face of a rodent and a moustache that seemed alive. Surely he must be dreaming? They were still in the country lane, and the terracotta late-afternoon light had turned to ashy dusk, but that . . . that man at the car window . . . He felt that the spinning of the earth was carrying him like a ball in the slot of a roulette wheel and delivering him to destinations that were endlessly repeatable, each ever so slightly different from the other, all more or less the same.

Encouraged by the unblinking gaze of father and son, the bear-wallah tapped on the glass again, and made a shallow bowl of his palm to beg. Those glittering, scaly eyes indicated a sickness that would finish him soon. Inside, he was too frozen to even shake his head in disapproval. At a signal from his keeper, the bear lifted its paw and replicated the human's begging gesture. The chain attached to the animal and run through the space between two of its fingers obliged clinkingly. He saw the head of a huge iron nail driven through the paw – or was it a callus? The claws at the end were open brackets of dirty gunmetal. The paw could easily smash the window, reach in, and tear out the child's entrails. He tried to ask the driver to shoo the man away but no sound emerged from his throat. He tried again.

'Driver, ask them to move on,' he said in a kind of low rasp. He couldn't bring up his arm to mime 'Go away' to the beggar.

The driver lowered his window and barked, 'Ei, buzz off.'

The man paid no heed; the begging from both creatures continued. Presumably at another signal from the man the bear nodded, then grinned. Where it met the teeth the gum was a bright pink, but further up the colour of cooked liver with a violet tinge. There were sticky threads of saliva gleaming whitely against all that dirty ivory and raw flesh. Then the animal started shaking, as if it was having a malarial fit. The boy screamed, once, twice.

He shouted, 'Driver, why isn't he going? Ask him again, now. Ask!'

The driver complied, his command issuing more forcefully this time. The traffic unclotted. As the car came to life, the pinning gaze of those scaly eyes receding backwards seemed to have become a solid, unfrayable rope. Then motion and the gathering dark severed it.

The boy coughed all night and kept him awake. Occasionally, he cried out in his sleep loudly enough for him to turn on his bedside lamp, get out of his bed and go to his son's to see what was wrong, to soothe his nightmares away.

Towards the end of the night, the child woke up with what he could only call a howl and continued to cry with an abandonment that brought back to mind the inexplicable and seemingly endless runs of crying during infancy. He couldn't establish now if the boy was still lodged in his world of dreams during this fit or whether something in the real world, an onset of some sickness, was making him scream like this. Questions had yielded nothing. Should he ring for room service and ask for a doctor? Surely a hotel of this class would have one? The boy's forehead and neck were not hot.

'What is it? Tell me, what is it?' he asked over and over again, reaching the edge of anger on the other side of his helplessness.

Then, a tiny chink in this wall of repetition: 'I feel afraid,' the boy managed to articulate.

He bobbed afloat on a swell of relief. 'Afraid?' he asked. 'Afraid of what? There's nothing to be afraid of, I'm here with you. Here, I'll sleep in your bed, my arms around you. Everything will be all right.'

But the child wouldn't stop. He caught something in his son's gaze, a brief focusing of his eyes on something behind his shoulder, as if he had seen something behind his father, something that made him wail louder, before the focus dissolved.

He turned his head to look. There could be nothing outside the wall of windows – they were on the sixteenth floor of the hotel. The dark glass reflected back at him a dramatically lit and shadowed scene of his staring face, twisted around on the stalk of his neck; his son lying on the bed with his mouth open in a rictus of horror and pain; the white bedlinen twisted and roped and peaked in the great turbulence that was being enacted upon it; the whole tableau shading off into the darkness that framed it. As his vision moved away from that sharp chiaroscuro foreground of the reflection he could see, in the refracted light from the hotel grounds, the skeleton of the skyscraper on the other side of the road. On the very top few floors, he could make out the scaffolding – was it still the bamboo and coir rope of his childhood or had they moved on to something more reliable and advanced nowadays? – and the billowing pieces of sackcloth or plastic or whatever it was that the workers had set up there. He wondered, not for the first time, what purpose those sheets served. A safety net, perhaps? They had certainly not prevented one of them from meeting a terrible end yesterday.

By the early hours, not far off from dawn, his son exhausted himself to sleep. He drifted off too, one arm around the boy. The light woke him; he had forgotten to draw the curtains in the night. Next to him, the child was dead. ■

© G.R. IRANNA
Untitled, 2013

GHACHAR GHOCHAR

Vivek Shanbhag

TRANSLATED FROM THE KANNADA
BY SRINATH PERUR

I didn't put up a fight when the family began efforts to get me married. None of my attempts at romance had got anywhere. It was only Chitra with whom I'd got as far as having long conversations, and that too was over. My sister Malati's marriage had ended badly, so Amma was more circumspect when it was my turn. 'Let's not get entangled with rich people,' she said, and so when we received word about the daughter of a college lecturer in Hyderabad, she was inclined to pursue the matter. The alliance was brought to us by a family friend named Sripati.

It was a Thursday, at around ten in the morning. I was about to leave home for the day when Sripati arrived. 'Wait, wait, wait, don't go!' he said. 'It's you I've come to talk to.' He chatted with Amma about mutual acquaintances, reported on his visit to the Raghavendra Swami temple, delivered gossip from the attached monastery, ate dosas, proceeded by stages to make himself at home and finally broached the subject. 'Look, this girl is good as gold. She's done her BA. The father is well respected. He has made his name in the university. We were actually looking at her for my sister-in-law's brother, but he never turned up from the United States. There's some talk he might have married there, but who knows . . . Anyway, if you all agree I can put the matter to the girl's father. Of course, I can't

261

guarantee they'll say yes. Times have changed, it's not like the old days . . .'

I looked at her photograph and found her prettier than the other girls I had seen. I decided to make her mine before other proposals came her way. It all went quickly from there. When we came to the matter of seeing the girl, I corrected Sripati with what I had picked up from Chitra's feminist talk. 'We should speak of the boy and the girl both seeing each other.'

He said, 'Yes, yes! Of course! I meant exactly that. Is it even possible these days to arrange a marriage with only the boy's consent? I must say you are both well matched. Her father too thinks along these lines.'

A couple of days later, on Sunday, we booked a car and set off for Hyderabad. Sripati accompanied us. We met Anita and her parents at the hotel we were staying in, and it wasn't long before the match was agreed upon. I took Anita down to the restaurant for a coffee; that was the only time we had to ourselves. The wedding date was fixed before we left Hyderabad. It had all gone by like a dream.

On the journey back, Sripati told us at great length about Anita's father's idealistic views. This was probably meant to soothe Amma, who had taken offence to something he said. When Anita and I were away having coffee Amma had announced grandly that we didn't expect a dowry. It seems Anita's father said, 'I wouldn't give my daughter to you if you asked for one.' Amma, who'd been enjoying her own magnanimity, was not pleased.

As we were returning to the room from the restaurant, Anita had told me she would visit Bangalore soon so we could meet again. But her father had a heart attack shortly after, and she couldn't leave Hyderabad. We met next at our wedding. I did call her on the phone before that, though. 'When are you coming here?' I would ask, trying to sound flirtatious.

I wanted her to say, 'Now,' but only received a matter-of-fact, 'The day before the wedding.'

I'd persist. 'Come right now.'

'Don't be silly,' she'd say, and douse my ardour with cold water.

I couldn't help wondering at times if she was truly enthusiastic about the marriage.

Our wedding day was a momentous one for me – a woman entered my life for the first time. Until then I had never even held a woman's hand. That day I discovered the exhilaration of getting married in the traditional way. What I'm saying might be incomprehensible to couples who have spent time together before marriage and for whom the wedding comes as a formality. They'd probably just laugh and call mine a case of sour grapes. And maybe they're right – it's true that things didn't happen this way because I particularly wanted them to. But a few details from the wedding day might help explain what I mean.

In the days leading up to the wedding I couldn't resist gazing at her photograph from time to time. That's when I'd call her on the phone. I had two photographs of her, both brought by Sripati when he first proposed the match. One of them showed her standing in a pink sari. Somewhat curly hair. Thick eyebrows. Broad shoulders. She seemed to be glowering at the camera, but there was something hypnotic about those wide eyes. I found it hard to turn away. She was in profile in the other photo, wearing a shalwar kameez, looking out through a window. She held a window bar with one hand. Her face glowed with light from the window. This photo would drive me wild. That slightly upturned nose, the swell of her breasts discernible through the fabric of her dupatta. I suppose Chitra was right when she'd say men were incapable of seeing beyond the bodies of women.

On our wedding day, Anita managed to look more beautiful than I'd been able to imagine her. She carried herself with poise. Her thick braid hung down to her waist. She was wearing lipstick. The first chance I got I stole a sideward glance at the blouse under her dark blue sari. We had few chances to speak during the ceremony, and these went in saying things like 'So much smoke', 'Who's that teasing you? A classmate?' There was a strange charm even in exchanging inanities. The ceremony required me to hold her hand at times, or touch her arm with my index finger, and these brief moments of contact would be the cause of an immense thrill. When it was time to tie the *taali* round her neck I leaned in close and a whiff of fragrance went straight to my head. The scent of flowers and her close presence were almost too much. For a brief instant I felt unsteady on my feet. She stood there with her head bowed; flecks of turmeric dotted the down on her cheek. My fingers brushing against the back of her neck, I tied the knot.

At lunch, when we had to feed each other sweets, the tips of my fingers touched her lower lip for a moment. The jolt this produced took a while to subside. I was still helpless when she brought a piece of jalebi to my mouth. I seized her hand and pretended to bite off her fingers. A few girls nearby went, 'Aww, so sweet,' and I felt embarrassed by my own antics. The wedding photographer, hankering for such moments, made me feed her again.

While we were still at lunch, a large group from Anita's side came up to us and introduced themselves one by one. Then in the afternoon, an army of elders from both sides took turns sitting on a chair so we could fall at their feet and seek blessings. In the evening we went home exhausted. Fortunately the more annoying relatives didn't follow us home. We could have dinner in peace and retire to our room upstairs.

I had on a white cotton kurta bought especially for the night. My mind swirled with the possibilities that lay ahead as we made our way to the room. I found it hard to even look at her. I tried to act casual as I closed the door behind us, but slid the bolt in slowly so the others at home wouldn't notice. When I turned round she was standing by the bed. The light switch was next to the door and I turned it off. The room was now faintly lit by the haze from the street lamp outside. I walked to her. I took a step closer. I could smell her scent now. I didn't know what to do next and I paused for a moment. Then I raised my right hand and placed it on her shoulder. One thing alone gave me the courage to touch her: we were now married. My hand lowered itself along her arm and stopped at her elbow. My left hand went to her waist and drew her closer. She moved towards me as well and we embraced. Her touch, her smell, the fragrance from the flowers she was wearing, the press of her chest on mine, her lips against my neck.

That single moment's intensity hasn't been matched in my life before or since. A woman I didn't know had chosen to accept me, in body and mind. Perhaps it is this instant that forms the basis of traditional marriage – a complete stranger is suddenly mine. And then, I am hers too; I must offer her my all. I want her to wield her power over me as an acknowledgment of my love. The rush of these feelings all together is too much to describe. Language communicates in terms of what is already known; it chokes up when asked to deal with the entirely unprecedented.

Similar feelings must have welled up in her too. Her face was buried in my chest. Her arms around me tightened. I could feel the bangles on her arms pressing into my back. Through touch, through the giving, yielding closeness of our embrace, this unknown woman began to be known to me. I've longed often for a comparable experience, but there seems to be none. That sense of strangeness, surrender, dependence, compassion, entitlement and a hundred other sentiments bundled together cannot possibly be relived.

I held her tighter still, then relaxed. I raised her face and through her lips gained my first taste of her world.

Three days after the wedding we left for Ooty for our honeymoon. A cliché, it is true, especially considering we were well off and could have gone anywhere. But Anita said she didn't particularly care where we went, and Ooty had been a prominent setting for my amorous imaginings since I was an adolescent. We might as well go there, I felt.

We were to arrive early in the morning, but the bus broke down on the way and it was noon before we checked into the hotel we had booked, a place named Green Valley. With our room's door closed, we were away from home and truly by ourselves for the first time in our marriage. Not knowing what to do, but aware this solitude was too significant to be wasted, I began caressing Anita haphazardly. She shied away, played coy, and we ended up laughing and chasing each other around the room like children.

We washed, had lunch and took a van to one of those sightseeing 'points' on top of a hill. Afternoon was turning to evening. The air was crisp and our breath had begun to fog. As we strolled about, Anita occasionally took my hand in hers or I would hold her lightly round the waist. Before long I was aroused and wanted to take her back to the hotel. But there were four other couples sharing the van with us, and we had to wait for them. It was dark when we returned. The wait had driven me half mad. I closed the door and pounced on her. I tore off her sweater, her sari, her blouse. I yanked at her petticoat's drawstring but only managed to jam it up. My impatient hands couldn't get anywhere with the stuck knot. She tried too, but to no avail. 'Tchah,' she said, 'this string has become all ghachar ghochar. Wait.' I stood there as she sat up, bent over the knot and carefully teased it apart.

It came to me later when we were lying there catching our breaths. 'What was that you called the petticoat string?' I asked her.

She giggled. 'Ghachar ghochar,' she said.

I'd never heard the expression. 'What's that?' I asked.

'Ghachar ghochar,' she repeated, her eyes shining.

'What does that mean?'

'It means just that. You wouldn't understand . . .' she said. I poked her bare side with a finger and began to tickle her, saying, 'Tell me now, tell me.' She rolled about, helpless with laughter, and then went quiet with mock gravity. She said, 'There are only four people in this world who know what it means. My parents, my brother and me.'

The expression had originated in their house, made up by Anita and her brother when they were children. They'd been on the terrace one evening, rolling kite string into a ball. Their parents were chatting nearby. The loose string strewn about had become so entangled at one point that her brother lost his patience, flung down the bit he'd been trying to separate and shouted, 'This has all become ghachar ghochar!' Anita had said, 'What language are you speaking?' From there it had entered the family's vocabulary, first used by the siblings and then by the parents. Anita couldn't stop laughing at the reminiscence; I joined her. She spoke of her family some more. She became grave when she came to her brother, who had lost a leg in a motorcycle accident. 'He got in with the wrong company and everything became ghachar ghochar,' she said. 'Otherwise he wouldn't have been roaring around on motorcycles.'

The next morning we woke up in a hopelessly rumpled bed. I entwined my legs in hers and said, 'Look, we are ghachar ghochar now.' She did not laugh. She must have thought I was making fun of her. Of course, those words could never mean to me all that they meant to her; nor would I ever utter them as naturally as she did. But she had shared with me this secret phrase that didn't exist in any language, and I was now one of only five people in the world who knew it. ■

from *Pizza in the Wild*

THE BACHELOR FATHER

Kalpana Narayanan

V enkat was afraid of saying something wrong. So he called his niece in the neighbouring town of Alpharetta, and she called the pizza shop from her cellphone and placed his order for him.

The delivery guy cleared his throat when Venkat handed him exact change – eight dollars and fifty cents. But Venkat, oblivious, took his pizza inside and spread paper towels on his lap and switched the television back on. He kept the classifieds open next to him. He had been told there was money in driving cabs, and he was going to look into it. But for now there was the question of whether Chithi's children would find out that she was their stepmother, not their blood mother – to be answered after the commercial break.

T he week before, Venkat had found a small, pretty Chinese girl at the front desk of the dry-cleaner's. For ten years, he had been the one to punch in the phone numbers of customers when they came in to pick up their lacy white lingerie and starched button-down shirts. He had been a good employee, except maybe for his poor English – and then, one month ago, his boss had fired him. From the sidewalk, Venkat had watched this girl bite into an apple as she laughed with a customer. His boss hadn't needed someone with more experience, or a computer – his Chinese boss had needed a small Chinese girl who looked like a daughter to make jokes with the regulars. Venkat had hoped to ask for his old job back, but at the sight of a scene that was complete without him, he'd returned to his house.

He lived in a one-bedroom shotgun shack. Empty soda cans lined the floor. Dishes were stacked in the sink and all over the counter. This – the smell, the bottles, the roaches – was a product of him. He was out of toilet paper, and was running out of paper towels, and there was no one to point this out. This was bachelorhood. His man-kingdom was off the beltway – a ride away from anywhere he would like to be. He could use paper plates to wipe his bum, and no wife would be there to whine about quilted double-ply. Though a little whining might have been nice.

Would Babu and Gita marry? Would Shakuntula find her missing prosthetic arm in the dumpster? He could sit naked as he determined the answers to these questions. Sun TV – the Tamil channel that he paid an extra ten dollars a month for – had become a good investment. 'I can't talk to you every day,' his daughter Sheila had told him recently after he'd called her two days in a row. 'It depresses me,' she'd said, and then he'd heard her husband Raj calling out to her in the background.

Venkat's parents lived in Bombay, and for the last ten years, he had rung them once a week. His sister always asked after Saraswati before his father took the phone and asked more pressing questions. 'Did you hear about the new direct flight? I'll never see Frankfurt!' 'How much longer do you think it will be?' Venkat's father planned on dying in Atlanta – he liked to gently remind Venkat of this in each of their conversations. Venkat regretted painting such a specific picture for him, of white-tiled floors and air conditioning, an intercom system and a happy wife's manicured finger pressing TALK. He also knew that by the time he had money to fly his mother and father over, he would no longer live in a house with an airplane-sized bathroom, that by then he would have convinced Saraswati to come back. For now, when he had no further answers to his father's questions – when the only thing left to say was yes, I bought you a ticket, Appa – he stretched the cord of the phone toward the front doorbell and rang it and told his father he had to run. It was better to keep him hopeful.

With his mother, it was easier, for theirs was a one-way interaction. Each week he penned her a letter on a thin, pale blue aerogramme, and each Saturday morning he went to the post office to post it and buy a new aerogramme. The large African American woman who sat at the counter joked that he could save himself time, mister, if he just bought a pack. 'I don't mind,' he would say, licking each sticky side. For he felt a better son walking those twenty blocks, as if that walk helped to close the long distance between them.

L ooking back on it, the accident came as a small stroke of luck. Venkat had opened a beer and was waiting for *Chithi* to end. He'd decided that if he was going to be unemployed, he might as well enjoy life. He was pushing the television stand toward the wall to clear a space to dance when he stepped on the thick extension cord. His foot turned in, and his ankle rolled out, and though he tried to catch his balance, he ended up on the ground. There was a thud and the television was on its side, next to his head. He reached over and plugged the cord back in.

Lying on his back, he listened to Chithi sitting her children down to tell them she had grave news. He lifted his head to find his left foot bent inward. He tried to stand, and he fell.

'You can do it,' he whispered to himself in the voice of an American sitcom actor. Crawling along the carpeted floor to the fridge, he found a family of small pink onions and one soiled brown banana. His stomach rumbled. He tugged on the phone cord, which dangled down the counter. His daughter Sheila was three hours behind and would still be at the office – he would be clicked straight to voicemail. No use calling Saraswati. The phone fell on top of him, and he dialled his brother Lakshman.

'Hold, sir,' Lakshman said.

There was a clatter, and he was met with the sound of clothes being brought busily down a ceiling conveyer belt. Lakshman owned a dry-cleaner's one town over in Alpharetta. He also owned a small white-panelled house whose shutters had been painted a fresh forest green just last month. There was dinner-table talk of buying a golden retriever puppy and naming it Cheerio. Lakshman was five years his junior.

'Yes, hello, your phone number?'

'Lakshman?' Venkat said.

'Always something,' Lakshman said after a pause.

Venkat's niece was at his door one hour later, with a small green suitcase that she clenched with both hands. A brown bag of groceries rested between her feet. She smiled a tight smile. Venkat was using a broom to prop himself up, and he straightened his shoulders. His first wife, Meera, had been his niece Shweta's age – twenty-two – when they'd met in the pale pink kitchen of his parents' flat. She'd brought him a tumbler of water, had spilled it and started to cry, and he had filled with love – for he could see himself playing this role, comforting this woman over these small grievances. Here was a woman helpless enough to turn to him for support. When he'd found Meera crying uncontrollably each day, though, he'd wondered if he'd misinterpreted the sign. It was as if he had married a child. It had not come as a surprise when, two teary years into their marriage, Meera had returned to her parents in Madras, and had not rejoined him.

'Will you be comfortable?' he asked Shweta now.

'Sure,' Shweta said, at his leg.

Her eyelids sparkled with gold. She had long, thick eyelashes and a puff of bangs that almost hid her eyes. This girl had no fuzz on her upper lip, and the fat had fallen away from her round face. She was more beautiful than the niece he had seen months ago – more beautiful than his own daughter. The realization shamed him.

'Venkat,' Lakshman yipped from behind Shweta.

Venkat shifted his focus to his brother.

'She has to be in bed with brushed teeth at nine,' Lakshman said, and went back to his car.

Venkat glanced at Shweta, and Shweta blushed.

'I can get it,' Shweta said and lifted the suitcase and bag, and only then did it occur to him to reach out.

His niece had been here once before. Venkat followed after her. She kept her sandals on, and in his bedroom she scrunched her nose, so he scrunched his nose. He knew a mix of sweat and Bengay rose from the sheets, but he hadn't been able to wash them yet.

She threw her suitcase onto the bed and pulled a bottle of Tylenol from her red leather purse. Easing out the cotton, she handed the bottle to him as if to say she was ready to be alone now. When he closed the door he thought he heard her speak. He leaned against the door but was met with silence. Collapsing onto the couch, he popped two pills and fell asleep to the sound of late-night Tamil on the television. He imagined his niece nestling under his thin sheets, and he slept dreamlessly. He had forgotten it was easier with another person close by.

An uncomfortable routine descended upon them. Shweta yanked his leg onto a pillow the next morning – a wine-coloured bruise had formed above his ankle – then made him a breakfast of eggs and cheese on toast. It was 'only' a second-degree sprain, she said, as she forked eggs into her mouth. There was no need to go to the doctor. She drove his car to the drugstore and brought home a roll of cream-coloured gauze. He watched her unravel wide circles until a messy heap of bandage lay on the table. Later that morning, he heard her on the phone as she told Lakshman it might take two weeks for him to walk. 'Until he's able to drive? But that could take a whole month,' she said, but she lowered her voice when she saw what Venkat imagined was a guilty look in his brown eyes.

In the kitchen, she made him a coffee thick with milk and Splenda, then sat down at the table and poured five spoons of sugar into her own chai. His niece was studying to become a nurse, and he watched her study hard. As if she had studied how to study, she furrowed her eyebrows and paced around, massaging her temples. Each time she turned a page in her large chemistry book, signalled by a loud swish of paper, he bit his lip and circled another classified. He did not want her to think he was lazy, his second wife Saraswati's favourite word. The problem was that there were no jobs for him. He was circling typing and fact-checking jobs, skills he did not have. For ten years, he had managed to hold a job that didn't require him to speak fluent English, and he was too old to learn the nuances of the language now. Saraswati had said his English was not the problem. She had pleaded with him to type up a CV, but there was an age a man was too old for ambition – for him, that age was fifty. He was at an age where he was ready to hike up his veshti and play rummy with grandchildren. He would rather smile as he handed down clothes to young customers as they chatted on about their lives that did not concern him. It was better for them to think he had no place in their world, for he felt the same about them. Yes, he preferred his Tamil serials about stepmothers to their sitcoms about loose teenagers and identical twins. When his boss had fired him, he hadn't asked the bold questions he would have asked if he were a prime-time investigative journalist ('Will you be rehiring when the economy improves?'). He'd stayed quiet and watched his silence reassure his boss of his decision.

When Shweta bathed his leg, he kept the words *thank you* from spilling out of his mouth. He did not want to sound so grateful that she'd feel she was giving more than was necessary. But his leg hairs stood on end as she scrubbed her washcloth between his toes that first afternoon. She did not cringe at his toenails, which had gone black when he was a child, something each of his wives had quickly pointed out. She did not insult his skinny legs. 'Chicken legs,' she said, smiling. She was obedient, something his own daughter had not managed to be. The role of the mother is not to be underestimated, he thought, grimacing, as she put his pinkie toe through physical therapy, bending it back and forth.

He had tried to be a mother to Sheila after Meera left – he had bought her stretch tights and mismatched earrings when she'd asked and he was able to afford it, and he had kept her from wearing lipstick and going on dates. But Sheila had left these things behind in a box when she'd moved to San Francisco. When she'd left, he'd drawn a knife through that box and found polka-dot socks and pink jelly shoes and a soiled white teddy bear that she had named Snowflake. Things he had given her, as if the sealed-up secret was that his daughter did not want to remember him. She had not let him toast her at her wedding, and she had not invited him to stay with her now that she was pregnant with his grandson.

Each afternoon, Shweta drove his beat-up car to her science class and came back with bags crammed full of items purchased with the allowance he had given her. The fridge filled with fresh spinach, cloves of garlic, gnarled ginger, egg-sized tomatoes – smells that began to fill the apartment as Shweta cooked. When he fell asleep with his face pressed into the couch cushions he could smell cumin and cilantro, the scent of a wife.

He tried not to notice the clean white underwear hanging from the towel rack in the bathroom. He picked up a pair of gold eyelash curlers and closed them in on his pinkie and yelped. He nudged a glittery black ballet slipper with his toe then circled his slippered foot over the newly cleaned floor. In handling these details of her life – in witnessing the ways his niece tried to make herself into a woman, unabashedly – he felt closer to her.

'Want to order pizza?' he said, after Shweta slammed her book shut and got up to make a third night's dinner.

'Green pepper?' she said calmly, turning to him.

He nodded. When he handed her the phone, she ordered an extra-large pie with cheese-stuffed crust and peppers and garlic sauce. They sat on far ends of the couch and bit off huge hunks as Chithi made her way through another treacherous day. When there were pauses in the dialogue, he translated. This was one thing he could pride himself on – Sheila was fluent in Tamil and English.

'That's Chithi's *pethi*,' he said, with his mouth full. 'She's trying to find the cure for Aids in those palm leaves.'

'She thinks she can just solve HIV?' Shweta demanded, but he was already thinking of his next words.

'I don't mind that you're not married yet,' he said. 'You should be free to live your life.'

Shweta shifted her long legs toward him and met his eyes.

'Am I free to see movies with friends?' she asked.

'Yes,' he said, hesitating.

'Thank you,' Shweta said, brightening.

When she turned back to the TV, he felt relieved and blocked out the pop-up image of Lakshman frowning. With Sheila, he'd felt the need to buckle down, to be twice as strict, as if he were speaking for himself and for her silent mother. But Shweta was an adult. She took care of him, and the home, in ways Sheila never had. What would Sheila do if she knew about his ankle? Send him a care package with some useless first-aid booklet?

Shweta reminded him more of Saraswati. He had missed conducting his life louder to drown out the sounds of someone else. When Shweta cooked, she banged around pots so that he had to turn up the television full volume. She chanted 'Healthy Little Beggar Boys Catching Newts or Fish' to the beat of clapped hands to remember the first line of the periodic table. His niece was more American than his own lonely daughter, but she was somehow more Indian too – like Saraswati, she cooked, she enjoyed the serials – and this was pleasing to him.

'Sweet dreams,' Shweta said, and he found her standing, looking down at him.

'Sweet dreams,' he whispered.

Saraswati was wrong, he thought as he reached out to the table and took the last slice of pizza. He could be a good father. But this required a good daughter.

Saraswati he had met online. She had responded to his personal ad. Sheila had helped him to place it in the *Times of India*. Suitable, elderly divorcee looking for soulmate. Saraswati was the last of ten women to respond – the others had been either too young, or too unattractive, or too attractive and eager for a visa. Saraswati had asked the right questions. How old? Station in life? She had thick hair and eyebrows that met in the middle. He'd responded – forty-nine. Sales.

They'd had a five-month-long Internet courtship (what's ur favorite thing to do? Pray 4 2moro – lol) that ended in a windy ceremony on a beach off the coast of Madras. Sheila had financed it, and had seemed happy at the prospect of his having a new family, until it became apparent that its members – Saraswati's two daughters – were not interested in a new family. There had been hints of something deceptive at the ceremony. What had looked like white teeth in the online photo were gapped and paan-stained in person. But he had been overjoyed, so Sheila had not objected when the daughters came back with them on his visa to attend the community college.

There had been fights. He blamed the daughters – all they did was complain about how his house smelled like grease, about how he should get a more ambitious job like their real father who they'd heard ran a TV shop in Goa, about how they couldn't believe how short he was, all while lining their narrow eyes with kohl. They called him baldy when they thought he wasn't listening, though he still had some hair and dog-perfect hearing. Once, he called them spoiled brats in the most imperious voice he could summon up. Four months later he and Saraswati separated. For the last two months, Saraswati had lived in her own flat in Alpharetta, a flat that he paid part of the rent for. Everyone seemed to have a happy home in Alpharetta except him.

When he'd called Saraswati to tell her he'd lost his job, Saraswati had repeated, 'You lost your job?' and then there had been a high-pitched yodel in the background. Saraswati had asked him, in an urgent voice, how he would afford to pay for her apartment. He had said that he would manage. For he was still hopeful that she would come back – that he could begin again a life just with her, that she would again separate carrots from celery into different Ziploc bags and stuff them into a brown bag for him to take to work, that she would again bring home surprise groceries like pistachio ice cream and that she would again wait for him under the sheets with just her head popping out.

'How much longer will it be?' he asked.

'Venkat,' she said, as if she had already answered that question.

'But I love you,' he said, embarrassed by the truth of his words.

'I know,' she said, after a pause, not unkindly, and hung up.

There was always something – the bathtub drain that got clogged by their thick hair. The leak above the bed that dripped on them. He had been raised in a community in which men with brains were not expected to use their hands. Now he was expected to have an enormous brain, two strong arms and endless money to buy love. These wives and daughters wanted a Tamilian Clark Gable to father and husband them – but not Shweta, he thought. He heard his niece's voice lift into the air. He was on the toilet and leaned toward the thin, mildew-stained wall that separated the bedroom from the bathroom. His niece was on her cellphone again, and he smiled as her sing-song voice picked up speed, raised and dropped octaves, as if for his benefit.

'Chithi's a slut,' Shweta said at the TV the next evening.

'All is fair in love and war,' he said, with an air of authority, but glanced nervously at her.

Shweta took the remote and turned down the volume.

'Is it fair for a wife to leave her husband?' she countered.

He turned and faced her.

'I said the wrong thing,' she exclaimed in a calm voice.

'No one said life is fair,' he said, after a pause. No one had referred to his situation with Saraswati so blatantly. 'It's been difficult, but I am managing,' he added.

'Dad said you brought this on yourself, but I feel for you.'

The camera zoomed in on Chithi's face registering shock, then anger, then regret. Venkat kept his eyes on the television, thinking about what his niece had said. Had he finally found someone who understood him? He looked at her with hope. Shweta smiled a half-smile and got up and disappeared into the bedroom. When the commercial break came, Venkat walked in what he imagined was a casual way toward the toilet. Inside the bathroom, he quietly shut the door and leaned against the wall. He moved his ear and heard Shweta cough, and then he pressed his fingertips to the wall. In this way, with his ear attached to the tiles, he tiptoed until he was climbing into the tub. 'I have this Q-tip and am trying to cover both ends in wax to make a candle.' He knocked over the purple bottle of shampoo on the ledge and hurriedly picked it up.

When he nudged open the door, he found his niece standing in the middle of the living room in one of her floor-length nightgowns. He must have looked unnerved, for she held up the roll of gauze as if to remind him of her purpose in being there.

He went to the couch and sat. Shweta wiped her brow and unwrapped layer after layer – they both looked away from the initial stench – and she rewrapped his ankle.

'You have a good knowledge base,' he said. 'But are you ready to save lives?' he asked, looking down at her sloppy work.

'I hope so,' she said in a sorrowful voice.

There was a pause.

'Do you ever feel like you're just waiting?' she said then.

'I do. For a job, for the news –'

'I feel like I'm waiting for my whole life to begin,' she interrupted. She looked troubled, and he wanted to help her.

'You're a very creative nurse,' he said meaningfully.

'That's what my teacher says,' she said, blushing. 'You're a creative patient,' she said generously.

'Thank you,' he said casually. But it did not feel casual. It had been a long time since he had made someone blush.

He had been trying not to say thank you, but then Shweta said thank you for everything. Thank you for washing your plate and thank you for letting me sleep in your bed. At the start of their second week together, Venkat splashed water onto his face and was at the kitchen table, circling classifieds, before Shweta woke. When Shweta emerged from the bedroom with her braid undone and spilling over her shoulders and with kohl smudged under her eyes, she looked surprised. It was the look Venkat's mother had worn when his father had come home early from playing rummy once. He smiled and returned his eyes to the newspaper and saw that the edition before him was a week old. He folded back the dated corner and continued to circle. When his eyes landed on the taxi driver ad that had been listed week after week, he starred it.

As his niece unwrapped his bandage that morning, he turned his ankle to the side, and peered up innocently at her. Earlier, he had been able to walk without putting pressure on his right foot. He watched Shweta pause at his normal-looking ankle and rewrap it so tight the blood rushed to his toes. Taping down the loose end of gauze, she asked if she could go out with a friend that weekend.

'Of course!' he said, and he removed his leg.

'It's fun here,' she said happily.

'It is?' he said.

'I wish I didn't have to leave,' she said. 'I'm going to move more of my clothes in this weekend. I'm out of socks and other things!'

When he opened his mouth to respond, a small nervous squeak came out. Shweta patted his head and got up to shower.

If Sheila could only see him. The last time Sheila had visited was when she'd been five months pregnant. He had made preparations to borrow an electric blanket from a neighbour, but she and Raj had booked a hotel. 'I'm married now,' she'd said. The three of them had gone to dinner at the local Chinese restaurant, and she'd asked him please not to cry as she and Raj had bundled up to head back to the hotel.

'Let's get an ice cream,' he'd said, but Sheila had declined. Just as the cab was pulling up, she had unzipped her puffy coat and let him place his bare hand on her stomach and feel for the kick. What he had felt was his daughter breathing fast.

According to the women in his family, to hold on to the past was to fail. It was why his own brother refused to hire him at his dry-cleaning shop. Lakshman's wife, Seeta, forbade it. Each time Venkat rang up Lakshman, he imagined Seeta standing next to him, motioning frantically for Lakshman to hang up. If Saraswati were still with him, then in a month they would be invited to stay with Sheila to bathe and feed her son that would be born, and Lakshman and Seeta would invite them to start a joint family with Cheerio in their white-panelled, green-shuttered house. But no one had a spare room for a bachelor father.

While Shweta was in class that afternoon, Venkat cleaned. He tried to think of ways he could be kind to her, to show her that he was serious. Maybe he could buy her a small token of his affection, a journal with a cartoon on its cover, or a pack of socks. Then he had an idea. He went back to the classifieds and tore out the taxi driver ad and, pacing, he called the number. He left a shaky message, spelling out the letters of his name, V as in Volvo, N as in Nancy. When he hung up, he felt a surge of immense confidence, and hope.

He beat the couch cushions together until he was surrounded by dust that sprang up in the light of the windows. In the bedroom, he casually opened the top dresser drawer and surveyed neat stacks of thrift-store shirts and nightgowns. He found an old chemistry test wedged between two shirts. '65' was written in red ink with 'Ouch! Week in Chem!' written in stern teacher letters. 'WEAK IN ENGLISH' was written underneath in Shweta's defiant handwriting. Stuck to the test was a Post-it note. *To do: check how many phone minutes r left 4 the month, pluck eyebrows, check times 4 Silver Linings Playbook, give B. ur final answer.* An awkward smile spread across Venkat's face. He'd never once found so much as a scrap of paper to suggest that Sheila had made a friend, let alone a life partner. Perhaps he would sit and have a conversation with Shweta, advise her not to rush into any alliance.

When the phone rang, he raced to catch it.

'Saraswati?' he answered, as Shweta walked in from class and put her books down.

'Venkat, let me talk to my daughter.'

It was Lakshman. Venkat reluctantly handed Shweta the phone and watched her trace her right hand over the table as she spoke, as if this were the most familiar thing – catching up with her real father. He heard her tell Lakshman that she got an A minus on her chemistry test and he heard Lakshman's voice rise in excitement. By the time she hung up, Venkat had put on the television, more loudly than usual.

'What do you want for dinner?' she came over and asked.

He could say he wanted sambhar, and she could say, do you mind if I add ginger, and he could say, no, ginger is good for digestion.

'Want me to cook?' he said instead.

That was one thing he had learned from being a bachelor father – he had cooked for Sheila for fifteen years.

'Cook what?'

'Spaghetti,' he said as if it were no big deal.

'I'm obsessed with meatballs,' she said, perking up. 'Don't tell Dad.'

'I won't tell,' he said.

'I'll make okra,' she said.

She went into the bedroom, so he went into the bathroom and shut the door. This was what a father–daughter relationship should be – playful with give and take, not so private that one had no idea how to make the other happy. What did it matter if your father knew you got your periods? Sheila had washed her bloody sheets without telling him, then asked him to take her to the store and give her five dollars. He had found the bloodstains and told her he would never give her five dollars without knowing what it was for, and Sheila had burst into tears.

'I call it Random Acts of Kindness – RAK,' Shweta whispered. 'Yesterday I gave a mutt a cookie. Tomorrow I'll drop a quarter on the ground. It's my form of religion.' Venkat stood on the edge of the tub. 'I love him,' she whispered, and he eyed his reflection as Shweta's voice dropped to a level he could not hear and then her voice rose again. 'My uncle's so sweet, he's going to cook!' Venkat met his eyes in the mirror. He lost his balance, surprised by the full-body feel of his laugh. In the empty tub, he looked up at the ceiling, which was dotted with the glow-in-the-dark stars that Sheila had stuck up as a child, and he was struck by how alone he had been and how quickly that could change.

That night, when he laid his leg on Shweta's lap, Shweta gently placed it back on the ground. The device that had brought them together was no longer necessary. She pulled a catalogue off the coffee table and opened it to a glossy page that showed a blond-wood desk with apples painted across the top. The desk sat in the middle of a room with thick white carpet and green walls. On top of the desk, red pencils were arranged like flowers in a mug.

'Don't tell Dad,' she said. 'I like writing. I want to die in this room.'

'I could buy you that desk,' he said earnestly. He squinted his eyes and saw the price in fine print – $179.99 – a third of his rapidly diminishing severance cheque.

'You could? I could never ask you to,' she said, but she put her arms around his neck. He kept his arms at his side as if afraid he might not let go if he tried to hold her.

'Let's discuss this weekend, when you're back from the movie,' he said, and a look of joyful surprise spread across her face.

The next day, Venkat spoke in a bold, confident voice when he put in his order with the furniture company. He was no longer as afraid of saying something wrong. He felt as if he were pressing himself back into the world as he read out the numbers of his debit card. Reluctantly, he agreed to pay extra for the overnight delivery too. This was what Saraswati had always wanted. For him to take responsibility. To take action, to be the hero of his own story. He would not be able to pay Saraswati's rent the next month, but it was more important that Shweta feel that this was her home.

The phone rang back, and Venkat rushed to pick it up. A bored-sounding woman asked if he could come in for an interview the following Wednesday. It was the taxi company. Venkat said yes, and took down the address. When he hung up, he straightened his shoulders. He felt as if he'd won the lottery.

The day after, when the delivery came, Venkat dragged in the two rectangular boxes. Ten minutes later, he was surrounded by nails and slabs of wood and bubble wrap. He pinched two bubbles, as if playing the part of a pensive man. He went to get the hammer, which was where he'd left it, years ago, under the kitchen sink. Back in front of the boxes, he stood with his hands on his hips, like a cowboy surveying the land. One hour later, he had lined up the different nails to match the images of nails in the instruction manual. Two hours later, he was sweating, hammering. Four hours and he was standing in front of a wobbly desk with apples on top. He laughed, in disbelief, with joy. As he smoothed his hand across the apples on top, he imagined Shweta doing the same and then looking at him with love.

He pushed the desk toward the front door so Shweta would see it first thing, when she came back from the movie that night.

Five hours later, car headlights appeared in the driveway. Venkat hurried toward the window. He saw Shweta sitting in the passenger seat of a tan Toyota, next to an African American boy. She moved closer. The two kissed. He felt surprise and then disappointment, as he watched.

When Shweta walked in, smiling a secret smile, he felt deceived.

'Oh,' she exclaimed, as she ran right in to the desk. 'You got the desk?' she said. She did not smooth her hand over the apples.

'How was *Silver Linings Playbook*?' Venkat asked stiffly.

'Perfect,' Shweta said eagerly. There was a pause. 'How did you know what movie I was seeing?'

He did not have a response, but he was thinking of his next words, which he had rehearsed: *I got you the desk because I want you to stay.*

'Be careful what types of people you're friends with,' Venkat said instead.

He felt his heart breaking as Shweta's face closed off. She did not put her arms around him, but pushed up her sleeves as if to say she'd wished he'd said something different. She walked around the desk, almost as if it weren't there, and she sat down on the couch.

'I'll be sad to leave,' she said suddenly, more to herself than to him, though she didn't sound sad.

'I thought you liked it here?' he asked. He felt his breath quickening when she did not respond.

'I do,' she said finally, studying her hands.

'Do you want to stay for one more week? You are free to see movies here.'

'Sheila was right about you,' she said mysteriously.

'What did Sheila say?' he asked hopefully.

She shook her head, and he felt every muscle in his body clench.

'She said you gave her things to make her stay. But you didn't actually want her to be happy.'

I want you to be happy, Venkat thought.

'You never listened to what Sheila wanted,' she said, her eyes filling with tears.

How could he have known what his daughter wanted? Everything had been a secret with her.

What he saw then, instead of Shweta, was his daughter, a shorter, puffier version of Shweta with kinder eyes. Sheila. She had been such a lonely girl. His thoughts went back to that box of things that Sheila had left behind. He had given her so much. But he had not loved her, not truly. He had kept her home, inside, because he had had no one else.

'Give me a chance,' he said to Shweta.

'I did,' she said, as she disappeared into the bedroom.

'Dad?' he heard her say into her phone, as she shut the door behind her.

An hour later, from his car, Lakshman waved to Venkat, so Venkat waved, and for a moment the brothers' hands were raised in just the same way. Lakshman pressed the horn then, and Shweta hurried out. Lakshman forced a smile, and Venkat could almost see what his younger brother was trying to smile at: his older brother, a man nearly identical to him, but shorter, waving against the silhouette of a smaller, emptier, vinyl-sided house – a less certain fate. ∎

CONTRIBUTORS

Katherine Boo's *Behind the Beautiful Forevers: Life, Death and Hope in a Mumbai Undercity* won the 2012 National Book Award for Nonfiction and has been translated into thirty languages. She has been a staff writer for the *New Yorker* since 2003.

Upamanyu Chatterjee is a civil servant in India. He has written six novels, including *Fairy Tales at Fifty*. He is married and has two daughters.

Amit Chaudhuri is the author of five novels, including *The Immortals*. He is Professor of Contemporary Literature at the University of East Anglia, and has contributed fiction, poetry and reviews to numerous publications. 'English Summer' is an extract from his forthcoming novel, *Odysseus Abroad*.

Michael Collins is a photographer, writer and curator. His work was featured in *Granta* 76: Music and *Granta* 79: Celebrity.

Tishani Doshi is a poet, novelist and dancer. Her latest book is *Fountainville*, a medieval Welsh tale recast among opium dens, gang wars and a surrogacy clinic.

Vijay Gadge spent three years assisting Katherine Boo in her reporting for *Behind the Beautiful Forevers*. He is now a high school student in Mumbai.

Gauri Gill is a Delhi-based photographer best known for her portraits of people in rural Rajasthan. Her work has been exhibited in venues across Asia, Europe and North America.

Anjum Hasan is the author of the story collection *Difficult Pleasures*, the novels *Neti, Neti* and *Lunatic in My Head* and the collection of poems *Street on the Hill*. She is Books Editor at *The Caravan* and lives in Bengaluru.

Anjali Joseph was born in Bombay and now lives in Guwahati, Assam. She is the author of the novels *Saraswati Park* and *Another Country*. 'Shoes' is an extract of a forthcoming novel.

Devo Kadam is featured in Katherine Boo's *Behind the Beautiful Forevers*, and spent three years assisting in her reporting. He is now a high school student in Mumbai.

Deepti Kapoor was born in Moradabad, in northern India. She is the author of *A Bad Character*. She lived in Delhi for many years, and now lives in Goa.

Raghu Karnad is a writer and journalist and the author of *Farthest Field: A Story of India's Second World War*, which will be published in 2015. He lives between Bengaluru and New Delhi.

Arun Kolatkar was born in Kolhapur, Maharashtra in 1931. After earning a diploma in painting at the J.J. School of Art, Bombay, he worked in advertising as a visualizer. His *Collected Poems in English* was published in 2010.

Amitava Kumar is the author of several works of non-fiction, including *A Matter of Rats: A Short Biography of Patna*. He teaches English at Vassar College in upstate New York.

Hari Kunzru's most recent book is *Gods Without Men*. He lives in New York City. 'Drone' is an extract from a forthcoming novel.

Arvind Krishna Mehrotra is the translator of *The Absent Traveller: Prakrit Love Poetry* and *Songs of Kabir*. His *Collected Poems: 1969–2014* was published in 2014.

Sam Miller was born in London but has spent much of the last twenty-five years in India. He is a former BBC reporter and editor, and the author of *Delhi: Adventures in a Megacity* and *A Strange Kind of Paradise: India Through Foreign Eyes*.

Neel Mukherjee was born in Calcutta. He is the author of *A Life Apart* and *The Lives of Others*, which was shortlisted for the 2014 Man Booker Prize. 'The Wrong Square' is the prologue to his third novel, *A State of Freedom*. He lives in London.

Karthika Naïr is the author of *Bearings*, a poetry collection, and *The Honey Hunter*, a children's book. 'Shunaka: Blood Count' is from her forthcoming collection, a reworking of the Mahabharata in multiple voices.

Kalpana Narayanan was born in New Delhi and raised in Atlanta. In 2011, she received *Boston Review*'s Aura Estrada Short Story Prize. She lives in Brooklyn.

Srinath Perur translates from the Kannada and is the author of the travelogue *If It's Monday It Must Be Madurai*. He lives in Bengaluru.

Sudip Sengupta is a Mumbai-based cinematographer. He shoots features, ads and documentary films.

Aman Sethi is a journalist and the author of *A Free Man*.

Vivek Shanbhag is the author of five story collections, two plays and three novels, including the forthcoming *Ooru Bhanga* (*Hometown Breaks*). He is an engineer by training and lives in Bengaluru. 'Ghachar Ghochar' is an excerpt from a novella of the same title.

Vinod Kumar Shukla lives in Raipur, Chhattisgarh, where he has taught at the Indira Gandhi Agricultural University. He has published several collections of poetry and four novels, including *Deewar mein ek khidki rehti thi* (*A Window Lived in a Wall*).

Samanth Subramanian is a New Delhi-based journalist. He has written for the *New Yorker*, the *New York Times*, the *Guardian* and the *Wall Street Journal*, among other publications. His second book, *This Divided Island: Stories from the Sri Lankan War* will be published in the UK in February.

Unnati Tripathi researches for documentary film and academic projects. From 2008 to 2012, she was primary translator and investigative researcher on *Behind the Beautiful Forevers*.

Rajesh Vangad received his initial training in Warli painting from his parents. His work has been exhibited in London, Barcelona and across India.